Sensing Willa Cather

Modern American Literature and the New Twentieth Century
Series Editors: Martin Halliwell and Mark Whalan

Published Titles

Writing Nature in Cold War American Literature
Sarah Daw

F. Scott Fitzgerald's Short Fiction and American Popular Culture: From Ragtime to Swing Time
Jade Broughton Adams

The Labour of Laziness in Twentieth-Century American Literature
Zuzanna Ladyga

The Literature of Suburban Change: Narrating Spatial Complexity in Metropolitan America
Martin Dines

The Literary Afterlife of Raymond Carver: Influence and Craftsmanship in the Neoliberal Era
Jonathan Pountney

Living Jim Crow: The Segregated Town in Mid-Century Southern Fiction
Gavan Lennon

The Little Art Colony and US Modernism: Carmel, Provincetown, Taos
Geneva M. Gano

Sensing Willa Cather: The Writer and the Body in Transition
Guy J. Reynolds

Forthcoming Titles

The Big Red Little Magazine: New Masses, 1926–1948
Susan Currell

The Reproductive Politics of American Literature and Film, 1959–1973
Sophie Jones

Ordinary Pursuits in American Writing after Modernism
Rachel Malkin

The Plastic Theatre of Tennessee Williams: Expressionist Drama and the Visual Arts
Henry I. Schvey

Exoteric Modernisms: Progressive Era Literature and the Aesthetics of Everyday Life
Michael J. Collins

Black Childhood in Modern African American Fiction
Nicole King

Gertrude Stein and the Politics of Participation: Democracy, Human Rights and Modernist Authorship, 1909-1939
Isabelle Parkinson

Visit our website at www.edinburghuniversitypress.com/series/MALTNTC

Sensing Willa Cather

The Writer and the Body in Transition

GUY J. REYNOLDS

EDINBURGH
University Press

Edinburgh University Press is one of the leading university presses in the UK. We publish academic books and journals in our selected subject areas across the humanities and social sciences, combining cutting-edge scholarship with high editorial and production values to produce academic works of lasting importance. For more information visit our website: edinburghuniversitypress.com

© Guy J. Reynolds, 2021, 2023

Edinburgh University Press Ltd
The Tun – Holyrood Road
12(2f) Jackson's Entry
Edinburgh EH8 8PJ

First published in hardback by Edinburgh University Press 2021

Typeset in 10/13 ITC Giovanni Std Book by
Servis Filmsetting Ltd, Stockport, Cheshire

A CIP record for this book is available from the British Library

ISBN 978 1 4744 3825 4 (hardback)
ISBN 978 1 4744 3826 1 (paperback)
ISBN 978 1 4744 3827 8 (webready PDF)
ISBN 978 1 4744 3828 5 (epub)

The right of Guy J. Reynolds to be identified as the author of this work has been asserted in accordance with the Copyright, Designs and Patents Act 1988, and the Copyright and Related Rights Regulations 2003 (SI No. 2498).

CONTENTS

Acknowledgements vi
List of Abbreviations viii

1. Willa Cather in the Realm of the Senses 1
2. Cather's Bodily Art and the Emergence of Modernism 31
3. 'Sense-dwarfed': Cather, Aestheticism and a New Corporealism 60
4. Pale Shades and Living Colours: Cather's Looks 86
5. Sound Affects: Music, Voice and Silence in *The Song of the Lark*, *My Mortal Enemy* and *Lucy Gayheart* 114
6. Touch: Haptic Narrative in *The Professor's House*, *Shadows on the Rock* and *Sapphira and the Slave Girl* 137
7. Cather, Taste and National Cuisines: *The Professor's House*, *Death Comes for the Archbishop* and *Shadows on the Rock* 162
8. Cather's Smellscapes: Perfumes and Flowers, Disgust and Seduction 186
9. Conclusion: The Body of the Author 209

Bibliography and Further Reading 228
Index 241

ACKNOWLEDGEMENTS

Many people, places and organisations have informed and inspired this book. At the University of Nebraska–Lincoln (UNL), Cather's alma mater, a succession of colleagues have encouraged my work. I am particularly grateful for the support of my former chairs – Linda Pratt, Joy Ritchie and Susan Belasco – and to my current Head of Department, Marco Abel. Cather research at UNL is centred on the Cather Project and the online Cather Archive. The former's Director, Melissa Homestead, and the latter's Editor, Andy Jewell, are researchers whose work underpins my thinking.

As General Editor of the *Cather Scholarly Edition* and also *Cather Studies*, I have worked closely with many other editors and scholars, notably Kari Ronning. The *Scholarly Edition* and *Cather Studies* led me to fruitful collaborations with the following: Anne Kaufman, Mark Madigan, Ann Moseley, the late David Porter, Ann Romines, Robert Thacker, Richard Millington, John Murphy and Françoise Palleau-Papin. These scholars have opened new research pathways, and have mapped Cather's literary and cultural worlds in invaluable ways.

Beth Burke has been central to my work over seventeen years at UNL. I have benefited throughout from her guidance in terms of research and editing.

Through my association with the Cather Foundation (Red Cloud) I have known many Cather aficionados whose enthusiasm has encouraged me. This book thus owes a debt to Ashley Olson, Chuck Peek and Tracy Tucker. Fellow scholars Eric Aronoff, Marilee

Lindemann, Susan Naramore Maher and Catherine Morley have all offered encouragement at various stages of this project. In its earliest stages, my thinking grew out of conversations with Katy Gardner; and in its later phases suggestions from Peter Capuano and Stephanie Tsank proved invaluable. Brad Morrow and Alex Ross reminded me of Cather's centrality to American literary culture. I am grateful to Kyla Garrison for hints and tips about the significance of jewellery, flowers and perfumes.

Mark Whalan, Martin Halliwell and the two anonymous readers of my initial materials provided important feedback; the diligent and vigilant Robert Lipscomb shaped the manuscript as it moved toward production.

Sensing Willa Cather grew out of work and conversations from the early 2000s, when I moved from the UK to Nebraska. Former colleagues Fred Link, Chuck Mignon and Susan Rosowski were often in my mind as I drafted these pages. Our collective work has benefited from significant endowments (from Charles Cather and James Woodress) that have supported travel and research assistance. And UNL's Board of Regents helped create the Cather Project as a long-term investment in literary scholarship – a rare and wise decision in these times.

Finally, a shout-out to my children – Jamie, Izzy and Zac – whose annoyance with my research encouraged me to *stop* doing the research and then get 'the thing' published.

LIST OF ABBREVIATIONS

In order to keep this book's scholarly apparatus relatively simple, I cite Cather's novels, and some of her other writings, within the text, using the following abbreviations. Full details of the texts are then given in the bibliography.

AB	*Alexander's Bridge*
ALL	*A Lost Lady*
DCA	*Death Comes for the Archbishop*
KA	*The Kingdom of Art: Willa Cather's First Principles and Critical Statements, 1893–1896*
LG	*Lucy Gayheart*
MA	*My Ántonia*
MME	*My Mortal Enemy*
OOO	*One of Ours*
OP!	*O Pioneers!*
OW	*On Writing*
PC	'Paul's Case'
SL	*Selected Letters*
SOL	*The Song of the Lark*
SOR	*Shadows on the Rock*
SSG	*Sapphira and the Slave Girl*
TPH	*The Professor's House*
YBM	*Youth and the Bright Medusa*

CHAPTER 1

Willa Cather in the Realm of the Senses

Willa Cather grew up at a time and in a place at a sensory crossroads, a historical juncture where different geographical and temporal orders of sense co-existed. On the prairies, sod houses and the early homesteading settlements presented a 'primitive' world of touch and smell: the touch of frozen earth, or cold wind against skin; the ache of hard physical labour; the feel, memorably caught in Mr Shimerda's fate in *My Ántonia*, of gunmetal against finger or mouth. The Frontier world of late nineteenth-century Nebraska possessed a fierce physicality, a world of snow, churned earth, rawly built cabins – of amazing heat and bitter cold.

Yet the world of Lincoln, Nebraska, to which Cather moved in her mid-teens, presented a more scopic experience, a modernity built around late Victorian performativity and modern urban culture. Lincoln was notable for its theatres, known as a crucial stop-off for musical and dramatic companies moving between the bigger Western metropolises. In Lincoln, Cather became a listener and viewer, a participant in the unfolding and radical performative spaces of theatre and opera. Here, the gaze was paramount, and the framing of the body on a stage central. Cather's earliest writings, produced as a student critic of theatre and music, were relentlessly obsessed with moments of looking and being looked at – were, in fact, sketches for a new form of writing, partly journalistic and partly fictional, that would position spectators and performers in intriguing geometries of the visual.

In 1928 Rebecca West summed up Willa Cather's work in terms

of sensory accomplishment: 'The most sensuous of writers, Willa Cather builds her imagined world almost as solidly as our five senses build the universe around us.'[1] In this study, I open up West's statement by using the five senses as a means to reflect on Cather's work – to see her as a narrative artist whose writing turns again and again to moments where taste, touch, sight, sound and smell are crucial. I read Cather as an artist moving from late Victorian to proto-Modernist modes of representation: a creative figure engaged with the sensorium in complex and varied ways. My Cather is a writer whose works focus on bodies in transition (especially as late Victorian culture gave way to the twentieth century and the advent of Modernism); on embodiment in all its thrilling diversity; on disabled, ageing and performative bodies; on varieties of American bodies. Such an approach returns us, too, to the complexities of Cather's representations of whiteness, and of non-white bodies. As we shall see, Cather's writing was often violently conflicted when her narrative gaze (and it was often a *gaze*) turned to these others.

Revisiting Cather's vast and diverse range of writing (fiction, both novels and short stories; poetry; reviews and occasional writing; journalism; and, now, the letters that, for the first time, can be consulted, analysed and cited in their original form), we see how body-writing shapes so many areas of her work.[2] Whether writing about illness and death, ageing, disability, or food cultures and performance, Cather was primarily a creative artist immersed in the representation of the human body, and – through her fascination with drama and opera – a reviewer and critic whose earliest touchstone was *corporealism*. Once established, many apparently tangential aspects of Cather's writing career begin to align around this central preoccupation. Seemingly marginal works that Cather produced as a journalist become significant. Writing about food policies during World War One, or about the training of ballet dancers, or about the voices of her favourite opera singers, she explored tropes of embodiment and body-writing. In the study that follows, I create a complex weave of sources where these accounts play a direct role in what I term as the 'making' of the Cather reader, a reader attuned to exploring performances (of theatre or opera), or primed to think of writing not only as textuality but also as an encounter with the writer's own body (as in Cather's accounts of A. E. Housman or Katherine Mansfield). The journalism and occasional writing become a form of acculturation into a distinctive mode of writing that turns repeatedly on the body, its representation, and the corporeal foundations of literary, dramatic and visual art.

Willa Cather, the Habitus and Body Studies

Writing in 1934, French ethnographer Marcel Mauss coined the term 'habitus' or 'the habitus', a term which is now synonymous with the later French theorist Pierre Bourdieu. Bourdieu's habitus conceptualises social practices that are immanent, largely unconscious – the 'way things are done'. Focusing, for instance, on questions of prestige and cultural capital, Bourdieu's formulation is a way to explain how certain artistic products might be reflexively and unconsciously accorded value. However, Mauss's original conception of the habitus focused exclusively on the body and its deportment, and read culture in terms of embodiment, or what he called 'techniques of the body'. A number of his examples focused on comparisons between British and French soldiers (Mauss served alongside British troops during the First World War). The culture of each nation is literally written on to the way an individual's body might move or act. French troops and British troops dig, or march, differently, Mauss observed. 'Each society has its own special habits.'[3] Mauss then went on to look at 'societies, educations, proprieties and fashions', examining differences in such simple and apparently universal human activities as walking, dancing or digging.[4] His aim: to suggest the ways that humans and their cultures create 'physio-psycho-sociological assemblages of series of actions'.[5]

Mauss's intense corporealism and his fascination with embodied experience have had a formative impact on ethnography – from his work one can trace an intellectual genealogy which leads to recent anthropological study such as Kathryn Linn Geurts's writing about the Anlo people of West Africa. She argues that

> in addition to its social, political, economic, and moral dimensions, the habitus is eminently sensuous. The web of sensory experiences and

sensory meanings in which everyday life takes place, in which engagements occur with other persons, other beings, inanimate objects, and landscapes (also sound-scapes, smell-scapes, touch-scapes, etc.) forms a critical foundation for conditions of interaction, well-being, and health.[6]

For Geurts, 'My argument begins with the claim that *sensory orders vary based on cultural tradition, and hence sensoriums may be different from one cultural group to the next.*'[7]

The habitus is a useful concept to deploy when we think about Willa Cather's fiction. Frequently, in her work, Cather creates tableaux or vignettes where we witness body cultures suddenly shifting; or we watch as one form of embodiment (perhaps associated with a particular national culture – say, that of France) encounters another (say, that of indigenous American cultures). Later chapters will thus deal with such disparate but interlinked episodes as: the varied competing food cultures of *Death Comes for the Archbishop* and *Shadows on the Rock*; the cultures of tactility (violent; healing) in *Sapphira and the Slave Girl*; and the representations of musical performance and dancing in *My Ántonia*. In all these cases Cather bases narrative in stylised aspects of culture (for instance: cuisine, performance, dancing, nursing), and explores how cultural change then registers at the corporeal level. Mauss, if he had read Cather, would recognise her as a kindred thinker who had chosen fiction for her closely observed, neo-anthropological thinking about techniques of the body.

Using Mauss and Geurts to rethink Cather's fiction, one begins to sense the centrality of bodily deportment, movement and action in her work. The anthropologists' sensitivity to cultural difference as it appears through embodied practices has clear parallels with Cather's fictional world. Working as an ethnographer, Mauss sensed these unconscious bodily practices emerging in the turmoil of conflict, as troops of different nationalities were thrown together. Analogously, Cather had met as a child an array of different nationalities as they encountered one another on the Nebraskan prairies. Mauss drew his examples from the interdependent and cross-cultural realities of European conflict, Cather from immigration and settlement. But both were, in their own ways, trying to create maps of bodily encounters in the contemporary era, encounters across national, cultural and ethnic boundaries. In Mauss's essay and Cather's fiction, observation of the body is the way to gauge cultural encounter and contrast: digging and marching in Mauss's account; dancing, eating or cooking in Cather. As I show in later chapters, some of Cather's finest vignettes and scenarios (Lena dancing with Jim in *My Ántonia*; the religious procession in *O Pioneers!*; the account of a Southwest mesa's indigenous cooking spaces in *The Professor's House*; the contrast between European and Amerindian dining in *Death Comes for the Archbishop*) grow out of close observations of embodied cultural difference: the Catherian habitus.

I would also argue that even Cather's stories set in the performing world ('A Gold Slipper' or *Lucy Gayheart*) stage encounters of the habitus, since they are so often about an individual looking into, or meeting, a highly corporealised world that seems far from their own habitual ways of bodily being. These encounters often have a gendered aspect, as – for instance – the Midwestern everyman, Harry Gordon, looks with fascination at the running, skating Lucy Gayheart, a character who, in her very idiosyncratic physicality, might almost come from a different species.

Another way to read Cather and the habitus is to think about *disrupted* habitus, about the ways that she shows encounters between bodies in such a way that we think not of a single, steadily evolving habitus but of abrupt disruptions of the habitus: moments of unsettling. In the chapters that follow I often discuss just such moments in Cather's work – moments when a character might encounter a very different habitus, or sense a very different form of embodiment to what he or she is used to. Cather wrote about French settlers in Quebec (*Shadows on the Rock*); about European Americans exploring the Southwest's ancient cultures (*The Professor's House*); and about slavery in its most intimate domestic configurations (*Sapphira and the Slave Girl*). In all these narratives Cather presents encounters between bodies, and how one habitus (for example, the cooking practices of Native Americans) might be understood (and misunderstood) by figures from another cultural habitus. As a writer fascinated by music and performance, Cather also explores the distinctive moments when a viewer or listener might encounter the habitus of the artist – as we shall see, in stories such as 'A Gold Slipper' and *Lucy Gayheart*, Cather focuses on the bodily meetings of singers and audiences, performers and fascinated onlookers.

Considering how the five senses are represented, it is obvious that Cather wrote during a vast transformation of the sensorium. The foundational technological, cultural and social shifts of the late nineteenth and early twentieth centuries (roughly from around 1880 to 1920) were transformations felt at the level of sight, sound, taste, touch and smell. The automobile, electricity, cinema and radio: all these technological innovations impacted the individual at a sensory level. The mid-1920s presented a very different sensory experience to that of the 1890s, as cityscapes and landscapes changed, but also, on a bodily level, as 'skinscapes' (how the body presents itself and is then represented) changed as well. Media theorist Friedrich Kittler has shown how recorded music and the greatly expanded performative realms of theatre and cinema radically changed what an individual would hear or see on a daily basis. Technological changes drastically altered sight and sound – perhaps the senses most deeply transformed by these shifts. Our representative Midwesterner – Cather herself, perhaps – had, by the 1920s, a proliferating array of visual and auditory technologies (telephone, cinema, gramophone, photography) that had, as Kittler demonstrated in *Gramophone, Film, Typewriter*, fundamentally uprooted the primacy of the written word.[8] These technological additions transformed and ruptured earlier forms of signification, bringing into play far more fragmented and fractured models of representation. In silent cinema one sees the actors mouthing their words, the script emerging as writing on the screen. In a telephone conversation one hears another's voice; but that individual might be many hundreds of miles away. Patterns of intimacy and distance, absence and presence radically reordered themselves. As Julia A. Walker notes,

> the messages transmitted through these new technologies must have seemed strange because so unexpectedly distant from the moment of their communicative intent. The act of communication – once experienced as a relatively integrated process – must have felt as if it were suddenly rent apart, splintered into the newly separable elements of bodies, voices, and words.[9]

This historico-materialist framing of the body offers a new and compelling way to think about Cather's *œuvre*. Consider the historical development of Cather's career. As a writer bridging the late Victorian, Modernist and pre-Postmodernist ages, Cather worked during a sweeping era of changes concerning representation of the corporeal. Her career, beginning as it did in the 1890s and stretching on into the 1940s, offers a fascinating record of a major writer's responses to the shifts that successively reframed the body over this revolutionary period.

Mary Baker Eddy and Randolph Bourne: The Progressive Era Body

As an artist, Cather grew to maturity at a time when decisive shifts took place in body culture. As journalist and editor, then as a creative writer herself, Cather had an early career that intersected decisively with a number of these developments. Her connections with two early twentieth-century figures are worth revisiting in the new context that I am describing: first, Mary Baker Eddy, the founder of Christian Science, whose biography (written by Georgine Milmine and published originally in *McClure's Magazine*) Cather edited: *The Life of Mary Baker G. Eddy and the History of Christian Science* (1909); and second, Randolph Bourne, an early, vociferous advocate for Cather's work, and the pioneering author of an account of disability, 'The Handicapped – By One of Them' (1911). Placing these works together enables one to see how Cather's fictions responded to, imaginatively engaged with and entered into a creative dialogue with some of the Progressive Era's debates about a new American body.

The Life of Mary Baker G. Eddy and the History of Christian Science stands in remarkable contrast to the creative career that followed for Cather. She edited a book that was about a religion founded upon anti-materialism and a defiant denigration of the physical, bodily basis of human life. Chapter XI of *The Life* encapsulates Eddy's philosophy (the text here refers to Eddy as Mrs Glover – her original married name) in all its anti-sensory and anti-corporeal fundamentalism: 'she asserted that there *is* no matter and that we *have* no senses. The five senses being non-existent, Mrs. Glover pointed out that "all evidence obtained therefrom" is non-existent also.'[10] As I demonstrate in this study, this statement is about as 'un-Catherian' as one could imagine. In Eddy's anti-material reading of human selfhood, the physical basis of life has to be overcome: 'He must ignore his physical body and the material things about him, and he must no longer depend upon the laws of nature or of man, but be governed by spiritual law only.'[11] Milmine (and her editor, Cather) then describe what we might call the 'Eddy body' as 'sensationless'. 'It can have no sensation whatever, and in Mrs. Glover's system, this spiritual man, whose body is sensationless, is the only man that exists.'[12] For the most part, the *Life of Mary Baker G. Eddy* consists of biographical materials and summaries of her central ideas. But at the end of Chapter XI, there is what seems to be an overtly judgemental overview of these ideas about the corporeal self. Eddy had constructed a system that constituted 'the revolt of a species against its own physical structure; against its relation to its natural physical environment; against the needs of its own physical organism, and against the perpetuation of its kind'.[13] At this point, the Cather scholar would dearly love to know whether this is Georgine Milmine writing, or whether this actually is an editorial intervention by Cather herself.

A few years after editing the Eddy biography, Cather embarked on her full-time career as a creative writer. That career became a long, trenchant riposte to Eddy's ideas. While Eddy advocates the anti-materialist transcendence of the body, Cather's work is relentlessly embodied and embedded in the corporeal. While Eddy claims to have found devotional and 'scientific' means to find physical wellness, Cather's characters, even if they are themselves devotionally ideal (as is, quite naturally, Father Latour in *Death Comes for the Archbishop*), find themselves within a world of physical constraint. And while Eddy had begun by rejecting sense-impressionism, thus constructing a 'sensationless' body, Cather began with – and relentlessly returned to – the senses as the basis for a narrative art preoccupied with corporealism. So, while Christian Science had as one of its aims the transcendence of death itself, Cather constructed narratives (*The Professor's House*, *Death Comes for the Archbishop*, *Lucy Gayheart*, *Shadows on the Rock* and *Sapphira and the Slave Girl*) which take death as the inevitable and central *telos* of human existence.

In contrast to Mary Baker Eddy, the public intellectual and writer Randolph Bourne – a major Cather interlocutor – created one of the Progressive Era's most radical accounts of the physical body. In his brief and brilliant 1911 essay, Bourne outlines the physical, social and psychological impacts of disability. For Bourne, there is no way out of his physical disability as it is the ground of everything he experiences. Yet the essay is astonishingly confident to the point of being ebullient.

Bourne's essay was intensely bodily, and relentlessly attuned to disability's social and cultural dimensions. Bourne points to the immediacy of his physical discomfort: 'No one but the deformed man can realize just what the mere fact of sitting a foot lower than the normal means in discomfort and annoyance.'[14] The account that follows blends this corporealised rootedness with a keen awareness of how disability manifests itself in the complex rhythms of social life. Bourne is fascinated by what he calls the 'impressions' of social interchange. He explored the possibilities for a figure 'bearing simply a crooked back and an unsightly face' who is none the less 'drawn into all the currents of life'.[15] He envisions a society where such a figure might actively belong in society, rather than being on its margins: at present 'I was truly in the world, but not of the world.'[16] And as the essay unfolds, it moves from its autobiographical focus on Bourne himself to a wider sense of how 'the handicapped', that 'horde of the unpresentable and the unemployable, the incompetent and the ugly, the queer and crotchety people who make up so large a proportion of human folk', might become part of society.[17] This process would necessitate recreating what Bourne called 'interpretations of life', which tended not to be fashioned, as he noted, by the 'queer and crotchety people'.[18]

Bourne, that is, wrote about the body, about disability, about the social performance of selfhood, about how 'interpretations of life' shape culture. He writes about embodiment and narrative, focusing his explorations on the 'deformed man'. 'The Handicapped' is, then, the absolute reverse – in terms of its conceptions of selfhood, narrative and society – of the Mary Baker Eddy volume. He foregrounds the disabled body (rather than suggesting a transcendence of physical materialism), suggests that narrative constructs social and cultural identities (rather than narrowing narrative down to schematised readings of scripture), and responds to the whirl and exchange of the modern city, notably New York (rather than taking the church as his chosen community). Bourne's fascination with the 'queer and crotchety', with 'interpretations' and with embodiment, suggests ways to think about Cather through their shared envisaging of the Progressive Era body.

To place Eddy alongside Bourne is to encounter two very different – in fact, opposing – visions of the human body in sickness and health. Eddy sought to transcend the body by means of an idiosyncratic and idealised application of 'science'. Bourne, on the other hand, accepting the foundational significance of corporealism, situates the body socially and psychologically in order to emphasise what is now termed the resilience of the disabled self. Read across the range of Cather's work – from its origins to *Sapphira and the Slave Girl* – Cather clearly established, even at the start of her career, proto-Bournean positions that she would then explore over decades of writing. Her first publication was a sketch of disability – 'Peter', an 1892 story published in the University of Nebraska's journal, *The Hesperian*, when Cather was still in her teens. Peter is a Bohemian immigrant, a one-time musician now lost on the Nebraskan Frontier. The story sets out, with predictive precision, familiar Cather narrative binaries: Nebraska/Europe, metropolitan/provincial, immigrant parents/American children. Even here, Cather places charismatic voice at the centre of narrative. Paul keenly remembers a French singer: 'And her voice, he thought he should know that in the other world.'[19] Having been a violinist in Prague, Peter now ploughs the Nebraskan prairie, a job he hates. But what is perhaps most interesting about this brief narrative is the grounding of narrative in embodiment. Peter 'had a stroke of paralysis, which made his arm so weak that his bowing was uncertain'.[20] He commits suicide, but the frozen body is too stiff to fit in a coffin, and so his family uses a pine box instead.

The story seems to blend a grotesque – and historically conventional – reading of the disabled body (as, basically, fated and troubled) with a more sympathetic reading of that body within a social matrix. The circumstances of Peter's death, his drinking and despair, are set against Cather's delineation of his cultural loss. He is a suicide with a sense of beauty (as will be Paul, in 'Paul's

Case'). The 'doubled' nature of this portrait would remain a feature of Cather's writing about disability, a form of tacking between traditional grotesquerie and a contemporary Bournean reading of bodies within their social milieux.

Later in this study, I look closely at patterns of disability and suffering in *Shadows on the Rock* and *Sapphira and the Slave Girl*. In both, I argue that we see further developments of this initial Cather modelling of the disabled body: at once rooted in inherited patterns on the grotesque and the uncanny (I discuss Cécile's first glimpse of the facially damaged Blinker in *Shadows on the Rock*, and Sapphira's seemingly embittered immobility in *Sapphira and the Slave Girl*), and reaching forward to a more nuanced and enriched understanding of human variety. These fables of infirmity might be read as transitional tales. They are at first seemingly regressive (Cécile's shock at seeing Blinker's face), then become, as one reads and rereads across the panels of the narrative, juxtaposing the sections of the narrative tapestry, micro-narratives that might hold clues to an entire society.

In *Sapphira and the Slave Girl* Cather constructs a story about racially inflected psychological vengeance on the bedrock of a character's disability. Sapphira can barely move: her body is swollen by oedema. Around her is the intimately connected 'family' of the slaveholders and their slaves. Sapphira is a kind of damaged, embodied putative panopticon, always trying to sense and react to the movements and actions of these other agents. Seemingly trapped by her illness, and deeply suspicious of her husband's fondness for the slave girl, Nancy, she sets in motion a desperate act of vengeance against her nemesis. That, at least, might be one reading. Yet the novel, as I demonstrate in my final chapter, is filled with sick, disabled and damaged bodies in tableaux that focus on healing and nursing. Looked at socially, then, Sapphira's resentments might be said to emerge less from her own bodily pain than from an inability to recognise the communality that we all share, and will share, as bodily beings fated to sicken and die.

And so one way to think about Cather's *œuvre* is as a long experiment in writing about bodily variety – including the ageing body and the disabled body. Having edited a book that programmatically attempts to abjure corporealism, Cather relentlessly and creatively turned her writing toward varieties of corporeal experience. It is notable how her writing became *more* 'Bournean' as she worked forward, often returning to issues and questions raised early in her career and creating increasingly complex maps of the embodied world. In *Lucy Gayheart*, a novel (like *Sapphira and the Slave Girl*) about physical service and help, Clement Sebastian's accompanist, James Mockford, is lame (a planned operation on his leg is the reason why Lucy takes over from Mockford), and Lucy's ambiguous reaction to his disability becomes an early index of the complex and potentially dangerous world she will now live in.

> For some reason she didn't like the way he moved across the stage. His lameness gave him a weak, undulating walk, 'like a rag walking,' she thought. It was contemptible to hold a man's infirmity against him; besides, if this young man weren't lame, she would not be going to Sebastian's studio tomorrow, – she would never have met him at all. (*LG* 41)

That is, Cather wove disability into her plotlines: all of the later major novels are, in one way or another, about characters reacting to, or against, disability. All grow plotlines out of characters barely comprehending (and thus misreading) disability. In *Shadows on the Rock* it is Blinker's facial disfigurement and Cécile's responses to his appearance that focus, at the novel's very inception, those issues of charity and philanthropy (and their limits) that become central to Cather's mapping of the French colony's emotional landscape. In *Lucy Gayheart*, it is James Mockford's lameness that, ironically enough, moves the plot in decisive directions, notably in the drowning, where the presumably incapable figure wraps himself around Clement Sebastian and takes both men down to watery death. In *Sapphira and the Slave Girl*, it is Sapphira's crippled and immobile body that sits at the heart of the web of emotional (dis)connections that eventually lead to Nancy fleeing to Canada. And at the very end of her life, as Sarah Clere notes, Cather was working on a novel about the fourteenth-century Avignon papacy, a manuscript that 'was to treat two children who have been brutally disabled' (one with a tongue cut out, one hung by the thumbs).[21] In so many ways, Cather remained a novelist vitally engaged in dialogue with Bourne's experimental ideas about the body.

Cather's Narrative Architecture: Storylines of the Body

Although Cather never produced a manifesto with the programmatic intent of Yeats's statements about the gyre or Eliot's 'Tradition and the Individual Talent', she did in fact repeatedly theorise her artistic practice. Since Cather was rooted in many late-Victorian forms and genres, these commentaries often turned back to that late nineteenth-century world. But as a commentator on fiction and narrative, opera, music and art, Cather often arrived at proto-Modernist positions. In particular, her principles (which came in the form of letters, interviews and essays about her works) often focused on that very sense of embodiment and corporeal aestheticism which I see as central to her work. Thus, Chapter 5 deploys Cather's 1925 Introduction to Gertrude Hall's *The Wagnerian Romances* as a way to understand voice, listening and national culture in Cather's portrayals of singers. Chapter 6 focuses on 'The Novel Démeublé' (1922) and its relation to the tactility presented in *The Professor's House*. And Cather's commentary on 'Anacoluthon' (a term for grammatical incompleteness) becomes the basis of my analysis of the narrative shape of *Shadows on the Rock* and its imaginings of colonial bodies in Chapter 7.

The 'Critical Studies on Writing as an Art' that were collected after Cather's death and published as *On Writing* (and later reprinted as *Willa Cather on Writing*) make for an eclectic and idiosyncratic collection, one that is vital for understanding how Cather wanted to make the body the very ground of art. The collection includes four letters (primarily written in response to enquiries about her works), miscellaneous essays (such as 'The Novel Démeublé') and four Prefaces (to works by Sarah Orne Jewett, Stephen Crane, Daniel Defoe and Gertrude Hall's *The Wagnerian Romances* – the latter a quixotic anthology summarising the plotlines of the major operas). This book references these essays, letters and Prefaces so as to elucidate Cather's fiction. But for the moment, I will outline some of the critical positions Cather developed, since we can then see how her career as a whole contained a distinctive underpinning:

a corporeal aesthetic shaped her work, and Cather's commentaries then provided a framework for understanding her modelling of the body and narrative, and (especially) the body *in* narrative.

Cather's writings on her own fiction are deductive, post-hoc explanations of her compositional process – less manifestos than technical explanations – that situate her work within a distinctive vision of art and literature. For the most part, Cather eschews explanations of writing as a moral or political act; as many critics have noted, she is far from being an *engagée* writer – a broadside first aimed at her work by Granville Hicks in 1933.[22] Nor is she interested in complex mythological or quasi-religious justifications of art – a typical Modernist 'solution' to the apparent dead-end of late Victorian realism. Instead, Cather circles around the enduring value of art (the so-called 'kingdom of art'), meditates on the body and writing's ability to capture human presence, and reflects on the distinctive formalism of her novels and the idiosyncratic narratives fashioned by writers such as Crane and Defoe. The 1927 letter to the *Commonweal* – about *Death Comes for the Archbishop* – demonstrates Cather's deep commitment to lived (physical and material) experience as the basis of writing (the letter is largely about travelling in the Southwest, and draws parallels between Cather's experiences there and the fictionalised lives of priests in the book). The letter on *Shadows on the Rock* features Cather's famous (and politically contestable) claim that 'a new society begins with the salad dressing more than with the destruction of Indian villages' (*OW* 16).

Travelling, cooking, making pottery: such is the recognisably physical world that Cather used to fashion her ideas about art and culture. In the 1936 letter 'Escapism', Cather trenchantly foregrounded the body as the ineluctable frame within which art has always been created. She imagines the artistry of Pueblo villagers: 'Hundreds of years ago, before European civilization had touched this continent, the Indian women in the old rock-perched pueblos of the Southwest were painting geometrical patterns on the jars in which they carried water up from the streams' (*OW* 19). In this recognised work of bodily classicism, she recalled 'The Hebrew prophets and the Greek dramatists' and their recognition of 'the unfairness of the contest in which beings whose realest life is in thought or endeavour are kept always under the shackles of their physical body, and are, as Ulysses said, "the slaves of the belly"' (*OW* 22). Art, then, is about the conflict between human idealism and the constraints forged by the body. Thus, 'the themes of true poetry, of great poetry, will be the same until all the values of human life have changed and all the strongest emotional responses have become different – which can hardly occur until the physical body itself has fundamentally changed' (*OW* 28). The grounding of the 'strongest emotional responses' in the body became, in late Cather ('Old Mrs. Harris' and *Sapphira and the Slave Girl*), the basis for a complex art which took the classical conservatism of this position and then evolved an experimental understanding of the interchange between ageing bodies, slave bodies and disabled bodies.

Cather developed aesthetic ideas out of sensory thinking. *Sight* – especially – plays a foundational role in these commentaries. Two moments when Cather compared her work to art, or explored the vital act of simply *looking*, are particularly significant. In her Letter to the *Commonweal* magazine (1927) she used the works of Puvis de Chavannes as an analogue for the formalistic design of *Death Comes for the Archbishop*. And in an undated fragment, 'Light on Adobe Walls', Cather explored sensory impressionism.

Puvis de Chavannes

The French painter and muralist Pierre Puvis de Chavannes was beloved by Cather, celebrated in his own lifetime, but then overlooked until a recent wave of art history recovered his reputation. The 'newness' of Puvis was an issue for some of his earliest critics. An anonymous review in *The Art Critic* (1894) concluded, 'Whether Chavannes' frescoes will some day represent the beginning of a new art of painting, I cannot say, but I firmly believe that it is one of the phases which will eventually lead to a new art.'[23] For Aimee Brown Price (the pre-eminent scholar working on this figure), this is in fact what happened: 'Puvis's work leads to that of both Picasso and Matisse.' His work, she writes, was 'superbly original and strong enough to draw more than a generation of artists in one way or another after him'.[24] A certain lineage connecting this late Victorian figure to major Modernists is now clearer than it has been before.

Cather deployed his aesthetic as a way to understand her

1927 novel *Death Comes for the Archbishop*. In her letter to *The Commonweal* about the book, she wrote: 'I had all my life wanted to do something in the style of legend, which is absolutely the reverse of dramatic treatment.' And added that,

> Since I first saw the Puvis de Chavannes frescoes of the life of Saint Geneviève in my student days, I have wished that I could try something a little like that in prose; something without accent, with none of the artificial elements of composition. (OW 9)

Cather here refers to Puvis's 1879 'La Vie pastorale de Sainte Geneviève' (a mural painted for the Parisian church which is now the Panthéon, and an image Puvis also reproduced as an oil triptych). Puvis's mural presents a series of discrete scenes: as one's eye moves across the mural, one encounters a series of highly stylised bodies caught in groups, posed, emphatically staged. Furthermore, it would be remarkable if Cather had not also seen the Puvis de Chavannes mural 'The Muses of Inspiration', installed in the Boston Public Library (1895–6).

What does Cather's interest in Puvis tell us about the proto-modernity of her narratives? Tapestries and murals fascinated Cather. The movement across and between panels, or tableaux, suggested movement and a form of pictorial narrative. Looking at the Boston Public Library mural, one's eye tracks across panels, or glimpses tableaux from different perspectives and levels, and then moves through oblique and direct viewings: 'Progression is given by the movement of the viewer from panel to panel. Puvis himself implies such by referring to the first panel as a Prologue.'[25] Although 'flat' in composition, the combination of panels asks the viewer to think across and between each section, thereby creating a form of narrative three-dimensionality. How do we link each section? What connects one panel, a visual vignette, to another? The flatness of the panels also draws attention to surface – especially the surfaces of the body. Cristina Giorcelli, writing about Cather and Puvis, draws attention to this 'panel method' where there is a concentration on 'stiff human figures in neo-classical poses' and 'an apparent lack of psychological depth and conflict'.[26]

'I have wished that I could try something a little like that in prose,' Cather wrote, 'something without accent, with none of the artificial elements of composition.' And: 'it is as though all human experiences, measured against one supreme spiritual experience, were of about the same importance' (*OW* 9). I read these statements, and Cather's interest in Puvis de Chavannes, as important signposts to how she created bodily narratives – a scenic form, if you like, that shaped her narratives. If all 'human experience ... were of about the same importance', then the artist has to pay attention to the ephemeral, the apparently trivial, the insignificant and the marginal. And this, indeed, is what the Cather who was influenced by Puvis de Chavannes did when she constructed a narrative such as *Death Comes for the Archbishop*. Looking at bodies in their quotidian circumstances (eating, smelling flowers, looking at a painting, listening to song), Cather created a mural of American sensory experience, and she described that achievement in terms of a 'new form' – as in a 1927 letter. 'I had a glorious year doing it,' she said of writing the novel, 'and working in that new form with no solid drama' (*SL* 396).

Looking at a Chavannes mural (say, from different vantage points in the Boston Public Library), the eye moves across panels, and a narrative emerges from a mobile gazing. The eye shifts between one perspectival plane and the next, or between panels or separate tapestries that form part of a narrative whole. Cather thus used quite unfashionably pre-Modernist analogues to fashion a way of describing her visual aesthetic in terms that suggest movement. This is a typically Catherian solution to a problem solved by the culture around her. Cather's career coincided more or less absolutely with the rise of a medium that would decisively foreground movement as the cornerstone of visual representation: cinema. In the years that the Lumière brothers and then Edison were inaugurating their filmic revolution, Cather began a career which used opera and late nineteenth-century art for inspiration when it came to looking – especially for creating forms of visual movement which, while not 'cinematic', certainly suggested that to gaze was a kinetic act.

'Light on Adobe Walls'

It seems fitting that one of Cather's major commentaries on the sensory world, 'Light on Adobe Walls', emerged only after her death as 'An unpublished fragment' (and was then published in the collection *On Writing*). What could be more fugitive, ephemeral and apparently insignificant than an 'unpublished fragment'? This short essay is, in fact, an exploration of the limitations of art and the paradoxical plenitude that arises within an art formed by sensory limitations. In 'Light on Adobe Walls' Cather is far from the heavy machinery of high Modernism, far from a theorised melding of aesthetics and Myth or History. The artist's awareness, instead, trains itself on the ephemeral sensory world we live in. 'Nobody can paint the sun, or sunlight,' Cather writes, and then finds a liberating subjectivism in this failure:

> He can only paint the tricks that shadows play with it, or what it does to forms. He cannot even paint those relations of light and shade – he can only paint some emotion they give him, some man-made arrangement of them that happens to give him personal delight – a conception of clouds over distant mesas (or over the towers of St. Sulpice) that makes one nerve in him thrill and tremble. (*OW* 123–4)

What is interesting about this curious statement is that failure ('Nobody can paint the sun') leads to investment in artistry ('some man-made arrangement') that is also, finally, a bodily success: 'that makes one nerve in him thrill and tremble'. This is Cather finding nervous plenitude in artistic limitation – as we shall see in later chapters, her fiction would model (repeatedly) similar turns toward a bodily affirmation or corporeal renewal (as in 'The Ancient People' section, which I discuss in the next chapter).

Cather's Impressionism thus led her toward what we might call 'sensorism': the experience of the world as a series of impressions, and an aesthetic founded (though that might seem too solid and permanent a word) on the senses themselves.[27] In 'Light on Adobe Walls', Cather sounds at first like an Impressionist, and then like a sensorist, or the aesthete–writer who shapes art around the five senses. 'At bottom all he can give you is the thrill of his own poor little nerve – the projection in paint of a fleeting pleasure in a certain combination of form and colour, as temporary and almost as physical as a taste on the tongue' (*OW* 124). From the nerve to the tongue; from form and colour to taste.

Cather's Sensory Fiction: Three Instances

Three illustrative examples of Cather's sensory fiction introduce my investigation, suggesting as they do how narrative, for Cather, had become, above all, a place to register sensory cultures and their transformations: an early review; the story 'On the Gulls' Road' (1908); and then 'Coming, Aphrodite!' (1920). Throughout Cather, fiction powerfully responds to, explores and represents the sensory world. Across nearly three decades of her early writing Cather explores modes of realism that focus on 'character' (in fiction) in terms of the meeting of selves through sensory contact.

Cather's Early Reviews

Cather's prodigious start as a writer was as a journalist and critic working for local papers in Lincoln, Nebraska. As a columnist for the *Nebraska State Journal* (the distant forebear of today's *Lincoln Journal Star*), she reviewed theatre and music, but also had the space and licence to construct sketches and vignettes that, when viewed from the vantage point of her long career, emerge as experiments where she began to develop situations and discourses that became reiterated motifs in her fiction. Writing under her own name or under pseudonyms, the undergraduate author created extended collages whose recurrent elements show her already modelling the body in transition. Her representations of embodied experience looked back to her Victorian idols while charting proto-Modernist modes of representation. And in particular, the early writing remodelled and adapted Aestheticist motifs and tropes.

From the start, Cather was embedded in the embodied world of performance and sought ways to take spectatorship out of the theatrical space and into the everyday world of provincial life. The early journalism possesses a distinctive formalism that ultimately gestures towards future fiction: it demonstrates little unity as such, being instead a collage of varied forms of writing – some fictional, some journalistically rooted in the actual culture of Lincoln. At times, Cather is clearly writing out of observed experience, composing a neo-journalistic account of the 'real life' around her, while in others a fictional remaking of experience is in play. One of the recurrent critical problems presented by her work had emerged: namely, what is the status of a fiction so directly rooted in actual experience, to the extent that prototypes might be found for fictional characters?

Thus, this early journalism is as significant for its distinctive formalism as it is for content or subject matter. There is no clear centre to this writing; it is highly improvised (in the sense that Cather is responding to the week-by-week goings-on of Lincoln); it is tonally and discursively heterogeneous. Compared to the typical newspaper piece of our own age, a column might seem highly experimental in its loose-limbed and open-ended structure. Late Victorian provincial newspapers and journals gave Cather a platform, but their own structures were sufficiently porous to allow a certain degree of experimentation within columns that had as yet few protocols. Cather found ways to fold an intriguing doubleness into even the simplest narratives so that a slight sketch or vignette, apparently improvised, might contain a creative plenitude of ideas about self and society.

In one of her very earliest pieces from 1893, Cather sketches a young man looking at himself, framing himself as if he were a picture and then asking his family to join in an act of spectatorship:

> The young man was standing before the glass putting the finishing touches on his toilet. When he cast the last earnest look at the glass, he opened the door and called in the family to admire him. They gazed at him as gravely and seriously as they would examine a painting. All their remarks and suggestions were made with the utmost gravity. When they had finished their adoration he pinned in his button-hole the red carnation he habitually wore and went forth.[28]

Rooted in *fin-de-siècle* Aestheticism, this short paragraph nevertheless incorporates proto-Modernist elements of performativity and spectacle into a smidgeon of journalism. From the very start of her career, Cather used bodily descriptions in a neo-theoretical way, placing in her sketches an additional level of signification that goes beyond a simple pictorial rendering to suggest more complex levels of representation. In particular, even as a teenage apprentice (Cather was barely twenty when this piece was published), she folded together embodied experience and cultural representations of the body: a figure caught in a pose, and simultaneously *represented* in such a pose. Thus, in this paragraph we see a moment replicated in later fictions: a figure framed, seen in a mirror, or imagined as a picture. Such turns in Cather's early work are significant in terms of narrative technique, providing a distinctive way of representing corporealism in terms of a conflated moment where the body is simultaneously described straightforwardly but also framed in a neo-Modernist manner that draws attention to modes of representation. Cather's early stories thus became a laboratory where she fashioned the narrative patterning and dramatic staging of the early reviews into fiction. The best, the most experimental, of the reviews became micro-narratives of bodily encounter: gazing at the body; the registering and evaluating of voice; the fascination with gestural movement; the sensing of dress and costume in all their textural diversity; the awareness of audience and how spectatorship might be staged. Cather's micro-narratives of encounter had already begun to explore these preoccupations.

Throughout her career, Cather created highly confined settings for looking and viewing (the railway carriage at the beginning of *My Ántonia* being but one example), as if echoing her early theatrical experiences. She returns again and again to confined spaces that allow a certain (limited) mobility and a criss-crossing of compelled gazing: theatres with their boxes and foyers; ocean-going ships with their decks and compartments; and journeys by train, which invoke walks down aisles and glimpses of strangers in other carriages. Often, such highly modern spaces feature at the start of a narrative, establishing a laboratory for modern spectatorship. For Cather, what such places seemed to offer above all was the complex combining of inner imaginative space (of reading or reflection) and social encounter within a confined space. In a discussion in my final chapter of essays from *Not Under Forty* (1936), I show how Cather developed this apprentice model of body-writing right through to the end of her career, as seen in the essays on Katherine Mansfield and Flaubert's niece, Mme Grout.

'On the Gulls' Road'

In the early story 'On the Gulls' Road' (1908), Cather transposed the intimacy of viewing within theatre to the confinement of viewing on an ocean liner. At the start of this story, a painter comments on the narrator's sketch of the female cynosure, Alexandra Ebbing: an opening sequence patterned with gazes, interrupted looks, and a strange mixture of fascination and shame.

> We returned to the object of his visit, but when he bade me goodbye at the door his troubled gaze again went back to the drawing, and it was only by turning sharply about that he took his eyes away from her.[29]

These sentences reveal traces of the covert glances and sideways looks of theatrical space – a mannered ballet of gazing that masks but continually reveals desire. But elsewhere, Cather's prose moves toward the much more explicit visual revelations also associated with her work: 'Her splendid, vigorous body lay still and relaxed under the loose folds of her clothing, her white throat and arms and red-gold hair were drenched with sunlight.'[30] Note Cather's interesting deployment of 'vigorous', a term more typically associated with the Progressive Era's male bodies. This blending of heightened renderings of encounter with an increasingly open frankness regarding the body marks Cather's early short stories. Cather shapes her micro-narratives by an abiding sense that meetings are always framed, always 'cultured': tropes and patterns from art, drama and fiction might inform the meeting. For the Ambassador, Mrs Ebbing is a person, but also an image: 'My mind played constantly with her image. At one moment she was very clear and directly in front of me; the next she was far away.'[31] The final element moving within this story, the sensory possibility that Cather found by working with a male narrator, opens up a different, gendered register of sensory apprehension: 'I had been watching from the rail, and when she was left alone I threw my cigar away and wrapped Mrs. Ebbling up roughly.'[32] Not only could Cather position herself wrapping up a female character, but she could also do so 'roughly' (after cavalierly throwing away a cigar). Changing the gender of one's narrator shifts sensory orders so as to imagine (as here) movements 'decisive' in their masculine immediacy and harshness.

'Coming, Aphrodite!'

'Coming, Aphrodite!' (1920) was, intriguingly, subtitled 'A Complete Novelette' when first published as 'Coming, Eden Bower!' in *Smart Set*; it certainly has an imaginative latitude and range belying its length. This captivating, idiosyncratic short story encapsulates the distinctive entwining of narrative experimentation with body-pictures that became the hallmark of Cather's major works. In particular, it deployed one of her favoured techniques: the inset or embedded narrative/micro-narrative. Cather often employs such inset narratives to reinforce the bodily thematics of her stories. In fact, one might almost generalise that if Cather deployed an inset narrative, or 'nouvelle' (the term she applied to 'Tom Outland's Story' in *The Professor's House*), then it was more or less certain that inset narrative would become a bodily insertion into the master narrative – and an even starker delineation of the body's sensory embeddedness in the world. These inset tales, apparently diversionary, even distracting on a first reading, work as both counterpoints and reinforcements of the central narrative. In Cather's storyworld, to move out of a main narrative is simply to move aside from and then back toward the senses. The impression is of something like a feint – the story moving toward another story, another level of fictionalisation, which in turn routes us back toward the sensory, the body. Each narrative level becomes, as it were, another form of re-embodiment, a reinstantiation of Catherian materialism.

In 'Coming Aphrodite!' the strangest turn in the story comes when the protagonist Hedger relates a tale from 'Ancient Mexico' about an Aztec king's daughter – a story based on a folkloric narrative she had heard from her guide, Julio, in the Southwest in 1912. For Cather, listening to Julio was 'like hearing a new language spoken' (*SL* 158).[33] The violent, erotic tale that follows shows how Hedger, painter and voyeur, is none the less a teller of tales (and able to turn his female cynosure, Eden, into a listener), and a fashioner of narratives possessing great sensory power. This is a tale of taste, touch, smell. The Princess falls in love with a captured chief, tattooed with 'the figures of wild animals, bitten into the skin and coloured', and she herself then 'submitted herself to the bone needle'(*YBM* 51). The chief then ravishes the Princess, and is captured, gelded and made her slave. So far, so physical. In the next stage of the narrative the Princess is married off to become Queen of the Aztecs. But she takes lovers, unknown to the King, though abetted by the Captive who continues to serve her. As each lover departs, the Captive makes sure they fall into an underground river, until one day when the Queen keeps the Captain of Archers with her for four days. Discovered at last by the King, the Queen now meets her fate – 'put to death by fire' along with her lover (*YBM* 54). Intense physicality runs like a thread through this narrative: the Princess is initially attracted to the Captive because of his tattoos; then there is her own tattooing; the castration; the endless seductions; the eventual *auto-da-fe*. It would be hard to imagine a tale more intensely focused on the body. The Aztec universe Cather imagines is relentlessly corporeal: a realm of scored skin, ripped-out flesh and burnings.

My three hermeneutic outlines suggest some of the ways that Cather used sketches, vignettes and inset narratives to remodel narrative. Whether writing about the local Lincoln scene, or creating an orientalist fantasy about ancient Aztecs, Cather reconfigured the basic building blocks of her narratives to foreground embodiment, and then to create fascinating conjunctions and juxtapositions focused on corporeal experience. In these three cases, Cather was working with short forms (stories and vignettes); her major fiction would build out from this model, accumulating and accreting body-sketches into larger narrative structures. As my later chapters show, this technique would establish templates for creating fictions encompassing the sensory diversity of American experience: the food worlds of colonial Quebec and the Southwestern mesas; the tactile world of slavery; the auditory cultures of the Midwest's performance spaces; the mapping of folk cultures surrounding flowers and their meanings.

The Body Studies Context

Recent work in Disability Studies has helped shape my thinking. Writers such as Rosamond Garland-Thomson (*Staring: How We Look*), Lennard Davis (*Enforcing Normalcy*), Tobin Siebers (*Disability Aesthetics*) and Michael Davidson (*Invalid Modernism*) inform this book's discussions on a very local level (for instance, the analysis of the visualised interaction between Blinker and Cécile, in *Shadows on the Rock*, that forms part of Chapter 4). And this scholarship also establishes a more general critical context for my work, demonstrating that 'invalid' bodies (Davidson's pun being highly intentional) or 'extra-ordinary' bodies are often central to writing (and to cultural representation in general).

'Body Studies' covers a wide range of interdisciplinary work that has emerged during the last three decades. Most scholars would probably see writings by Michel Foucault, as well as those of Deleuze and Guattari, as the foundation of this new field. David Hillman and Ulrika Maude introduce their collection of essays in this subject area as being 'broadly speaking historico-materialist in their approach'.[34] One might see the current scholarly field as being characterised by the application of such historico-materialist paradigms to specific instances of representation, where one begins to see the aesthetic creating new forms of embodiment, new ways of representing the human form. Thus, Peter J. Capuano's recent study of nineteenth-century fiction and its scientific contexts, *Changing Hands: Industry, Evolution, and the Reconfiguration of the Victorian Body*, looks at the ways that the Industrial Revolution and Darwinist evolutionary theory led to novelists reimagining the human hand and what it might do. Abbie Garrington's *Haptic Modernism: Touch and the Tactile in Modernist Writing* is another such work where historical contextualisation aids in understanding literature in terms of representational shifts that 'reconfigured' (to use Capuano's term) the body. Recent work in Cinema Studies (which I draw on in this study) has been particularly important in showing how technological shifts create representational remodellings that often focus on the human body: hence the suggestive title of Jonathan Auerbach's *Body Shots: Early Cinema's Incarnations*, and hence Jennifer Barker's exploration of how cinema not only works on a visual level but also suggests other forms of sensory experience, notably touch, in *The Tactile Eye: Touch and the Cinematic Experience*. This willingness to look at aesthetic experience through a range of sensory models has become a feature of very recent scholarship, such as Peter Dent's collection of essays on the tactile experience of sculpture (rather than the more obvious *viewing* of forms).[35] What we seem to be witnessing is a blending of the 'historico-materialist' analysis with a poly-centred attention to how the senses (touch as well as sight, notably) inform modes of representation and aesthetic experience.

Alongside this large-scale conceptual framing, *Sensing Willa Cather* draws on recent Cather criticism that helps us understand the specific contexts of her representations of the body. She wrote widely about art, performance and opera, not to mention a vast range of literature (from the United States, but also Britain, France and Russia) – and this journalism and occasional writing often took the body as its focus, as many of my chapters show. This study deploys a diverse range of scholarship that has mapped these corporealised connections and intertextualities. In particular, I often draw on *Cather Studies*, the central venue for publishing work in this area.

Second, the growth of queer studies of Cather and her work has generated a range of important readings of performativity, selfhood and sexuality – and these analyses underpin my overall approach to understanding her sensory narratives. The body is, typically, central to these readings. For Marilee Lindemann, 'Exemplary or abject, revelatory or duplicitous, the looked-at body in Cather's fiction is . . . a "queer" body because . . . it is made ec-centric – off-center in the sense of not fully belonging to the person who inhabits it.' Lindemann then goes on to read Crazy Ivar, the isolated eccentric in *O Pioneers!*, in terms of queerness: he is a figure seemingly outside the normative societal order, 'terrorized by the specter of the queerness within himself'.[36] This study locates Lindemann's understanding of Cather's queer bodies at a sensory level: in fictional discourses microcosmically alert to how characters see or hear or taste otherness and difference.

Conclusion: Reading This Book

I have organised this book both contextually and (in a very loose fashion) chronologically. The opening two chapters deal with two of the main cultural contexts that framed and fashioned the early parts of Cather's career: the emergence of proto-Modernist ideas at the end of the nineteenth century and the importance of Aestheticism in her early thinking about culture. These two chapters trace the significance of figures such as Ibsen, Oscar Wilde and George du Maurier for Cather. I look at how she reviewed and commented on them, and trace a network of tropes and representative figures (for example, the figure of the male aesthete, or the female artist, or the 'living statue') that Cather then developed from her understanding of 1890s Aestheticism. In these initial archaeological forays, I argue that Cather was very much a child of Aestheticism and the 1890s, and that she nevertheless explored questions raised by that movement in her work, which was written largely during Modernism's heyday.

Loosely (but not entirely) chronological, the subsequent six chapters address the five senses (sight, sound, touch, taste, smell) in her work. The initial chapters tend to focus on early works, the latter on later works such as *Shadows on the Rock*. A final chapter concentrates on Cather's own image (in Edward Steichen's famous portrait of her, for example) and then ties that self-imaging to patterns of looking in *Sapphira and the Slave Girl* and the broader sensorium in that narrative. I finish with Cather's own physical entry into the concluding pages of that novel (Cather imagining herself as a young girl, entering into the drama), a *deus ex machina* moment which I read as the conclusion to a creative career built on narrativising corporealism.

Although the argument steadily progresses through Cather's writing, I am also concerned with complex patterns across and between stages of Cather's writing. Cather circled around a cluster of preoccupations (themes, tropes, figures, situations, questions) throughout her career. In the 1890s she was writing about the figure of the diva and the psychological and cultural impact of the female voice on listeners; in *Lucy Gayheart* (1935), decades later, she continued to map and remap questions surrounding musical charisma.

I think of Cather's career as taking the shape of an extended tapestry or mural, an extended imagining that embraces novels, journalism, short fiction and even her own interviews. Her own *œuvre* should be considered the written counterpart to a Puvis de Chavannes mural: a narrative broken into panels but with linkages across the separate parts.

In order to trace those linkages, I also endeavour to read as widely as possible across Cather's remarkably heterogeneous range of writing. The novels themselves remain my overall focus, but to read those novels alongside the reviews or – as we now can – the letters is to sense holistically how Cather (as much as any major novelist) worked to create a body of work contoured around a nexus of interests. Thus, to read an early theatre review, written when Cather was a student, alongside episodes from *Sapphira* is to see how Cather continually used complex geometries of social viewing in her work. *Sensing Willa Cather* draws on what might be called the 'new Cather archive' – that assemblage of letters and manuscript materials now concentrated at the University of Nebraska–Lincoln and other institutions. Such materials add a biographical foundation to Cather's preoccupations with the body and its representations (my footnotes contain a number of such references). The manuscript materials (including a relatively recent discovery of a draft fragment of *Sapphira and the Slave Girl*) also enable one to see how Cather rewrote and edited key sentences, such as those describing the black body, thus demonstrating how as a (self-)editor she paused and reconsidered descriptive sentences.

Cather said of the Southwest's churches in her 1927 letter about *Death Comes for the Archbishop*: 'They are their own story, and it is foolish convention that we must have everything interpreted for us in written language' (OW 5–6). I have tried, in the studies that follow, to read Cather as a narrative artist fascinated by what might be 'interpreted for us in written language'. Writing about sight and sound, touch, taste and smell, Cather created narratives that emerged from late Victorian culture but anticipated Modernism's fascination with body and text, and therefore with representation itself. Cather became a 'body artist', a 'body teller', a reshaper of narrative forms she had inherited from the nineteenth century (the vignette or sketch, the review of performance, the journalistic account of a meeting with a writer) – a complex project driven by her fascination with the sensory grounds of human experience.

Notes

1. West, *The Strange Necessity*, 215.
2. Changes in the literary executorship of Cather's estate, followed by a review of her will, led to the publication of the *Selected Letters*. 'And now we flagrantly defy Cather's will in the belief that her decision, made in the last, dark years of her life and honored for more than half a century, is outweighed by the value of making these letters available to readers all over the world,' note the editors, Andrew Jewell and Janis Stout (*SL*, vii).
3. Mauss, 'Techniques of the Body', 71–2.
4. Ibid. 73.
5. Ibid. 85.
6. Geurts, *Culture and the Senses*, 243–4.
7. Ibid. 17.
8. Kittler, *Gramophone, Film, Typewriter*.
9. Walker, *Expressionism and Modernism in the American Theatre: Bodies, Voices, Words*, 1.
10. Cather and Milmine, *The Life of Mary Baker G. Eddy and the History of Christian Science*, 179.
11. Ibid. 180.
12. Ibid. 199.
13. Ibid. 209.
14. Bourne, 'The Handicapped – By One of Them', 320.
15. Ibid. 320.
16. Ibid. 322.
17. Ibid. 324.
18. Ibid. 324.
19. Cather, 'Peter', 11.
20. Ibid. 11.
21. Clere, *Troubling Bodies*, 17.
22. Hicks, 'The Case Against Willa Cather'.
23. Anonymous, 'Puvis de Chavannes', 31.
24. Price, *Pierre Puvis de Chavannes I: The Artist and His Art*, 167.
25. Keeler, 'Narrative Without Accent: Willa Cather and Puvis de Chavannes', 122.
26. Giorcelli, 'Willa Cather and Pierre Puvis de Chavannes', 73.
27. For an account of Cather and impressionist painters see Asad Al-Ghalith, 'Cather's Use of Light: An Impressionistic Tone'. Al-Ghalith discusses Cather's interest in figures such as Gari Melchers, Alfred Sisley, Camille Corot and H. O. Tanner.
28. Cather, 'One Way of Putting It' (17 December 1893), 13.
29. Cather, 'On the Gulls' Road', 145.
30. Ibid. 145–6.
31. Ibid. 147.

32. Ibid. 150.
33. This letter (to Elizabeth Shepley Sergeant: 21 May 1912) is perhaps the first formulation of that dual movement into an archaic, non-white American past and a 'new language' of body-writing that then animated texts such as 'Tom Outland's Story' and *Death Comes for the Archbishop*.
34. Hillman and Maude, *The Cambridge Companion to the Body in Literature*, 3.
35. Auerbach, *Body Shots*; Jennifer M. Barker, *The Tactile Eye*; Peter Dent, *Sculpture and Touch*; Capuano, *Changing Hands: Industry, Evolution, and the Reconfiguration of the Victorian Body*; and Garrington, *Haptic Modernism: Touch and the Tactile in Modernist Writing*. Connor's *The Book of Skin* is another example of a pan- or multi-sensory reading of culture. See also: MacDougall, *The Corporeal Image: Film, Ethnography, and the Senses*; Marks, *The Skin of the Film: Intercultural Cinema, Embodiment, and the Senses*.
36. Lindemann, *Willa Cather: Queering America*, 35–7.

CHAPTER 2

Cather's Bodily Art and the Emergence of Modernism

Cather was very much a child of the late nineteenth century and its literary–artistic cultures. Her fascination with opera and Romanticism, her highly Eurocentric aesthetic, her deployment of Gothic motifs and her ambivalent relationship to literary Decadence: these are all well-known aspects of an 1890s mind shaped by voracious reading and a phenomenal appetite for culture.[1] But Cather then had many years of apprenticeship (essentially the two decades from her time as a 'college prep' student at the University of Nebraska from 1890 up to her leaving *McClure's Magazine* to launch a full-time writing career). That career, in its broadest configuration, was a remarkable experiment where a provincial late Victorian sensibility – shaped by figures such as Ibsen, Wagner and Puvis de Chavannes – was then kept *in utero* until she transitioned to a very different time and place: New York City on the very cusp of Modernism.

Cather's Ibsen

Henrik Ibsen fascinated the young Cather, his work remaining a lodestar for her conceptions of Realism for decades. A key figure in the literary culture of the 1880s and 1890s, Ibsen was central to arguments about a 'literary drama' that would create a more socially responsive, artistically complex and ethically alert form of theatre. Writing about the transformation of late Victorian theatre, John Stokes notes,

Change, when it came, was belated and partial, with Ibsen largely responsible. In his middle and later periods Ibsen inaugurated a theatrical debate into the great issues of the day: the claims of women, the call for leadership, the function of religion, the nature of creativity and, above all, the need to engage with the future.[2]

Henry James's 1893 essay 'On the Occasion of *Hedda Gabler*' read Ibsen as a figure whose work had come to encapsulate the Zeitgeist, as a 'barometer', a figure in whose writings current preoccupations reached their most powerful crystallisation:

> Whether or no Henrik Ibsen be a master of his art, he has had a fortune that, in the English-speaking world, falls not always even to the masters – the fortune not only of finding himself the theme of many pens and tongues, but the rarer privilege and honour of acting as a sort of register of the critical atmosphere, a barometer of the intellectual weather.[3]

For James, Ibsen was a form of master mapper, a figure whose work helped to shape critical debate (because critics would have to respond to him in one way or another) and who showed 'the prospect' of where playwriting might now go: 'He has cleared up the air we breathe and set a copy to our renouncement; has made many things wonderfully plain and quite mapped out the prospect.'[4]

James's comments from the early 1890s help frame Cather's referencing of the Norwegian during that decade. A tyro critic, Cather was keen to show her familiarity with the edginess denoted by his work. At the start of her career, she repeatedly alluded to Ibsen in ways that show she had identified him as a cultural signifier, a symbol of the progressive and experimental forces in modern theatre. Generally, Ibsen took his place in Cather's early writing as one of those names she deployed to show her familiarity with the people who would have been on the lips of London's or New York's most *au fait* theatre-goers: Sarah Bernhardt, Eleanora Druse, Henrik Ibsen, Ellen Terry. Her early reviews reached back into the longer-term history of drama but showed a thoroughly journalistic edginess in her willingness to shape a sense of the cultural present, the 'now' where the spectator would find the latest productions and performers.

Cather certainly nailed her colours to the mast in her earliest writings, pledging allegiance to one of the late 1800s' most controversial, radical figures. 'Realism is a protest against lies' was the flat assertion made in an essay she wrote for the university's paper, the *Hesperian*, in 1892. The still-teenage Cather lauded Ibsen for his Bohemian independence from bourgeois values and his ability to see through ideals that had become masks:

> By ideals he does not mean that progressive series of elevated types, which lives in our imagination, and without which progress would be impossible in this world. To Ibsen, the ideal man is the man without ideals. But he means the mass of false, conventional, inorganic conceptions of goodness to which we are all slaves. The courage to live our lives without idea[l]s is the sum and substance of all earthly wisdom.[5]

She nearly repeated this assertion six years later when working as a professional journalist for the Pittsburgh *Leader*. Confidently addressing George Bernard Shaw as if she were his peer, Cather wrote: 'Let Mr. Shaw turn him to his master, Ibsen, and read *The Wild Duck* over again, and he will find that it is a dangerous business, this tearing our life-lies away from us.'[6]

Cather's responses to Ibsen confirm her 1890s fascination with aesthetic and philosophical radicalism, with artists who saw through 'conventional ... conceptions of goodness'. She also registered this impact using an idiosyncratically physical and bodily language: ideas embodied, quite literally. By 1894, Cather had already developed a critical language that interpreted art in terms of intense physical contact. Ibsen's plays, she wrote in the *Nebraska State Journal*, have been 'thrilling and chilling us for so long'; 'Ibsen has already sent a shiver over the bare shoulders of the theatrical world.'[7] The image is characteristically Catherian in its flamboyant physicality, its sense of audience and cultural reception, and its dedication to a certain shock value. The theatrical world she imagines metonymically in terms of the bare shoulders of the female theatre-goer thrilling to the cold touch of the radical outsider Ibsen. The 'five senses' (of Cather) lauded by Rebecca West are already coming into play in images of art's impact that privilege physical encounter and tactile encounter.

The key to grasping Cather's long evolution as a writer is to read through and along the arcs of commitment that link the 1890s to the 1920s and 1930s. Cather remained remarkably consistent in many of her literary–cultural passions, but within that matrix of devotion and fascination she found great creative plenitude. Considering Cather's 1890s fascination with the 'chilling' and 'thrilling' outsider figure of Ibsen, the 1891 writer is not that distant from Cather in 1925, imagining Professor St Peter's disillusion, his near-suicide, and his thoroughly Ibsenesque resolve to live on the 'bloomless side of life' (*TPH* 280).

As a writer with a strong interest in Scandinavian culture that had been fostered largely by simply growing up amongst so many immigrants, Cather found herself drawn to these Northern artists and writers.[8] Receptivity to the Northern experimenters placed her at the leading edge of late Victorian art and aesthetics. Arnold Weinstein groups figures such as Ibsen, Strindberg, Munch and Hamsun under the umbrella term *'Breakthrough'*, describing 'a generation of writers appearing in the last few decades of the nineteenth century, linked loosely together against the bourgeois values and assumptions of their age'. Weinstein argues against the 'slightly stolid' received image, for instance, of Ibsen's realism, pointing to the 'stunning acrobatics and the destabilizing – indeed revolutionary – energies at work in many of these plays'.[9]

But Ibsen had other telling points to make about the relation of literature to society and the roles of women as protagonists in art and drama. He was also the figurehead of the 'literary drama' being championed by *fin-de-siècle* critics such as William Archer. In place of pure spectacle and the commercial theatre, the literary drama offered a more complex, more highly verbal and denser aesthetic. Drama, for proselytes such as Archer, might now aspire to the sophistication and public status of the novel. In 'The Free Stage and the New Drama' (1891), Archer deployed Ibsen's work as one sign of the shift toward this more resonant dramatic form.[10] Archer advocated for Ibsen both in his critical writings and as a translator. Broadly speaking, his campaign for a more literary, a more aesthetically complex drama, and a drama with a strong public role, placed Ibsen at the centre of a theatrical revolution.

Cather knew William Archer well; they met during her tour of

England in 1906. It was, perhaps, Archer who suggested to Cather that she might live in England. As late as 1939, Cather was writing detailed accounts of her relationship with the Scottish translator, critic and drama theorist. In a 1939 letter to Ferris Greenslet, Cather was at pains to discount Archer's play, *The Green Goddess* (1921), while praising his translations of Ibsen – 'The man who first translated and popularized Ibsen in English, did a great service to the English stage' (*SL* 573). Here we can see the quixotic nature of Cather's receptivity to influence. Her statement that the 'world broke in two in 1922' is often cited by scholars who want to stress her 'stern antimodernism', to quote Michael North.[11] Yet if Cather was not a high Modernist of the 1920s, she remained committed to the pre- and proto-Modernist aesthetics of the 1890s. Her fascination with Ibsen, and her close friendship with his translator and advocate, Archer, demonstrate a kind of 'trace' that deserves note, a buried genealogy of influence that suggestively creates an image of Cather as a radical remodeller of Realism in the Ibsenesque sense, a diagnostician of bourgeois life keen to strip away its artifices to find a more nuanced (and perhaps brutal) form of social realism. If we think of the chamber realism that Cather created in the 1920s, we can see how *My Mortal Enemy* (with its plaintive bitter cry, 'Why must I die like this, alone with my mortal enemy?') used an Ibsenesquely astringent form of Realism to refashion the marriage plot.

Cather as Reviewer: The Reviewer as Creator

Cather's entry into culture was through performance: first, as a high-school actor (sometimes playing the male roles in productions in her home town, Red Cloud), then as an orator (her high-school commencement address is often seen by biographers as her first serious piece of critical writing), and then as a reviewer of music and theatre during her undergraduate career.[12] Cather was a performer and a reviewer of performance first and foremost during her teenage and student days, and then as a journalist it was also performance that preoccupied her and provided the initial testing-ground for her ideas about the 'kingdom of art'.[13]

Cather had come of age at a time when performance was the

centre of debates about female artistry, about the struggle between high and low/literary and popular forms of production, about the identity of the playwright, not to mention ongoing and often legalistic arguments about censorship. Some of the *fin de siècle*'s dominant cultural motifs found embodiment on the stage, most notably through the emergence of the New Woman. And the increasing internationalism of literary culture – a process aided and accelerated by the growth of literary and cultural journalism – was symbolised by what can be called the 'Ibsen wars': the debates over the Norwegian playwright's works and their significance, debates which preoccupied British, continental and American commentators.

As a viewer and reviewer of performance, as well as a performer herself, Cather was at the centre of a contested cultural matrix, monitoring the metropolitan debates from afar and then, increasingly, entering into the conversation herself. By the time she had established herself as a journalist by 1900, Cather, still under thirty, had already mapped out the preoccupations that she would then transpose into her fiction. Thus, performance became central to her fictional representations of social encounter, while her fiction often centred on a female artist's body (then viewed, contested and celebrated). In myriad ways, Cather's fiction of the early twentieth century was, in fact, an elaborate answer to questions posed by the theatrical culture of the late nineteenth century, a thinking-through of debates that had preoccupied critics and writers in the 1880s and 1890s.

Cather had come of age at a remarkably propitious moment for a young writer, especially one with her interests. Superficially, she seemed on the edge of culture, far from the metropolitan centres of performance. In fact, Lincoln had a thriving and expansive theatre culture, and Cather seems to have arrived in the town at a transformational moment in the development of that theatre culture. In 1885, the refurbished Funke Opera House opened. In 1891, the massive Lansing Theatre opened in the centre of town (it had 2,000 seats plus room for hundreds of standing customers).[14] These major theatres were close to the university campus in a town that was still relatively compact. The train network, a constant feature of Cather's Nebraskan novels, enabled touring companies to use Lincoln as a convenient stopping point on journeys that might be taking them to the bigger cities of Omaha, Denver and Chicago.[15]

Oscar Wilde's famous 1882 tour of the United States included a stop in Lincoln (his hotel was a handful of blocks from the recently established university). Cather always used the materials available to her, and prominent amongst those materials were the opera houses, theatres and concert halls that dotted even the rawest of Frontier states (it is estimated that Nebraska at one point had 500 opera houses – this term being the preferred one since it associated performance with the classier world of opera rather than the more risqué world of theatre, with its painted women).

Cather's early novels map in their imaginative topographies a keen sense of the proximity of performance spaces to the everyday world of business or education. In her *fin-de-siècle* cities, going to the theatre is always a possibility. In the section of *My Ántonia* where Jim moves to Lincoln to study at the university, Cather creates a quite distinctive modelling of young peoples' lives in Progressive Era America. Both Jim Burden and Lena Lingard leave liminal lives, beginning to make their own way after leaving their family homes. Jim has a mentor, Gaston Cleric (and much like Tom Outland in *The Professor's House*, he lives in a kind of homosocial education world made up of young men and their male mentors). Lingard works as a seamstress; Jim studies hard (and will move on to Harvard). But their social milieu is a performative one as much as it is entrepreneurial and educational. Jim and Lena also go to the theatre, a glimpse into Cather's sense of just how deeply interwoven theatre life was into the ordinary textures of towns such as Lincoln. The compact centre of a rapidly developing provincial city such as Lincoln brought education, transport, commerce and entertainment together within a ten-block downtown. A young person such as Cather, recently arrived from the raw prairies, might really feel she was at the centre of things. For the spatiality of Cather's novels, in terms of their urbanism, is very distinctive: the reader is continually made aware of just how close, how sheerly proximately the performative, the domestic and the business worlds exist. One might say that Cather is simply making an obvious, realistic point. In Cather's late nineteenth-century cities, the bourgeois world of commerce and family was deeply intertwined with a performative space that could sometimes offer a quasi-Bohemian alterity within the cityscape.

In Cather's exploratory reviews of the early to mid-1890s, when she was still an undergraduate in Lincoln, the young critic mapped a distinctively new social space: the stage, with its distinctive new personae and the scopic world of the theatre-goer gazing down on a performer who might, Medusa-like, return the stare. Cather reviewed theatre but she also used theatre-going as a laboratory space to imagine new forms of identity, new forms of social and cultural exchange. Issues of class, taste, cultural status and gender identity were always in play, mapped out in the performative exchanges played out on provincial stages. Cather fiercely condemned or valorised productions and performers. But she also used theatre-going as a narrative laboratory, a forum where minimalist narratives of viewing and bare human contact might reverberate into deeper, extended stories of recall and affect.

'One Way of Putting It' was published in the *Nebraska State Journal* on 3 December 1893, when Cather was still nineteen. A 'review', it is also a sketch, a brief vignette of theatre life focused with an unsettling sense of the modern on cross-gazing between members of an audience as a performance unfolds before them. It started with a look:

> The man had a white face and a rather serious, pained expression between the eyes. He sat alone in the dress circle, looking over the audience with his opera glasses. He came almost every night to the theatre, and he was always alone. Sometimes he left at the close of the first act, even when the play was particularly good, and when he remained he appeared to be more interested in the audience than the play. That night he was watching a woman sitting on the other side of the house.[16]

On one level this short vignette is filled with a fairly shopworn language of romantic desire, an operatically idealistic language that seems over-familiar, the romantic glance and so on. On another, it represents a startlingly experimental entrée into narrative itself. The expected romantic scenario has been fragmented, its narrative split and reshaped by the intersection of performance and memory. In the new space of theatre the viewer becomes crucial, the viewer's dreams and reveries as significant as the performance itself. Desire moves in strange circuits, not only toward the performer but also across and between members of the audience. The gaze has become fractured and is remade. Instead of looking at the actress, the male viewer (envisaged by the female author) now looks upon another member of the audience, another man's partner. There is recklessness and compulsion in Cather's imaginary encounter (he had 'seen it come to pass night by night'), and also a sense that the bourgeois world (theatre visits, marriages) contains complex vectors of contact and desire that work relentlessly within the putatively placid structures of everyday life. Note, too, the dreamlike quality of the scenario, the blending of the fictional and the real, the interpenetration of performed drama and everyday life:

> The curtains rose and the play began, but still he kept his eyes fixed upon the woman and the man beside her. There was no particular mystery about his watching her, that was all he came there for, to see another man do what he had failed to do to see a girl come into the glory of her womanhood.
> The passionate tones of the great actress on the stage fell lightly upon his ear, for he saw two other people who were not watching the play very intently. It seemed to him then that she grew more and more beautiful and radiant with every rise of the white lace on her breast. At the end of the third act she and the man beside her rose and went out because the thousand other men and women were de trop. The lonely man on the left, in the dim light that was made for the heroine to die in, leaned his head on the rest in front of him and wondered why he had been created.[17]

Late Victorian American provincial culture had, in other words, a more complex scopic configuration than we might at first imagine. Even the most provincial of towns had their performative spaces where new modalities of encounter were emerging. Cather's sense of performative space is one where the audience is always significant, and where the gaze has become splintered, fractured and reconfigured. Male spectators might gaze at female performers but, Medusa-like, the performer might also exert a countervailing power, a reverse gaze that might hold, contain and control the male viewer's agency.

The Nethersole Kiss

The actress's corporealism had become a locus for late Victorian debates about gender identity and the unsettling shifts (for many) in the representation of the female body. Actresses whose careers Cather knew well, whom she had seen and whose writings she knew had also begun to widen the role of the actress, becoming businesswomen who produced their own plays, acted as (self-)publicists and then wrote their own life stories (for instance, Sarah Bernhardt's *My Double Life* appeared in an English translation in 1907).

The actress now had an autonomy and a celebrity status that might overshadow the authority of the writer himself. As Cather's friend, William Archer, observed of Sarah Bernhardt, 'she does not dream of taking a great piece of literature and bending her genius to its interpretation. It is the playwright's business to interpret *her*.'[18] A greater diversity of female characters had begun to appear on the stage; many were controversial, sometimes transgressive. 'In the second half of the nineteenth century, new spectacles of feminine suffering began to appear on the fashionable French and English stages as audiences were mesmerised by the figure of the fallen woman and the actresses who played her.'[19] The courtesan, the disgraced wife or the prostitute: theatre was incorporating figures from the edge of respectability. The most significant courtesan role was, of course, that of Marguerite Gautier, the protagonist of *La Dame aux camélias*. The latter was the 1852 stage adaptation of the 1848 novel by Alexandre Dumas, *fils*, the drama that became known in English as *Camille* and then became the basis for further adaptation as Verdi's *La Traviata* (1853). Sarah Bernhardt played Gautier in an 1898 production of the play.[20]

Another major figure, Olga Nethersole, the progenitor of the infamous 'Nethersole kiss' (which I discuss more fully in Chapter 5), was a figure that Cather saw on the Lincoln stage. As Katie N. Johnson writes, it was Nethersole's role as producer of the play that was crucial. The source was Alphonse Daudet's 1884 novel, *Sapho*, then adopted by the American playwright Clyde Fitch. But the British actress–producer Nethersole was heavily involved in steering the adaptation. 'Nethersole's name might not have been on the script, but she was instrumental in shaping the project.'[21] Nethersole brought together the female producer's business acumen and power with a subversive exploration and remapping of identity. In an 1899 *Cosmopolitan* article, 'My Struggles to Succeed', she wrote about her 'heart-wearing and spirit-breaking' theatre work, continuing to say that 'often it has seemed that I was rolling a stone up a hill only to have it fall back threatening to crush the spirit out of me'.[22]

Cather wrote about Olga Nethersole a number of times in 1894. In her 1 March *Nebraska State Journal* column, 'Between the Acts', she reported news from London, commenting on Nethersole's role in *The Transgressor*, a play written by A. W. Guthrie. The drama had a *Jane Eyre*-like plot about a man whose first wife is insane and who proceeds to commit bigamy. This mischievously typical Cather early review was an exercise in cultural appropriation, a re-formation and transmission. The student critic replayed and rewrote reports of the London stage (which she might well have gleaned from East Coast papers that had made their way to Lincoln). Reviewing thus gave Cather an entrée into culture, a way to report on metropolitan life from the provinces. Entering culture through reviewing, Cather must have used a tissue or palimpsest of sources to create her own sense of what the performance worlds of London, New York and Chicago must have been like, while running alongside those received narratives her own encounters with Lincoln theatre. This dynamic, where the provincial connoisseur or artist encounters culture alive on what Fitzgerald in *The Great Gatsby* called 'the ragged edge of the known universe', while also coming across accounts of culture shaped in the great cities of the East or Europe, would underpin some of Cather's creative works, notably stories such as 'A Wagner Matinée' or 'The Sculptor's Funeral'.

By 16 September 1894, Cather was still thinking about Olga Nethersole and using what she knew of Nethersole's reputation to make unfavourable contrasts with another actress, Julia Marlowe. Cather compared British-born Marlowe's classical style with that of Sarah Bernhardt, Nethersole and the famed Italian actress Eleonora Duse. She had pinpointed three of the most controversial actresses of the era and contrasted their expressive and Romantic styles against that of Marlowe. If Marlowe goes to London, that is still all a throb with the tragedy of Duse, of Bernhardt and of Olga Nethersole, she will not make a ripple in the troubled tide. Her classic tones will be literally drowned by the great passions that have surged over the London stage as by the roar of a torrent.[23]

This comment elevates Cather's paradoxical relationship with performance (the reviewer absent from the centres of performance but intimate with provincial performance to a fanatical degree) to a cheeky extreme.

Edith Lewis singled out the early reviews of the English actress Olga Nethersole's performance as *Carmen* in her account of Cather's Pittsburgh years. Cather had sensed the idiosyncrasy of Nethersole's performance:

> This strange English girl, with a physique neither powerful nor imposing, a face by no means beautiful, and a voice that in spite of its emotional range and its hundred unexpected tricks of flexibility, is always just a little harsh ... She is not pretty, not even good-looking, but she can make you believe anything.[24]

Cather had at last seen the new, expressive style that Nethersole had brought to the stage. She could now line herself up with the other critics whose responses Cather had been appropriating for several months. Witnessing Nethersole, Cather could fit her own responses alongside those of the metropolitan critics:

> I have noted with pleasure that in one thing all her critics are unanimous in lavish and enthusiastic praise of her first act. They say that in abandon, in recklessness, in the touch of pitiful bravado which characterizes Bohemia, in the true demi monde idea of Dumas, in the hundred details of that first act she is unsurpassed.[25]

The review is fascinating for its attempt to read acting style and female performance within a wide-frame cultural context. Cather argued that Nethersole managed to transcend the limitations of being English but needed to go much further to become a French coquette:

But if Miss Nethersole can play the Camille of the first act, can overcome her traditions, nationality, instincts, and be thoroughly and entirely a French coquet and a woman of the demi monde of Paris, then she has the ability to take unto herself the spirit of all times and lands, the power to 'live in all lives that are and love in all loves that be.[26]

As with a good deal of Cather's reviewing from Lincoln in the 1890s, this piece raises many captivating questions. While a student, Cather had seen an English actress play what might be thought of as one of the most French of roles. She focused her attention on the national identity of the actress, but also saw performance as a place where one might assume a different cultural identity. A vital space – the theatre – could become a laboratory where selfhood might be performed and reconfigured. There is a powerfully cosmopolitan edge to Cather's appraisal, a sense that the better an actress Nethersole can become, the more likely she will be to 'take unto herself the spirit of all times and lands'. Cather here sees theatrical culture in terms of female performance, but also in terms of national self-making or, even more significantly, in terms of 'un-self-making' and what might even be a form of passing into another national identity. What is important about the review is that Nethersole was renowned for the expressiveness and passion of her performances. 'As an actress,' a recent commentary has argued, 'Nethersole was of the Romantic School and emphasized physical abandon and the vivid display of passionate extremes.'[27] Cather, though, seems to have wanted a yet more expressive, passionate Nethersole, and then she reframed that debate in terms of nationality. Rather than locating Nethersole in a framework shaped primarily by the actress's expression of sexual independence, Cather re-places Nethersole into a cultural matrix shaped by different European identities. Now, the question is not 'has Nethersole gone too far as an expressive actress?' but instead 'as an Englishwoman, can she go as far as she needs to, in playing a French coquette?'[28]

Identity, then, was performatively cast and recast as Cather watched Englishwomen becoming French, or women seemingly become men. For although Cather scholarship has traced many of the connections between Cather and the theatre, it has not always been clear just how queer Cather's sense of the theatre was. As a student reviewing dramatic and operatic performances in the new town of Lincoln, she was none the less witnessing some of the major figures pioneering, sometimes in highly controversial ways, new forms of being a self, as they took on roles on the stage that were both unsettling and revelatory.

For Cather, then, Nethersole was an edgy figure, as she was for the broader culture: writing in Lincoln in 1894, Cather had caught some of the actress's distinctive and discomfiting power. Then, in 1900, a New York court acquitted Nethersole at an indecency trial brought against Clyde Fitch's *Sapho* (1900). Based on Alphonse Daudet's French novel of 1884, Fitch's play had it all: the adulterous heroine, a relatively explicit moment of staged sexuality (as the characters walked toward a bedroom), French origins and an English actress. This was a major episode in the performance wars of late Victorian and early twentieth-century America: cultural disputes focused on the staged expression of desire and on the scandals surrounding key performers such as Sarah Bernhardt and Olga Nethersole.[29] Theresa Saxon points out that the attempted censorship of *Sapho* might well have been directly related to Nethersole herself, who had a racy reputation as a transgressive performer. She cites a review in one of the New York papers, the *World*: the actress 'plays immoral women because she knows that such exhibitions excite a morbid curiosity which theatre goers as a class are always willing to gratify'.[30]

The links between *Sapho*, Clyde Fitch, Olga Nethersole and Cather are quite clear. Cather had studied Daudet during her university career.[31] In a later letter to the Emily Dickinson scholar George Whicher (19 December 1924), Cather thanked him for asking her to give the 'Clyde Fitch lecture' and then says she will do so in a year or more. Had such a lecture been given, the quite complex web of connection between Cather and the English actress would have been apparent.[32]

'They had never discovered their bodies': 'Three American Singers'

Katie N. Johnson states that Nethersole 'scandalised her audiences not only with a kiss, but with her whole body'.[33] The body of the actress or the singer was one of Cather's great subjects, a leitmotif of her work over many decades. Thus, the essay Cather published in *McClure's* after she had finished writing for that magazine, 'Three American Singers' (1913), might be read as the capstone of her early career as a theatre/opera critic, as well as a prologue to what would follow in that decade: 'A Gold Slipper', 'Scandal' and *The Song of the Lark*. This triptych of portraits – the arrangement of narrative panels pointing forward to the episodic narrative principles Cather used throughout her career – is deeply instructive when we begin to think about how Cather shaped a narrative of the self out of her intense engagement with female performance. In her sketches of Louise Homer, Geraldine Farrar and Olive Fremstad, Cather focused on certain features of the performative life: nerves and nervousness, public representations (particularly in photographs), stasis and movement.

Nerves and Nervousness

Cather had begun to read characters within a matrix shaped by concerns about nerves and nervousness – that emergent fascination (shared by many writers and intellectuals) with what was known as 'neurasthenia'. F. Scott Fitzgerald's essay, 'The Crack-Up' (1936), would position the artist's breakdown squarely at the centre of American popular culture (and would presage the more spectacular drugged and mental breakdowns of Burroughs, Lowells and Plath). But as Jackson Lears points out, George Miller Beard's *American Nervousness* (1880) had already 'identified "neurasthenia," or "lack of nerve force," as the disease of the age'.[34] Cather's writing of the female artist's body occupies what is now recognised to be more or less the midpoint between the late nineteenth-century clinical identification of nervousness by scientists and the mid-twentieth-century absorption of 'breakdown' into confessional narratives. Cather's language of the body thus became highly transitional.

Cather writes of Louise Homer as follows: 'Probably her physical poise has a good deal to do with the evenness of her work. Her physical equipment is magnificent . . . her nerves are hidden under a smooth and strong exterior . . . She was never harassed by nervous strain.'[35] The Catherian body is a nervous body, but also a body that can be controlled – its surface and its exterior literally 'smooth'.

The objectifying of the body, a recurrent feature of Cather's writing, becomes part of a complex, quasi-mechanistic dynamic of both eruptive nervousness and an exteriority that hides such disruptive energy for the sake of performance. There is also, in Cather's emphasis on the 'smooth and strong' exterior of the singer's body (we might think of her descriptions of Thea's strong body in *O Pioneers!*), a proto-Modernist emphasis on *surface* (Modernism as turn to the surface after the 'depth' of Victorianism).[36] In her study of Josephine Baker (and her skin), Anne Anlin Cheng notes a transformational moment within Modernism:

> for a brief period in the early twentieth century, before cultural values collapsed back once again into a (shallow) surface and (authentic) interior divide, there was this tensile and delicate moment when these flirtations with the surface led to profound engagements with and reimaginings of the relationship between interiority and exteriority, between essence and covering.[37]

It is, surely, within this moment that we can situate much of Cather's writing about the surface of the performer's body – moments when interiority and exteriority fuse, or enter into a productive dialectic where the singer's control and composure (her inner discipline) is literally written on to her skin.

Photography: Imaging the Singer

The heyday of the nineteenth-century *cartes de visite* had been earlier in the century, but even at the end of the 1800s, celebrity photographs, and their assemblage into albums, remained important parts of the circulation of icons within popular visual culture.[38] In her account of actress postcards in Australia, Veronica Kelly notes that 'the early twentieth century is predominantly characterized by the mass production of cards of the female performer – the actress', and 'Mass-produced photographic portrait postcards of theatre identities are material documents of a significant social articulation of early modernity: artefacts which derive from theatrical practice, but succeed in extending charismatic presence and signifying potency far beyond their theatre-industrial origins.'[39] Hence the popular visual culture within which Cather wrote, with its complex mixture of the 'charismatic' and the 'industrial', the portraits of singular starts circulated through mass production.

Cather's 'Three American Singers' positions itself on the boundary between these 'theatre-industrial origins' and 'charismatic presence'. Indeed, the essay might be said to be (like much of her creative writing) an investigation of female charisma. Her fifteen-page essay included eleven images of the three singers, many of them showing the performer posed in costume, in stylised enactments of key scenes. Cather comments in detail on these images, and such commentary is historically startling, if we consider how relatively late in the day a sophisticated cultural criticism focused on photography emerged. In her sense of the image, particularly her sense of how the portrait is sensed by a viewer but also changes over and through time, Cather's writing anticipates that of Susan Sontag's *On Photography* (1977) or Roland Barthes in *Camera Lucida* (published in English in 1981). As with these later works of cultural criticism, Cather's writing is attentive to time, to the transformation of the face and body through temporality, and to the new forms of visual intimacy and knowledge that the camera has brought into everyday life. She writes of the imaging of Geraldine Farrar, 'There are some photographs of Miss Farrar taken at about this time, in which she looks very much like the child elocutionist of the ice-cream social.'[40] Then the young American moved to Paris: 'those early Paris photographs show a face over which wave after wave of that kind of beauty had passed, marking it as with little knives'.[41] In its interpretative *looking* at an image, this comment belongs to a time much later than 1913. Technology has brought the reading of a face through time into the currency of everyday human contact. We are all now the viewers or the spectators of the face, or the subjects of such imagining, and most of us have our own personal image archives (that is, photo albums, analogue or digital). Cather had lived through the beginnings of this radical visual revolution as a late Victorian American with access to new technologies.

Strikingly, the manœuvre we see here, of Cather looking at a face for the marks of time upon it, sensing the corporeal change implicit within a single image, would become a recurrent feature of her fiction's attention to the body. Hence the ironic ending of 'Coming,

Aphrodite!' (1920), with its sense of mutability and masking, of the changing permanence, of the actress's face:

> Leaning back in the cushions, Eden Bower closed her eyes, and her face, as the street lamps flashed their ugly orange light upon it, became hard and settled, like a plaster cast; so a sail, that has been filled by a strong breeze, behaves when the wind suddenly dies. Tomorrow night the wind would blow again, and this mask would be the golden face of Aphrodite. But a 'big' career takes its toll, even with the best of luck. (YBM 73–4)

Embodiment: Stasis and Movement

The viewing of the female body was a major feature of the 1890s culture in which Cather first made her name as a critic. Gail Marshall has explored the classical female figure, very much a feature of plays such as Harry Pleon's *A Vision of Venus* (1893). This work was based on Frederick Anstey's *The Tinted Venus* (1885), a novel about a statue of Venus mistakenly brought to life. London's Palace Theatre of Varieties also featured 'Living Pictures', which Marshall describes as 'carefully staged replicas of well-known paintings and sculptures', some of which were dressed in flesh-coloured tights to give the illusion of nakedness. Frederick Atkins wrote of one reaction to such a tableau: 'Up went the opera-glasses ... English men in raptures over an exhibition of girls standing in the glare of the electric light with nothing but thin flesh-colored tights from head to foot.'[42]

The female body posed, the body in movement: shaped as it was by emergent technologies such as cinema, the visual culture Cather grew up in had at its centre the female body ambivalently poised between the static and the mobile. Cather deployed photographs that displayed the performer in theatrical dress, often in a representation of a climactic moment from the performance. We see Fremstad as Isolde, her arm outstretched; Homer in classical dress in *Orpheus*; Farrar elegantly robed as Juliet. The images emerge from the confluence of two nineteenth-century developments in staging and the representation of theatre. The costumes and appurtenances of the stage in these images (we can see painted backdrops and period-style chairs, for instance) emerge from Victorian pictorial drama: the careful historicising of drama through deeply researched work on set design and costumes.[43] As the century developed, images of the performer also became important in a culture of collecting and circulation that surrounded the image of the performer: *cartes de visite*, then cabinet cards and then postcards. In Cather's 1913 article the studio photograph marks the transition between Victorian historicism and modern celebrity culture.

What is particularly interesting is the way that Cather's writing about theatre captures, embodies and charts the movement of society from one stage of technology and culture to another. In Cather's account of Farrar's portrayal of Juliet, it is the relative informality of the performance which captivates: 'When she made her début as Juliet in New York seven years ago, her critics were greatly disconcerted because she sang much of the chamber scene lying down, in her night-gown,' Cather writes.[44] Farrar claimed to have struck out for a more informal, more expressive and bodily form of performing:

> People are often shocked because when I sing in concert I don't wear gloves. I can't sing in gloves. I can't sing if I feel my clothes. I don't wear stays, and I would like to sing without any clothes, if I could. Fifty years ago a singer had nothing to do but nourish herself and sing; they had never discovered their bodies. But with a singing actress it's different; I sing with my body, and the freer it is, the better I can sing.[45]

Farrar's words capture well the transition, noted by fashion historians, from the formal dress codes of the nineteenth century to the looser styling of the early twentieth century. Philipp Blom has drawn attention to the secret surveillance photographs of English suffragettes in prison during this decade, where women went corsetless, their hair down.[46] It is exactly this bodily freedom that Cather also points to in her use of Farrar's words. Compared to a time when singers wore gloves to perform in, Farrar (recumbent, gloveless, stay-less) is a bodily radical in her self-presentation. Cather then used the figure of the singer and the singer's self-imaging (in interviews and photographs) to explore the possibilities of a transitional culture where not wearing gloves or a corset might signal revolt through style. The semiotics of the clothing changes might seem tiny to us now, but Cather's 'Three American Singers' shows just how significant such modifications in female dress could be, seeming to herald new forms of expressiveness within the space of performance.

Cather's early twentieth-century essay sits on the juncture between late Victorian visual culture and early twentieth-century motion picture culture. In the late nineteenth century, the full-length view of the actress had gradually replaced the portrait. David Mayer dates such a move from around the mid-1860s. The body remained largely controlled, however: 'Gradually, the actress, her entire physical self invisible, begins to emote, but her emotion is aestheticized and controlled by the photographer and is unlikely to be as overtly theatrical as it would have been on a stage before an audience.'[47] 'Three American Singers' marks a further development in the increasing emotional fluidity surrounding the iconography of the actress. The body comes into play; it is expressive and less controlled, and the actress comments on her own expressiveness, having in Cather's piece the agency of self-definition.

Thea Kronborg: 'a driving power in the blood'

If we now look at an early example of Cather's body-writing, 'The Ancient People' section of *The Song of the Lark*, we will be able to see how she then explored some of these corporeal conceptualisations in her fiction. The downbeat and exhausted Thea, the diva whose creative evolution the novel traces, undergoes a form of renewal – creativity as expressed primarily through embodiment: 'She had begun to understand that – with her, at least – voice was, first of all, vitality; a lightness in the body and a driving power in the blood' (*SOL* 338). Cather then creates a rather 'masculinist' episode – young characters throwing rocks in a Western landscape – as if to explore the body of the future diva. It is hard not to read these sentences and not to think of how Cather must have pored over stylised images of her favourite singers. Here, she creates a prose parallel of the female body moving and also statuesquely posed. Note the ways in which this passage seems to create in words a sense of the posed-but-active body seen in images of the diva:

> Thea settled the flat piece of rock between her wrist and fingers, faced the cliff wall, stretched her arm in position, whirled round on her left foot to the full stretch of her body, and let the missile spin out over the gulf. She hung expectantly in the air, forgetting to draw back her arm, her eyes following the stone as if it carried her fortunes with it. Her comrade watched her; there weren't many girls who could show a line like that from the toe to the thigh, from the shoulder to the tip of the outstretched hand. The stone spent itself and began to fall. Thea drew back and struck her knee furiously with her palm. (*SOL* 341–2)

At this point, Thea is renewed, revitalised. 'The Ancient People' has become a fable of the body. Thea is not a member of the American elite, though she is journeying toward that echelon of society. She is an outsider figure, a woman artist from the provinces. But her parapsychological illness, her 'American nervousness', would be all too familiar to the Progressive Era Americans discussed by historian Jackson Lears. 'After 1900, amid new models of mind–body cooperation and psychological abundance, old prescriptions for neurasthenia continued to lose legitimacy,' writes Lears.[48] Compare Thea (with her activity, her energy, her bodily force) in 1915 to the narrator of Charlotte Perkins Gilman's 'The Yellow Wallpaper' (1892), spatially confined, nervously frayed, unable to find an outlet for her creativity. Two decades later, Silas Weir Mitchell's rest cure has become outmoded and energy is venerated. Thus Thea arrives in the Southwest burned out and nervously broken. But she is also sensorially open and receptive. Cather then traces in Thea's renewal a re-embodiment that enables her to reshape herself as a singer, while also forging a narrative that performs decisive cultural work. 'The Ancient People' deploys a native setting as a means to position the female artist's body as an iconic answer to the problem of national neurasthenia. The iconic framing and shaping of the performer's body here serves to channel and control 'nervousness': the images that Cather had written about in 1913, when she commented on figures like Farrar, now returning as a solution to a broader cultural crisis.

Thea's re-embodying of herself is also significant when placed against a cultural context shaped by how male commentators had begun to think about female performers. Thea, like all of Cather's female performers (such as Kitty Ayrshire or Lucy Gayheart), possesses a steadfast autonomy very much rooted in her own bodily independence. They might be mentored by a man (typically not by just one male mentor, but by a number of them), but these performers' creativity remains very much their own, and seems to be rooted in a powerfully physicalised sense of creative autonomy.

The Theatre of the Real: Cather, Modjeska, Sontag

Cather came to creative and critical writing even as she first entered into, then deepened her knowledge of, performance and performers. She began to write theatre criticism at the crest of that cultural wave when actresses were becoming celebrities and emerging as central to debates about performance. As many critics and biographers have noted, her fascination with figures such as Sarah Bernhardt proved a major and abiding feature of her life.[49] She wrote about many of the most famous performers of her age. And she placed, quite literally, a real-life singer, Helena Modjeska, directly into the narrative of *My Mortal Enemy*.

My Mortal Enemy (1926) uses encounters with 'real people' to fashion a narrative that is relentlessly alert to the reality of performance and the performativity of everyday life. The novel seamlessly integrates both real and historical figures into an imagined narrative. Without a basic knowledge of Cather's turn-of-the-century performance world, a reader might not know that Helena Modjeska was an actual historical figure (in contrast, the poet mentioned in the same chapter, Anne Aylward, is fictional). Modjeska (1840–1909) was a Polish–American singer who has come to occupy a curious but important place in American culture. After emigrating to the US in 1876 (there is a Modjeska Canyon in Southern California, named for her residence there), she became a celebrated interpreter of Shakespeare. Her 1910 autobiography, *Memories and Impressions of Helena Modjeska*, contains vivid portraits of her performing heyday. Decades later, in the 1999 novel *In America*, Susan Sontag would again deploy Modjeska, and use descriptive phrases that (in the eyes of some critics) were too close to Modjeska's own language, and that of Cather too.[50] Wherever one might stand on this plagiarism dispute, it is surely fascinating that Modjeska has

Bodily Art and the Emergence of Modernism / 53

continued to reverberate as a character and a performer, tantalisingly reappearing as a woman on the border between the actual and the imagined, a performer whose imitations created a form of 'actuality' that was then reimagined by authors such as Cather and Sontag.

Modjeska's own account of her life is vividly 'Catherian': a narrative of transatlantic migration, self-creation and performativity. *Memories and Impressions of Helena Modjeska* demonstrates that *The Song of the Lark* emerged from a popular culture where the female performer had become a significant figure within narrative. This Americanisation narrative might be placed alongside other texts of its ilk, such as Mary Antin's *The Promised Land* (1912). But it is perhaps more interesting as an intertext that sheds light on how Modjeska's friend, Cather, created stories out of performance and the observation of performance. Modjeska learns through watching other performers; she lives in a world of ceaseless observation and theatrical engagement. Her autobiography shows how the performative world of late nineteenth-century America, packed as it was with foreign artists working in English for the first time (or Anglophone artists singing in Italian or German), was a place to observe dramas of shifting from one identity to another, narratives of selfhood where being American or becoming 'English' might be the subjects of close critical scrutiny. Here are Modjeska's comments on playing Juliet:

> The critics were all fair, with the exception of one, who could not forgive my 'foreign appearance' nor my accent. To criticise my accent was quite justifiable, but I wondered what my foreign appearance had to do with the matter. Was Juliet an American? Or must all Shakespeare's heroines look Anglo-Saxon, though they belong to different nationalities? Well, never mind that – my chief object was to act Juliet to the best of my ability and I did so.[51]

Modjeska's account captures an exilic, peripatetic and impressionistic life that can seem presciently 'modern' in its mobility and transience. Within this peripatetic whirl, it is the identity (the national identity) of the performer that becomes crucial. As discussed previously in this chapter, Cather had asked similar questions of Nethersole in the 1890s: was she too English to play a Frenchwoman? At the end of her life, Modjeska looked back on similar moments when her identity (and the transformation of that identity) had become the subject of critical speculation. Gail Marshall argues that Modjeska's Polish identity left little for reviewers and commentators to hang on to – thus making her an elusive figure when decoded in terms of national typologies (one might contrast Bernhardt's French identity: an identity easily and enthusiastically decoded by reviewers): 'Modjeska's Polish identity offered few recognisable signifiers to her audience . . . critics simply rejected her as falling short in the qualities of "naturalness" and "charm" so beloved of English actresses, and particularly of Ellen Terry, at that time.'[52]

Within Modjeska's exilic Polish world, the figure of the Jew acts as a counterpoint to the singers and artists she meets. Modjeska is clearly fascinated by the Jewish: they are exoticised and 'othered' at a number of points, and Modjeska will typically refer to 'shabby Jews' or a 'thin scattering of Jews'.[53] However, one also notes that she rejects a friend's outright anti-Semitism: 'Like many Europeans, he had a profound contempt for the whole race, and was most unreasonable on the subject.'[54]

It was within this context (a space framed by questions of performativity and identity) that Cather created her representations of the body in performance. *My Mortal Enemy*, written in 1925 and published in 1926, thus becomes an act of testimony and remembrance in part focused upon a figure who died some sixteen years earlier. Cather's characters ceaselessly go out to see performances, and within their own homes the quotidian experience is woven from a ceaseless flow of sensory moments that make up self-presentation. In Chapter V, Cather deftly fashions an episode which, although 'fictional', is clearly rooted in her early experiences as theatre-goer and drama reviewer. The action is focused through the eyes of Nellie – a proto-Jamesian focaliser in the narrative (as a young person witnessing the complex and ambiguous world of adults), she bears witness to the constant flicker of performed social life.

My Mortal Enemy demonstrates both the possibilities of the proto-Modernism of Cather's operatic/performative world and the troubling undercurrents within her modes of representation. Cather's writing in Chapter V is about aesthetic finesse: Modjeska is summoned from the dead, as it were, to take her place as a figure of cultural sophistication and performative power. Cather writes short, clipped sentences that compress a whole world of aesthetic plenitude into highly sensory (and sensual) glimpses of beauty or sounds of transcendence. Thus Modjeska is a hieratic figure, caught in poses that are reminiscent of the potent bodily power Cather had sensed in the images of women in 'Three American Singers'. Nelly comments,

> How well I remember those long, beautifully modelled hands, with so much humanity in them. They were worldly, indeed, but fashioned for a nobler worldliness than ours; hands to hold a sceptre, or a chalice – or, by courtesy, a sword. (*MME* 58)

This is the posed singer of the early twentieth-century images discussed earlier. Similarly, we have the thoroughly Catherian (and Romantic) sense of song as a literal form of embodiment – a making manifest of the singer's interiority:

> For many years I associated Mrs. Henshawe with that music, thought of that aria as being mysteriously related to something in her nature that one rarely saw, but nearly always felt; a compelling, passionate, overmastering something for which I had no name, but which was audible, visible in the air that night, as she sat crouching in the shadow. (*MME* 60)

To recall that moment, Nellie sings to herself the title of the Bellini aria (from *Norma*) that Modjeska has just performed: 'Casta diva, casta diva!'[55]

Conclusion: Venerating Beauty

My Mortal Enemy translates the language of reviewing (of theatre and opera) into a form of impacted and condensed modernist writing where a detail might stand in for a whole world of hinted-at significance. While Hemingway was beginning his career at this time with stories where meaning might stand off-stage, as it were,

Cather had by now translated the late Victorian world of performance into a modernist arena where a single crisp detail might suggest a vast array of significances.

The aesthetic becomes a form of verbal precision and control in Cather's writing: the body in performance frozen and then recalled via shorthand of key phrases that embody in written symbols the ephemeral nature of that scintillating performance – a hand held in a certain posture or the utterance of *'Casta diva!'* Such is Cather's bodily writing, a writing of the female performer at its most exquisite – a precise rendering of the epiphanic moments of a performing life.

But the veneration of beauty – the aesthetic – might also mask a whole world of otherness, of messy ordinariness even, or of 'the real' – this is the space where Modjeska's memoir sits with its conflicted representations of the figure of the Jew and its strange mixture of cosmopolitan openness and provincial racism. What we see here is a problem with a certain form of Aestheticism – a problem that had emerged in late Victorian performative culture and which then reverberated into Modernist culture. Cather had developed, through reviewing, a way to represent moments of aesthetic plenitude: an utterance, a gesture, a moment of secular grace. Her fiction extended and deepened such a writing of Aestheticism into narratives that were, in many ways, highly progressive and experimental, enabling her to map beauty on to everyday performance, as in *My Mortal Enemy*, or to read the body in terms of aestheticised potential, as in *The Song of the Lark*. At the same time, the movement to isolate the Aesthetic moment sometimes served to exclude or screen out the historical and cultural cacophony that might include the anti-Semitism of Modjeska's world. It is to Aestheticism, and Cather's relationship to this vital late nineteenth-century movement, that I now turn in order to chart how she had begun to explore representational questions that would then serve as the ground for Modernism.

Notes

1. Rosowski, *Willa Cather: The Voyage Perilous*; Giannone, *Willa Cather and Music*. For an account of Cather and late nineteenth-century British writing, including

figures such as Wilde and Stevenson, see Reynolds, 'The Transatlantic Virtual Salon: Cather and the British'.
2. Stokes, 'Varieties of Performance at the Turn of the Century', 207.
3. James, 'On the Occasion of *Hedda Gabler*', 230.
4. Ibid.
5. Cather, 'Henrik Ibsen', reprinted in Colglazier, 'Willa Cather on Henrik Ibsen's Realism: The Protest Against Lies', 99–103, at 101.
6. Cather, 'Pittsburgh *Leader*'.
7. Cather, 'With Plays and Players', 9.
8. In 'Nebraska: End of the First Cycle', her 1923 historical overview of the state, Cather discussed the 1910 census figures, which had listed the state's population as being 1,192,214, including over 900,000 that made up the 'foreign population', of whom 103,503 were Scandinavians. 'Nebraska', 236–8.
9. Weinstein, *Northern Arts*, 1, 75.
10. Archer, 'The Free Stage and the New Drama'.
11. North, *Reading 1922*, 173.
12. The local paper, the *Red Cloud Chief*, published her oration. Biographer James Woodress describes it as 'a remarkable performance for a youngster of her time and place' (Woodress, *Willa Cather: A Literary Life*, 60).
13. Crane, *Willa Cather: A Bibliography*, lists 251 items (mostly reviews of performance) that Cather wrote during her Nebraskan years, 1891–6, for newspapers such as the *Nebraska State Journal*.
14. Cather's enthusiastically mentioned the opening of the New Funke in her 'Amusements' column (1894): 'The formal opening last night . . . was one of unqualified brilliancy.' Tactfully, she used the second part of her column to review a production at the Lansing, perhaps mindful of the need to please both sets of theatre owners. 'Amusements', *Nebraska State Journal*, 13 September 1894.
15. For an account of how railways helped shape the narrative terrain of her fiction, see Mark. A. R. Facknitz, 'Changing Trains: Metaphors of Transfer in Willa Cather'.
16. Cather, 'One Way of Putting It', *Nebraska State Journal* (3 December 1893), 13.
17. Ibid.
18. Archer, *The Theatrical 'World' of 1894*, 205. Elaine Aston cites Archer's observation in 'Studies in Hysteria: Actress and Courtesan, Sarah Bernhardt and Mrs. Patrick Campbell'.
19. Aston, 'Studies in Hysteria', 253.
20. See Coward, 'Introduction' to Alexandre Dumas, *La Dame aux Camélias*, vii–xx, for an overview of the novel's cultural significance.
21. Johnson, *Sisters in Sin*, 47.
22. Cited in Johnson, *Sisters in Sin*, 61. Johnson discusses Nethersole's role as a producer, and the controversy this engendered, 60–2.
23. Cather, 'Utterly Irrelevant' (16 September 1894), 13.
24. Lewis, *Willa Cather Living*, 44.
25. Cather, 'As You Like It', 13.
26. Ibid. 13.

27. Houchin, *Censorship of the American Theatre in the Twentieth Century*, 50.
28. Johnson, *Sisters in Sin*, 45.
29. Houchin, *Censorship of the American Theatre in the Twentieth Century*, 40–52.
30. Saxon, 'Sexual Transgression on the American Stage: Clyde Fitch, Sapho and the "American Girl"', 737. The review was in the New York *World* (7 February 1900), 14.
31. Woodress, *Willa Cather*, 72.
32. Stout, *Calendar of Letters*, 114.
33. Johnson, *Sisters in Sin*, 45.
34. Lears, *No Place of Grace*, 7.
35. Cather, 'Three American Singers', 34–5.
36. Debate about whether the photographic image might or not give access to interiority is very much a feature of contemporary discussions of modern photographers. See Sally O'Reilly's contrasting comments on Roland Fischer ('Our incursion into the life of the individual stops abruptly at their skin') and Rineke Dijkstra ('the human form cannot help but transmit emotions'). *The Body in Contemporary Art*, 30–1.
37. Cheng, *Second Skin*, 11. See also Clarke, 'The Body in Photography', for a useful introduction to many of the critical issues suggested by the imaging of the body.
38. For an account of the *cartes de visite* phenomenon and then the vogue for celebrity photographs, see Roger Hargreaves, 'Putting Faces to the Names: Social and Celebrity Portrait Photography'.
39. Kelly, 'Beauty and the Market: Actress Postcards and Their Senders in Early Twentieth-Century Australia', 99–100.
40. Cather, 'Three American Singers', 36.
41. Ibid.
42. Atkins, qtd in Marshall, *Actresses on the Victorian Stage*, 132.
43. A good place to sample this theatrical culture is via the extensive online collection of the Victoria and Albert Museum, available at <www.vam.ac.uk> (last accessed 26 October 2020).
44. Cather, 'Three American Singers', 38.
45. Ibid. 38.
46. Blom, *The Vertigo Years: Europe, 1900–1914*, 230–1.
47. Mayer, 'The Actress as Photographic Icon', 81.
48. Lears, *No Place of Grace*, 245. Lears discusses the transformation of treatments of neurasthenia, the switch from 'rest' to 'energy', 239–48.
49. Funda, '"The Crowning Flight of Egotism": Willa Cather, Sarah Bernhardt, and the Cult of Celebrity', 25–30.
50. Vulliamy, 'Sontag Pleads Poetic Licence in Using Uncredited "scraps of history"'.
51. Modjeska, *Memories and Impressions of Helena Modjeska*, 380. Stokes, *The French Actress and Her English Audience*, provides an invaluable context for thinking about Cather and figures such as Modjeska, not least because he places transcultural performance, and the figure of the internationalised actress, at the centre of his account.

52. Marshall, 'Cultural Formations: The Nineteenth-century Touring Actress and Her International Audiences', 63.
53. Modjeska, *Memories and Impressions of Helena Modjeska*, 69, 71.
54. Ibid. 264. The friend is a caricaturist, Paprocki. For a detailed account of Cather and 'the Jews', see Meyer, 'On the Front and at Home'.
55. Richard Giannone reads Myra Henshawe as a kind of 'version' of Bellini's heroine, Norma – 'the conception of a strong-willed heroine coming to grips with contending forces within herself and a hostile world outside is clearly at the heart of Willa Cather's creation of her protagonist'. *Music in Willa Cather's Fiction*, 181. Cather's blending of allusion (to the Bellini opera) and bodily immediacy (Myra's performativity) might also be related to certain forms of Modernist representation – a topic I will return to in later chapters.

CHAPTER 3

'Sense-dwarfed': Cather, Aestheticism and a New Corporealism

The cultural world of the United States in the 1880s and early 1890s, when the precocious Cather first began to write and to immerse herself in performance, was highly distinctive. Cather graduated from the University of Nebraska in 1895 – the year before the trial and subsequent imprisonment of Oscar Wilde. Not only did Aestheticism shape her earliest encounters with and contributions to culture, it also shaped the ways in which Cather imagined the body. To understand the body mapping of her early works ('Paul's Case' being the prime example), one must understand the complex archaeology of Cather's reading in Aestheticism, as well as her own very distinctive (and idiosyncratic) fashioning of narratives of the aesthetic that would be set in such unlikely places as Pittsburgh and Lincoln. Cather, I will argue in this chapter, created narratives of provincial Aestheticism that took the metropolitan tropes suggested by Wilde or (particularly) George du Maurier, but then adopted those motifs to settings far from Paris or London, resulting in the provincial aestheticised body of Thea Kronborg or Paul.

Cather's Dialogue with Aestheticism: The 'five avenues'

Cather's fascination with the broader field of nineteenth-century literary schools – and, in particular, French Symbolism – has also seemed central to her creative evolution, in the eyes of many critics. In fact, one of the earliest scholarly compendia of Cather's critical writing, Bernice Slote's *The Kingdom of Art* (1966), presented the

Nebraskan writer as the heir to these European movements.[1] Slote's Cather was a Midwestern aesthete, a writer whose secular religion echoed that of Verlaine or Wilde: the veneration of art above all, the creation of an aesthetic credo.

Cather's early writings are important because they suggest the ways that her critical writings and her fiction-making often grew out of the same field of enquiry into how the body might be represented. In these early critical writings, Cather engaged with late Victorian ways of representing the body (for example, in theatrical or in musical performances, or through fashion) and created touchstones that provided reference points for her later fiction. In order to understand the evolving complexity of Cather's work, it is necessary to search these early writings for such markers: the precocious Cather had identified representational nodes in late Victorian and Aestheticist culture which she would then turn back to repeatedly, turning these moments in a Modernist direction.

Revisiting those early reviews and essays, we now see that the encounter with Aestheticism was a way to engage with the body and with the senses. Cather's 1896 commentary on Paul Verlaine is a good place to revisit these arguments, and then to reread in terms of my central thesis: that Cather's work was a sustained meditation on how the body was in transition between late Victorian and Modernist eras, and that narrative itself might be a place to fashion compositions built around corporealism and shifts within the bodily habitus. For her account of Verlaine is a highly sensory one, focused on sight and sound in particular. After Verlaine's death in early 1896, Cather wrote an obituary essay for the *Nebraska State Journal*, a piece that praised the French artist for his highly sensory work. 'He called one of his greatest volumes *Romances Without Words*, and indeed they are almost that. He created a new verbal art of communicating sensations not only by the meaning of words, but of their relation, harmony and sound' (*KA* 395–6). The twenty-two-year-old Cather had identified 'communicating sensations' as a core principle of art.

French writing, particularly that broadly framed by the term 'Symbolist', appealed to Cather because it engaged with the sensorium – and to a degree this suggested the limitations of Anglophone writing. This is the implication of another early response to French writing: namely, her praise for novelist and travel writer Pierre Loti, particularly his *The Romance of a Spahi* (*Le Roman d'un spahi*). Writing for the *Courier* (9 November 1895), Cather condemned the 'lifeless' descriptions of English authors, then contrasted the French, especially Loti, and their sensory prose.

> All through this book one can smell the aroma of the tropics, see the palms and the tamarinds and the old white mosques, and the burning sandy water of the Senegal, hear the sound of the tom-tom and the epic chants of the griots.

She positioned Loti as an exemplary figure, 'a sort of knight-errant to bring it to us, who gives to (us) poor cold-bound, sense-dwarfed dwellers in the North the scent of sandalwood and the glitter of the southern stars' (*KA* 367).

That is, Cather found in French writing a sensorily enriched richness that contrasted with Anglophone literature's sensory depletion. At times, as in the praise for Loti, that contrast takes on self-punishing provincialism, as if to say that the Midwestern American world lacks the sheer sensory enrichment of European fictional worlds. But the imaginative turn Cather then took was a crucial one – and forms the focus for much of my ensuing discussion: the imaginative opening-up of her American terrains to incorporate forms of 'sense-expanded' writing that she had found in Loti's prose. Her central imaginative move was to learn the lessons of British Aestheticism and French Symbolism, but then fold those lessons back into narratives about pan-American experience, especially experiences utterly grounded in varieties of the American body. In effect, Cather's fiction read sensoriness back into novels about the Americas: French North America in *Shadows on the Rock*, or the Southwest of *The Professor's House*, or *Sapphira*'s ante-bellum Virginia. Her fiction might be read as an extended exploration of whether she was, in fact, correct about Loti, and about American culture: was her culture 'sense-dwarfed'?

Regarding British Aestheticism, the central figure is, of course, Oscar Wilde, with whose work and life Cather had a complex relationship. Wilde had been the central figure in bringing the Aesthetic gospel to the United States (and had lectured on 'The

Decorative Arts' in Lincoln in 1882).² By the mid-1890s, Wilde's trial in England had both overshadowed and undermined his original fame as the Aesthete provocateur – and his identity as a homosexual had moved decisively to the foreground. Cather's critics typically tie her interest in Aestheticism to her queer identity. Cather's engagement with British Aestheticism becomes a form of code, in these readings, for explorations of themes, characters and tropes where queerness manifests itself in complex patterns. 'Paul's Case', especially, is now commonly read as an early text where Cather transposed a figure who might have stepped out of a Wilde play into an American setting.³

Nevertheless, Cather's early comments on Wilde are at times amongst her most conservative and conventionally moralistic – we sense the young writer giving her readers and editors exactly what they wanted in terms of a neo-Victorian judgement. But Cather's fascinations with flowers, with music, with decoration, with art were all manifestations of her indebtedness to various forms of Aestheticism. The young Cather rejected Wilde, even as her work explored his legacy, positioning questions raised by the British writer in new American settings.

This aesthetic convolution or paradox – as we might call Cather's self-division when she wrote about Wilde – ran throughout her 28 September 1895 Lincoln *Courier* article on the Aesthetic Movement: 'The downfall of the leader of the aesthetic movement pre-figures the destruction of the most fatal and dangerous school of art that has ever voiced itself in the English tongue' (*KA* 389). Cather attacked Wilde's *Lady Windermere's Fan* for being a 'lie, a malicious lie upon human nature' (*KA* 390). Cather felt that Wilde had wasted his talents, and in a strangely foreboding phrase seemed to signal a fear of artistic potential destroyed: 'When one looks out over the chaos and confusion of wasted life and wasted talent, one wonders whether Oscar Wilde, and all the rest of us for that matter, will not have another chance' (*KA* 393). The aesthete's talents might be wasted (here the links between Wilde and Cather's Paul are clear).

But then, in a sentence that is central to her early criticism, and also to my study of Cather's sensory world, she invoked the five senses as a means to fulfil art's promise:

> Where the soul can feel as here the senses do, where there will be a better means of knowing and of feeling than through these five avenues so often faithless, that alike save and lose us, that either starve us or debauch us. Perhaps. (*KA* 393)

That is, a sensory art, an art rooted in what Cather called the 'five avenues', might act in a way to become the basis of 'a better means of knowing and of feeling'. This 1895 statement (Cather was still twenty-one) might be read as a pledge to answer the questions raised by Wilde's career through deploying a creative lexicon rooted in sensory exploration.

Cather's connections to the Wildean legacy remained firm throughout her life. Perhaps the most intriguing instance of this connection came in 1932, in the Preface to the Jonathan Cape edition of *The Song of the Lark*. Here, late in her writing career, Cather linked one of her earliest novels to Wilde's legacy, nodding to a genealogy of Aestheticism that she had rarely formally acknowledged: 'The life of nearly every artist who succeeds in the true sense (succeeds in delivering himself completely to his art) is more or less like Wilde's story, *The Portrait of Dorian Gray*' (*SOL* 617). Whether or not *The Song of the Lark* really is a quasi-*Dorian Gray* narrative is contestable. It is rare to find this comment impacting on critical readings of the novel. Yet *The Song of the Lark* might be read as an analogue or intertext to Wilde's novel in that both deal with artistry, performance, and the ageing – or not – of the artist's body. Certainly, the novel's last glimpses of Thea take on a new significance when read through the prism of Wilde's story – Cather presents artistic evolution as a process of keeping the body endlessly youthfully energetic, trained on the performative ideal.

> While she was on the stage she was conscious that every movement was the right movement, that her body was absolutely the instrument of her idea. Not for nothing had she kept it so severely, kept it filled with such energy and fire. (*SOL* 526)

Late Cather now explicitly repositioned herself as an aesthete, and allied her writing to that most bodily of *fin-de-siècle* narratives.

Mary Warner Blanchard describes Wilde's tour of the United

States in 1882 (he visited over a hundred cities to promote his aesthetic creed in general and the D'Oyly Carte production of Gilbert and Sullivan's *Patience* in particular) as the crystallisation of a cultural revolution – the 'invasion of aesthetic style into the rituals of everyday living'.[4] Blanchard begins her study by looking at *style* in its various manifestations, but like many other cultural historians who have worked on this period (Jackson Lears, most notably), she then sees the Gilded Age as a compelling mixture of cultural currents, an era of robber barons, certainly, but also of experimentation and cultural innovation, of modernism and anti-modernism. Her study compellingly points to four major areas where culture moves in radical and revisionist directions.

First, in terms of style and decoration, Aestheticism placed a great deal of emphasis on the introduction of the decorative arts into everyday life, the reconfiguration of the domestic by ideals of quotidian beauty and craft. A central part of Wilde's American lecture tour was 'The Decorative Arts', a version of which emerged as 'Decorative Art in America' in a volume published, intriguingly, in 1906 (the same year as 'Paul's Case'). Here, Wilde told his American audience they needed 'that which hallows the vessels of every-day use'.[5] Wilde's 1880s attacks on shoddy domesticity and his veneration of craftsmanship reverberate in Cather's satirical lampooning of suburban housing in *The Professor's House* (and that novel's veneration of Cliff Dweller domesticity). 'I found meaningless chandeliers and machine-made furniture, generally of rosewood, which creaked dismally under the weight of the ubiquitous interviewer.'[6]

Second, the post-Civil War era saw the rise of a stylised male figure: the aesthete. Blanchard sees such figures as staking out new forms of identity, as opposed to more traditional masculine ones such as the soldier, Frontier warrior or entrepreneur. Aestheticism made it possible for men to be interested in matters of style, dress and decoration. Above all, Wilde imagined a highly performative male self at odds with the strait-lacedness of the iconic Victorian male persona: 'What did clearly mark Wilde as divergent from Victorian norms', writes S. I. Salamensky, 'was his sheer performativeness.' Moreover, 'He stood in sharp relief to the high-Victorian context in which masculinity was defined by stringency, self-control, self-effacement, and "earnestness" – the term unmercifully mocked in Wilde's most famous play.[7] A fascinating, and charming, aspect of the 'Decorative Art' lecture is Wilde's identification of such characteristics amongst iconic Western American men, such as the miners he met: 'Their wide-brimmed hats, which shaded their faces from the sun and protected them from the rain, and the cloak, which is by far the most beautiful piece of drapery ever invented, may well be dwelt on with admiration.'[8] Wilde showed Cather a way to think of provincial or Western American masculinity in aestheticised ways.

Third, alongside this stylised male emerged the figure of the dynamic, artistic female. Writers such as Harold Frederic (*The Damnation of Theron Ware*) and Kate Chopin (*The Awakening*) created compelling representations of the empowered female artist figure. Aestheticism redrew gender typologies, momentarily offering a more diverse array of selves than mid-Victorian culture had done. Blanchard points to the emergence of images of the 'strong female artist' in the 1880s as, for example, in illustrated trade cards and other forms of advertising:

> Particularly popular was a stock card illustration of a woman artist painting vigorously at an outside easel, with an admiring gentleman looking over her shoulder . . . . Mythological renderings of the muses of art were not static classical forms but strong female figures, either as active creators or as discerning critics.[9]

Mid-1890s fictions explored the allure and danger of such figures, through narratives where the female aesthete disrupted and undermined masculine identity. In Harold Frederic's *The Damnation of Theron Ware* (1896), a pastor becomes hopelessly infatuated by the provincial aesthete, Celia Madden, a compellingly exotic figure whose cosmopolitanism stands in stark contrast to Ware's provincial Protestantism. Eventually, Ware escapes his seducer and imagines a new life further west in the state of Washington. Frederic's narrative posits a dangerously seductive Aestheticism assailing the solid provincial protagonist. The dangers posed by the aesthete and the need to escape Aesthetic (or 'de-Aesthetic') entrapment had become central to narrative. Later that decade, Kate Chopin's *The Awakening* (1899) traced another narrative line through the seductions of Aestheticism and a final escape from bourgeois conformity. Chopin's richly Aestheticised houses and landscapes immerse the reader in a decadent world, and Edna Pontellier's relationships with a series of lovers confirm the dangerous (a)morality heralded by Aestheticism. The novel's conclusion, centred on Pontellier's strangely luxurious suicide as she gives herself up to the sea, confirms Aestheticism's allure, while questioning its utopian possibilities.

Fourth, the late 1890s witnessed a reaction against the experimentation, revisionism and innovation of the previous two decades. Two landmark literary events marked out this conservative reaction and cultural *revanche*. First, Wilde's trial for sodomy in 1895 marked the fall of Aestheticism's most outspoken, flamboyant proselyte. Second, the shocked reaction to *The Awakening* signalled a further pushback against the countercultural explorations being pursued by the decade's major writers. In the domestic and sentimental sphere, writers whose lives and works seemed to endorse sexual and emotional experimentation quickly found themselves marginalised. By the end of 1899, Chopin's career as a novelist was over, while Wilde was in exile (and would die in 1900).

Signalled in the United States' imperial adventures against the declining Spanish empire at the end of that decade, a more renewed culture of traditional masculinity seemed to be emerging. Amy Kaplan couples American imperialism to the literal 'embodiment' of virility and strength in the masculine body. As celebrated by figures such as Theodore Roosevelt, the male body was retraditionalised as, quite literally, corporealised prowess:

> In a period of the New Woman, the New Negro, the New South, and the New Empire, the New White American Man was invented as a tradition ... as nothing new at all, but rather a figure from an enduring recoverable past.[10]

Considering figures such as Fitzgerald's men (Jay Gatsby, Dick Diver) or Hemingway's Nick Adams, it is easy to see how the next generation of American writers wrestled with what we might call the 'New White American Man', by contesting, questioning or creating their own quixotic variants of such figures. Particularly fascinating about Cather's writing is the fact that the era's most significant queer female novelist should also have been one of the authors also working with this figure. It was through Aestheticism, and the *fin-de-siècle* debates around Aestheticism, that Cather forged her first responses to this male body. Cather debated, argued and quarrelled with Aestheticism and its legacy. But it would take until the full flowering of her career as a professional writer for the terms of that debate to be set and for the full shape of her creative dialogue with the cultural legacy of the late nineteenth century to emerge.

'Plumed defiance': Cather and the Male Aesthete

Already in her early criticism, Cather revealed herself as actively engaged with Aestheticism. Her veneration of style, beauty and art were Romantic, as Susan Rosowski noted in *The Voyage Perilous*, but also highly Aestheticised in a later nineteenth-century sense – mainly because Cather, like Wilde and his followers, was keen to relocate ideals of beauty within the realms of domestic decoration, clothing and everyday life.[11] Cather's early theatre reviews were, for instance, intensely Aestheticised columns, sketches of the urban life of Lincoln, a setting that, in many ways, was a strange mix of raw Frontier town and culture centre, where the clothing of the audience, the stage set and the performers' costume designs might be as significant as the work itself. As addressed in the previous chapter, these columns position the young Cather as a tyro aesthete, a judge of beauty, style and form. But, like Wilde, Cather widens definitions and then exports 'beauty' to become a yardstick for everyday life.

'Early' Cather redeployed prominent Aesthetic tropes and figures, placing them in unlikely settings before creating fables that testified to the movement's apparent failure. By the time she began to write short fiction, Wilde had been tried and the high-water mark of Aestheticism had passed, but her work registered its impact through a marked fascination with clothing and decoration.

Cather's early critical writings often saw her celebrating figures who had explored and extended the cultural implications of Aestheticism. One particular touchstone was George du Maurier's *Trilby* (published in *Harper's Monthly* in 1894, then as a novel in 1895). 'She has come to us at last in book form – Trilby the much talked of, Trilby the well-beloved,' wrote Cather in September 1894. 'For six months the English-speaking peoples have talked of little else . . . with her pretty foot, her army coat and taint of Bohemia.'[12] Her November 1896 elegy for du Maurier, a British–French illustrator who had found fame late in life with *Trilby*, deployed a highly Aestheticised vocabulary to imagine his observational powers. Du Maurier

> was one of the followers of that white armless lady in the Louvre, one of her knights-in-waiting, her loyal retainer. He even gave to his 'La Svengali' the pose and bearing of that immortal marble woman. With the pencil and the pen, first in one form, then in another, he pursued that radiant spirit that is at once the artist's unrest and his great joy.[13]

Du Maurier's tale of British and French Bohemianism, his fascination with voice and performance, and his rendering of the defiantly artistic New Woman left imaginative traces in Cather's writings. Understanding this formative genealogy (of influence and inspiration) helps us see how Aestheticism shaped her body-picturing. In particular, du Maurier's racy Gothicism decisively focused late Victorian culture's preoccupation with voice and gender. Set in Paris's Bohemian *demi-monde*, *Trilby* surrounds its performing heroine (as *The Song of the Lark* will) with a circle of male allies, aficionados and mentors. The novel is initially an exuberantly comedic account of Bohemia, but as the narrative thickens and develops, disturbing questions of power come to the fore. At the centre of the novel sits the relationship between Svengali (voice coach and singing master) and the uproariously charismatic female protagonist, Trilby. Female performance and the woman's voice obsess Svengali (and the character, of course, gave his name to a generic figure exercising manipulative control). What will men do with female performance? How to control and discipline the woman's voice?

In an opening scene, we witness his imperious desire to exert control over the female performer. Svengali himself cannot sing:

> He was absolutely without voice, beyond the harsh, hoarse, weak raven's croak he used to speak with, and no method availed to make one for

him. But he grew to understand the human voice as perhaps no one has understood it – before or since.¹⁴

Consumed with a passion for music but unable to sing, Svengali hatches his plans to manipulate the female singer.

Trilby might be suggestively juxtaposed against *The Song of the Lark*. Both novels construct plot out of the dynamic encounter between female performer and a male circle of acolytes, supporters, teachers. But whereas Trilby is entrapped by Svengali (and both characters will eventually die, as du Maurier fashions a narrative of vampiric fatedness), Cather's heroine transcends the male circle's influence, achieving a success which, although ambivalent (Thea is a solitary figure when we last see her), is defiantly autonomous.

Thus, Cather learned from, and adopted, plots and character types she found in her early literary passions. But she also used her journalism to create sketches drawn from the life around, sketches that often focused on culture, the Aesthetic and Aesthetes. As early as 1894, the year of her twenty-first birthday, Cather was creating vignettes or sketches of life on the Lincoln street – sketches where visual display and sartorial ornamentation had become part of quotidian provincial life. The young Cather had lived most of her life in Red Cloud, Nebraska, and then Lincoln, but her writing showed a metropolitan fascination with street fashion, as in her portrait of a downtown Lincoln hipster, a *flâneur* abroad on the streets of the *fin-de-siècle* Midwestern town. She described Lincoln's Tenth Street, the 'Lincoln Bowery', and then deftly sketched one of its inhabitants, a Wildean figure:

> He may be seen almost any day at one of the cheap restaurants. He is very young in all senses of the word. He is tall and blonde and wears his hair curled. He comes down to breakfast about 10 o'clock, attired in patent leather house slippers, checked trousers, a shirt with flowers embroidered on the front, a light blue tie, a watchchain disappearing in each of his trousers pockets, a light felt dressing gown hanging open, and a tall silk hat thrust on the back of his head. In this strange garb he comes down the street to the restaurant. He hangs up his hat and cane, settles the cluster of diamonds in his scarf and yawns wearily as he throws himself into a chair and taps for the waiter.¹⁵

Read in the light of Cather's later career, such sketches are revelatory. The fascination with surface, with material culture, the provincial anxiety about distance from metropolitan life (leading Cather to rename Lincoln's Tenth Street as its 'Bowery'), the mapping of everyday social custom, and the monitoring of what might make a person utterly distinctive: Cather had already created an aesthete's idiom. From this Lincoln hipster one can draw a line to the Paul of 'Paul's Case' and then on to her stories of musical performance. It is particularly fascinating that Cather begins by claiming that her young man is from the 'Lincoln Bowery' (the real-life Bowery Boys were a notorious nineteenth-century New York City gang), but then softens and aestheticises her hoodlum (he is a 'still milder species' of the city tough). The reader senses the influence of Jacob Riis (*How the Other Half Lives* was published in 1890), but then recognises Cather's provincial aestheticising of street culture. This is that 1890s moment, pinpointed by Jon Savage in his history of youth culture, when urban America's young people began to become the nexus for defiant style: 'Never mind what reformers or journalists thought, they would get what they wanted by fair means or foul: intoxicants, weapons, clothes . . . In doing so, they broadcast the very plumed defiance that their exposure was attempting to curtail.'[16]

Cather examines 'plumed defiance' in the celebrated early story, 'Paul's Case', which appeared in *McClure's* in 1905. That tale exemplified her ability not only to assimilate influences, but then to inflect them in order to create a distinctively provincial, Western American slant on *fin-de-siècle* transatlantic literary–cultural themes. Paul is a hyperbolic aesthete, a near-parodic walking embodiment of the ultra-sensationalism that Wilde had ushered in. In particular, 'Paul's Case' links Aestheticism to crime: he steals money from his employer to fund his escape from Pittsburgh to New York City (and then commits suicide – another kind of crime – rather than allowing his father to take him back to Pittsburgh). Wilde had also linked crime to Aestheticism in *Dorian Gray*, as Lord Henry says of crime and the 'lower orders': 'I should fancy that crime was to them what art is to us, simply a method of procuring extraordinary sensations.'[17] 'Paul's Case' is 'post' *Dorian Gray* in that it shapes a narrative around this connection. In fact, the distinctively lower middle-class Paul might be said to be a figure who out-Wildes Wilde in his fusion of the Aesthetic, the criminal and the ordinary.[18]

Paul is a hyperactive, twitching, neurotic figure; he is all sensation, a nervous decadent. The story's full title signals Cather's interest in the pathologies of Aestheticism: 'Paul's Case: A Study in Temperament'. This is one of the major American tales of turn-of-the-century performative masculinity. Restraint, discipline and earnestness seem to have melted away, leaving a self on edge, looking for sensation and aesthetic stimulation. The fact that the story was written and published while Cather was a teacher at Pittsburgh Central High School (Paul is a student at 'Pittsburgh High School') only adds a frisson to a reading of the tale, as if one were reading a racy account by a young writer (Cather was just over thirty) of the doings of the teenagers.

Paul is insolent and confrontational, blending the aesthete's fascination with appearance with the teen rebel's instinctive sense of defiance. His school barely knows what to do with him; Paul himself moves through Andrew Carnegie's Pittsburgh looking for imaginative release from a world of utilitarian and constrictive puritanism. The worlds of music and performance offer the obvious escape; Paul's evening job is working as an usher at Carnegie Hall. Paul feels his uniqueness, his outsiderdom, in thoroughly bodily ways. As with other Decadent and Aesthetic figures from *fin-de-siècle* culture (think of Dracula), Paul's strangeness is literally embodied in a corporeality that might be both young and old, one that disorders chronology itself:

> The drawing-master had come to realize that, in looking at Paul, one saw only his white teeth and the forced animation of his eyes. One warm afternoon the boy had gone to sleep at his drawing-board, and his master had noted with amazement what a white, blue-veined face it was; drawn and wrinkled like an old man's about the eyes, the lips twitching even in his sleep, and stiff with a nervous tension that drew them back from his teeth. (PC 75)

Paul's love of the Aesthetic then grows from a highly bodily, highly sensory receptiveness to music. This bodily response to music seems to offer him a way to discipline and organise his sensory impulses:

He needed only the spark, the indescribable thrill that made his imagination master of his senses, and he could make plots and pictures enough of his own . . . what he wanted was to see, to be in the atmosphere, float on the wave of it, to be carried out, blue league after blue league, away from everything. (*PC* 78-9)

Paul is a young vampire with Edna Pontellier's yearning for escape. The question is whether Paul's Bohemianism is sustainable: is there any way in which the world of provincial America might provide a way for Paul to *live*? The narrative's turn toward crime throws this dilemma into stark relief. Born into ordinariness, Paul wants to live an extraordinary life. But for that, he needs money.

Cather's fable curiously echoes 'The Dynamo and the Virgin' chapter of *The Education of Henry Adams*, with its opposition between the spiritual female figure and the mechanistic/technological ideal symbolised by the dynamo. In Cather's telling, it is the aesthete who meets the machine. Paul is the androgynously virginal figure poised on the edge of adulthood and sexual knowledge; he will die beneath the wheels of a train figured in terms of pure energy and force: The machine slays the aesthete. Thus, in terms of simple plot, 'Paul's Case' appears to be a monitory tale of Aesthetic failure. And yet, as in many of Cather's narratives, the sheer material plenitude of the story (the decorated rooms, the clothing, the relentless attention to colour and style) suggests a living world that will simply *go on* beyond the conventional limits of narrative closure. Even as the plotline follows a declensionist structure down toward catastrophe and death, the incidental details of the narrative offer the reader florid materialism and a plenitude of beauty. And the death of the Aesthete is never, in fact, the death of the Aesthetic, because to die Aesthetically might be to underline the power of the movement's ideals. Cather seems to construct 'Paul's Case' so as to end with a savage wiping out of the aesthete: crushing him utterly by means of a mechanistic brutalising. Yet there are two machines alluded to in the story's closing lines. There is the train that kills the protagonist and then there is the image of the human body. The final sentence functions imagines a film camera: 'Then, because the picture-making mechanism was crushed, the disturbing visions flashed into black, and Paul dropped back into the immense design of things' (*PC* 83). The story is subtitled 'A Study in Temperament' and it ends with 'a picture-making mechanism' and 'the immense design of things'. 'Temperament' and 'design': thoroughly Aesthetic terms. But it is fascinating, too, that Cather positions the dead aesthete's body in terms of his 'picture-making mechanism'. Paul is an aesthete in the age of the camera, just as Cather herself was an aesthete in an age increasingly dominated by the proto-industrialism of still photography and movie imagery.

'Paul's Case' established a narrative line or arc that recurred throughout Cather's career: the fable of Aesthetic failure, where a plotline of decline and failure, and even death, nevertheless unfolded through scenarios of stylistic, decorative and environmental beauty. The American aesthete fails or dies (these fables have a definitively *national* cast); his or her world lives on. Cather, too, imagined the dead or defeated or marginalised aesthete. In fact, this figure became one of her central and recurrent character types – a figure we can trace from early characters such as Paul right through to Professor Godfrey St Peter and Lucy Gayheart. The aesthete dies, often on the margins of the culture – on the slummy edge of the city or drowned in a frozen Nebraskan river. The cultural work of such narratives seems clear: to acknowledge the fragility of the Aesthetic in its American setting, while suggesting a plenitude achieved through memory and the commemoration of simply placing such figures at the heart of narrative.

The intense bodiliness of Cather's early writing, and the quirky male-centredness of much of her early fiction ('Peter', 'Paul's Case'), were further developed in the male crisis narratives of the mid-career, notably in *One of Ours* and *The Professor's House*. In the former, Claude Wheeler finds himself in an intensely physical job, farming, for which he seems to have no passion. Each book of the novel seems to present a blocked bodily narrative. Claude farms; it gives him little satisfaction or ends in failure (as when a blizzard causes him to lose his pigs). He marries; the marriage seems to give little sense of physical fulfilment (and his wife Enid embodies a de-corporealised spirituality that might recall Mary Baker Eddy). The narrative arc is akin to a male-centred inversion of *The Song of the Lark*: whereas Thea moves through successive episodes of bodily awakening and development, Claude's narrative is one of unfulfilled bodily potential. Hence the strangely lyrical moments of corporealism that punctuate the steady rural realism that is the novel's dominant mode. In one notorious sequence (it served as one of the tableaux in the PBS documentary film about Cather, *The Road is All*), Claude strips off and bathes in the horse tank – a moment with a deeply discordant tonality:

> The water had been warmed by the sun all afternoon, and was not much cooler than his body ... The sky was a midnight-blue, like warm, deep, blue water, and the moon seemed to lie on it like a water-lily, floating forward with an invisible current. One expected to see its great petals open.

Then he hears his wife returning and runs naked across the yard, a 'white man across a bare white yard' (*OOO* 277, 279). Claude's physicality, here luxuriously Aestheticised and furtive, creates a form of counternarrative in the text, an antiphonal subject placed against the routines of farm and family.

And thus when things *do* happen to Claude, they are highly corporeal, utterly physical. The courtship between Claude and Enid catches fire after he is badly injured in a farming accident – his mules run out of control and pull him into a barbed-wire fence. The bandaged, neo-mummified and bed-bound figure that we see echoes Thea at the start of *The Song of the Lark* and pre-figures the eventually sickened and prone figures of Father Latour and Professor St Peter. A point I will return to at several moments in this meditation is a simple but, I think, substantive one: Cather created fables of the male body in much of her work, inverting or seemingly parodying Progressive Era ideals promoted by writers such as Theodore Roosevelt. In place of vigour, strength, overt masculinism, Cather's neo-Aestheticist narratives sought out the fascination of sickness or illness, and the damaged body.

Modelling the Body:
'Coming, Aphrodite!', the 'Complete Novelette'

Now let's turn to the story 'Coming, Aphrodite!', first published as 'Coming, Eden Bower!' in *Smart Set* (1920), then as 'Coming, Aphrodite!' in the collection *Youth and the Bright Medusa* the same year. Cather subtitled 'Coming, Eden Bower!' 'A Complete Novelette': the story is indeed a world in miniature, containing, in little more than twenty pages, a narrative about looking, artistry, the female body (posed and in movement), taste and Aestheticism. In the story, Cather refracts her interest in the body and art through a series of intriguing vignettes: the young painter Don Hedger meeting Eden; Eden's ascent in a balloon, where she cheekily takes an acrobat's place before removing her skirt to show off her legs as she makes her descent; Hedger's commitment to a modern and experimental artistic sensibility; and a final dénouement where both artists have achieved differing forms of success. Each of these moments is a panel set within a fictional mural whose overall subjects are art and the modern body. Eden is impetuous and highly physicalised, intensely feminised and the fascinated cynosure for Hedger's look. In his or her own way, each artist is a modern; each tries to create a modern art of fluidity and flexibility. For the young Eden, it is sheer movement that seems to be the centre of her being: she exercises, takes fencing lessons, becomes an acrobat. Her very modern female mobility anticipates that of Lucy Gayheart. Hedger, a fledgling artist, lives in a boarding house into which Eden moves. He first watches her, drawn to her 'splendid figure and good action' (*YBM* 8). Eden Bower herself is a nineteenth-century living statue now brought to life; she is a model whose vitality and sinuous action point to the dynamic modelling of the female body in the age of cinema. In other words, she is 'glorious in action' and 'muscular energy seemed to flow through her' (*YBM* 20).

But success is entropic, and brings the stasis and rigidity that offset fame and money. As often in Cather's fiction, the ending of a narrative is the literal *stilling* of a body – either through death or through a process of maturation and success that is anti-kinetic:

> Leaning back in the cushions, Eden Bower closed her eyes, and her face, as the street lamps flashed their ugly orange light upon it, became hard and settled, like a plaster cast; so a sail, that has been filled by a strong breeze, behaves when the wind suddenly dies. Tomorrow night the wind would blow again, and this mask would be the golden face of Aphrodite. (*YBM* 73–4)

Hedger might be seen as an aesthete now faced by newly mobile modern women; he is a sensationalist in search of an aesthetic that might match his intensely embodied sensibility. He idealises 'woman as she existed in art, in thought, and in the universe' (*YBM* 25). He wants 'to paint what people think and feel; to get away from all that photographic stuff' (*YBM* 49). And as he draws close to Eden, he enters 'an invisible network of subtle, almost painful sensibility' (*YBM* 48).

In this narrative, Cather creates a miniature life story – or life stories – where the conventional features of behaviour and action are relegated below a sense of self based upon the five senses. 'Coming, Aphrodite!' is one of her most bodily tales, a narrative of sensory encounter shaped through a condensed short story. In Cather's tale of an encounter between young artists, the senses are foregrounded to the extent that sight, sound and smell are far more important than the fleeting dialogue between Eden Bower and Don Hedger, the singer and the painter.

The painter and the singer: the visual artist and the vocal artist form a binary from which Cather builds complex shapes. The painter Hedger is powerfully drawn to simply gazing at Eden Bower's body through a spy hole, a fetishistic moment of framed looking: Cather's painter is a voyeur. This impulsive, then obsessive viewing is also a highly Aestheticised moment. As so often in Cather, the instinctive or accidental point of human contact cannot exist 'outside' of culture but is immediately framed and shaped by cultural codes. In its fictionalising of the male gaze and its unabashed foregrounding of scopic fascination, Cather's story reminds me of much later cinematic representations of the gaze, as seen in Alfred Hitchcock's *Peeping Tom* (1960) or Jane Campion's *The Piano* (1993). And as with the male protagonists in those films, Cather's scopic hero cannot help himself, cannot stop looking; and as with Campion's film, Cather's story juxtaposes male viewing against other forms of sense in order to destabilise male viewing.[19]

Many cultural historians and theorists have highlighted the increasing visual-centredness – the sight-focus – associated with modern cities, urbanisation and post-Enlightenment society. Sight, above all, is the pre-eminent sense of the Enlightenment and modernity. Empirical observation became the principal modality of scientific exploration. In the Enlightenment, 'seeing was closely allied with knowing. Progressive thinkers often claimed that they were living in an enlightened age, when the bright flame of reason would dispel the dark clouds of ignorance and superstition,' writes Patricia Fara.[20] In the modern city, as Georg Simmel showed in his foundational essay, 'Sociology of the Senses: Visual Interaction' (originally published in 1908), within a community of strangers the individual looks rather than personally greeting one's fellow-villagers.[21] For anthropologists and cultural historians working within 'sensory studies', the last few centuries have, in fact, witnessed a steady privileging of sight above the other four senses. Our current theoretical preoccupation with 'the gaze' – famously crystallised in Laura Mulvey's 'Visual Pleasure and Narrative Cinema', with its analysis of the 'voyeuristic' and 'fetishistic' forms of the male gaze, and its deployment of a term such as 'scopophilia' – might thus be read as the logical outcome of an Enlightenment preoccupation with the scopic/visual.[22] Reversing the analysis, a number of commentators have noted how other senses became demoted within this sensory hierarchy. Smell, in particular, seems to have become part of an orientalist construction, often coming into play as part of an olfactory code which designates otherness. Within Western culture, smell has increasingly been demoted amongst the senses, while the use of deodorants has led to a uniformity of the aromatic environments where we live and work.[23]

Hedger's viewing of Eden is instantly transformed into a tactile sensing, as if to view is also to touch:

> The soft flush of exercise and the gold of afternoon sun played over her flesh together, enveloped her in a luminous mist which, as she turned and twisted, made now an arm, now a shoulder, now a thigh, dissolve in pure light and instantly recover its outline with the next gesture. Hedger's fingers curved as if he were holding a crayon; mentally he was doing the whole figure in a single running line, and the charcoal seemed to explode in his hand at the point where the energy of each gesture was discharged into the whirling disc of light, from a foot or shoulder, from the up-thrust chin or the lifted breasts. (*YBM* 20)

The painter's art frames experience, but even as it frames, the body of the observed seems to break the frame and the containment. Hedger looks through the framed knot hole within the wainscoting. But the curve of his hand round the pencil, unmistakably masturbatory, then seems to trigger nothing less than an upsurge of energy through the 'running line', ending with the charcoal seeming to 'explode' in his hand. Hedger is a typical Cather protagonist in that he thinks Aesthetically, reaching for his pencil, framing the body and mediating it through art. He is also typical in that these moments of framing or mediation are immediately broken, disrupted, contingently fractured by the body itself, and by desire for the body. Cather seems preternaturally, cinematically aware of how to stage a scene through the interplay of bodily surfaces. The shaped, Aestheticised viewing of Eden is broken up by Hedger's neo-orgasmic explosion, but then Eden views herself, in a moment at once quotidian and quietly amusing: 'When her gymnastics were over, she paused to catch up a lock of hair that had come down, and examined with solicitude a little reddish mole that grew under her left arm-pit' (*YBM* 20–1).

I argued in my opening chapter that Cather had learned from Pierre Puvis de Chavannes a way of viewing, or looking, that prized sequence and the movement of the eye across panels (say, in a mural). Sequencing accounts for everything, not only the momentary staging of a look, but in the ways that one moment of viewing is then counterpointed against the next. Cather's writing has a complex visual sequentiality. Very often, such sequences cannot help but remind us of her own critical training as a viewer of performance (one scene in an opera giving way to the next; one panel in a Puvis mural being placed next to another). A viewer like Hedger is brought into an involved, almost ecstatic viewing of a performance. That moment then dissolves into the trivial, the object of viewing turning to herself to gaze mundanely on the body's mundanities: a mole, not a 'whirling disc of light'. The movements, quicksilver and ironic, between different angles of perception and between different tonal registers, enable Cather to register the human body in ways that are both monumental and oddly inconsequential. After the mole, we return to Hedger's epically classic version of what has just happened: 'The spot was enchanted; a vision out of Alexandria, out of the remote pagan past, had bathed itself there in Helianthine fire' (*YBM* 21).

The Song of the Lark: Aestheticising Encounters

Cather's early writings explored the unlikely emergence of Aestheticism in American settings: a ragged Frontier settlement, the raw industrial city of Pittsburgh, lodging houses and Midwestern hotels. Wilde himself had famously travelled to dozens of cities throughout the country, and Cather's work pursued a Wildean tack, as it were, in mapping the Aesthetic ideal on to provincial American sites.

Space – American space – played a major role in the 1890s displacement of Aestheticism from its European, cosmopolitan birthplaces into new homelands, where it might flourish, or (so often) wither and die, or be defeated. In Frederic's *The Damnation of Theron Ware*, the Methodist minister finally plans to move to Seattle – the affair with the Catholic aesthete is over, and Ware will move deeper into the Protestant, anti-Aesthetic West. In *The Awakening* (1899), Edna Pontellier's death is certainly Aestheticised, but her suicide at sea seems peculiarly fitting, as if the new possibilities her life has offered can no longer be contained on land: she will have to leave, leave land, and die on the very borders of the nation. Cather's 1904 story, 'A Wagner Matinée', told a tale of internal exile: an ageing music devotee, who has lived for decades on the Nebraskan prairies, experiences (tearfully and perhaps for the last time) the delights of Wagner during a trip back east, to Boston.

Frederic, Chopin and Cather all tested the European gospel pioneered by Wilde and du Maurier by placing aesthetes in provincial American settings. Tellingly, these tales would focus on the body of the aesthete as if the struggle between culture and philistinism would literally work itself out on to flesh itself. *The Song of the Lark* deepens these meditations, standing out as a sustained exploration of what Aestheticism might mean in its new provincial American home. The novel's representations of late Victorian and proto-Modernist forms of Aestheticism make that early novel a particularly fascinating example of Cather's transitional art. One sees Cather taking a very Victorian narrative line (Thea Kronborg is almost Alger-esque in her provincial quest for success), then rewriting that plot to address the Aesthetic tropes I have been outlining: the power of the female voice (and how it might be controlled by male mentors), the place of the 'Kingdom of Art' in remote American places, the new bodies brought into being by the cultural shifts of the 1890s, and the sensoriness of Progressive Era culture.

The Song of the Lark emerges as Cather's transitional novel, a massive portmanteau in which she places many of her initial ideas about the body and its representations. Its sheer size (it is easily Cather's longest work) and its neo-Victorian machinery of plot devices (humble origins, fortuitous financial bequests, a rags-to-riches grand narrative) are deceptive. In very many ways, this is a remarkably experimental novel, a repository for thinking about embodiment and bodily contact, whose basic scenarios and dramatic situations would establish templates for much of Cather's later work. It was with *The Song of the Lark* that the initial impetus of Cather's career, seen in the reviewing and the short stories, shows its potential to serve as the imaginative spine of a much longer work – an imagined life-story not configured in terms of moral growth or characterological 'development', but through a complex mapping of the creative self's emergence from the sensory ground of the body.

Cather's first two novels, *Alexander's Bridge* and *O Pioneers!*, were hybrid narratives. *Alexander's Bridge* grafts the late nineteenth-century neo-Gothic narrative of doubles (Bartley Alexander is a Stevensonian or Wildean figure with two lives, notably a secret adulterous self) on to the Jamesian international novel. *O Pioneers!* hybridises the emergent narrative of female self-determination (as seen in the works of Kate Chopin or Charlotte Perkins Gilman) with immigration/Americanisation narratives (such as her mentor S. S. McClure's *My Autobiography*). Both were fascinating experiments, their manipulation of popular narrative shapes showing Cather working still with her editor's hat on, inflecting and splicing received narrative forms.

In *The Song of the Lark*, the hybridisation of narrative is more audacious, the artistic stakes are higher, and the results that much more compelling. The novel hybridises two forms (Cather using her typical binary model): the European *Künstlerroman* and the

American local colour form. But Cather opens up the spaces within these narrative forms to explore the aesthetic/bodily concerns that had preoccupied her for two decades.

A tramp plays a major role in Cather's mural – to use a Puvis term – of the West. Cather's tramps, in their dereliction and affront to conventional sensory codes, are important figures in her mapping of the body. She uses tramps and their deaths critically and interrogatively – superficially, they are figures drawn from the world of nineteenth-century sensationalism: dangerous hobos, wanderers, or figures from the rural margin or the urban underworld. But in Cather's (re)deployment, they occupy a liminal and critical position, challenging the sensory order of mainstream society. They focus that fascination with contamination and health that Susan Meyer has identified as a major Catherian preoccupation.[24] The anthropologist Mary Douglas referred to 'dirt as matter out of place', and one might add that, for Cather, dirty people matter because they are often out of place in the fledgeling Western communities she explored.[25]

The tramp arrives, bringing sensory disturbance. 'He looked over the fence . . . There was a terrible odor about him, too. She caught it even at that distance, and put her handkerchief to her nose' (*SOL* 150–1). The tramp smells bad but looks even worse: 'his bony body grotesquely attired in the clown's suit, his face shaved and white – the sweat trickling through the paint and away – and his eyes wild and feverish' (*SOL* 151). The tramp brings his smells and his wild look, his snakes (killed by the saloon-keeper): his is a stark, brutally immediate, affronting physicality. When he is thrown out of town, he 'left no trace except an ugly, stupid word, chalked on the black paint of the seventy-five-foot standpipe which was the reservoir for the Moonstone water-supply' (*SOL* 152). The tramp, feverish from typhoid, exhibits his sickening body before the town. Arrested by the marshal, he is charged for giving a show without a licence. He then, apparently, disappears. But the tramp has enacted and embodied the insult scrawled on the standpipe; he lowers his diseased body and corrupted belongings into the water supply, poisoning the town and thus killing 'several adults and half a dozen children' (*SOL* 152).

The outsider always registers in a bodily way for Cather – as a form of physicalised text that makes literal a community's anxieties and fears. Thea, like many other Cather protagonists, is haunted by the tramp's body, becoming an early version of Cather's artist-writer haunted or shadowed by the physically grotesque Other – we might also think of Tom Outland's intense response to Mother Eve in *The Professor's House*: 'She kept seeing him in his bedraggled clown suit, the white paint on his roughly shaven face, playing his accordion before the saloon. She had noticed his lean body, his high, bald forehead that sloped back like a curved metal lid' (*SOL* 153).

Cather places the tramp's entry into the town at a pivotal moment in Thea's narrative: she is about to leave, to take her vitality and potential to the big city (Chicago); the tramp wanders into the small town, bringing his death, and dies there while taking others with him. We have those who stay and those who leave, here reconfigured in terms of bodily exits and entries, highly physical forms of decayed decline, and vital ascent. The narrative is one of deep 'showing', not 'telling' – Cather's technique following that panelling mode that I have highlighted: an attention to surfaces and how the reader's eye traces episodic configurations across a series of vignettes or scenes.

Thus, in the next sections of the novel Cather explores Thea's burgeoning bodily strength – her development as a singer configured in overwhelmingly physical terms, as a bodily sequencing where potential is literally embodied, ready for artistic exploitation. In fact, it is remarkable how little is made, by her teacher's and mentors, of the cognitive, conscious aspects of becoming an artist. Instead, artistic potential is a highly physical instantiation, felt in sinew and blood. It is also profoundly social – as others respond to and relate to that physical embodiment.

Conclusion: Cather and the Body in Transition

To contextualise Cather's representations of the body, specifically a late Victorian body framed by Aestheticism, is to realise that her fiction traced cultural transformations of embodied experience. The figure of the diva was a 'new' figure, emergent in the late nineteenth century. Oscar Wilde decisively foregrounded, in the late decades of the nineteenth century, the male aesthete as a figure of fascination. Placing such figures (Paul, the Lincoln hipster, Thea Kronborg and Eden Bower) in American settings – often provincial ones – Cather then expanded the sensory range of American narrative. From her early lament that her world was 'sense-dwarfed', Cather's first decades of writing had found a paradoxical sensory richness and transition in the small town, the industrial city or the emergent world of American Bohemia.

Notes

1. Slote's 1966 compendia of Cather's earliest writings included her 1890s articles and reviews about such figures as Christina Rossetti, George du Maurier, Robert Louis Stevenson, Oscar Wilde, Pierre Loti and Paul Verlaine: all central figures in what one might call the 'post-Romantic' development of literature in Europe.
2. For useful accounts of Wilde's impact on American culture (for instance, during the 1882 lecture tour), see MacInerney et al., 'Oscar Wilde Lectures in Texas', and Freedman, 'An Aestheticism of Our Own'.
3. See, for instance, Marilee Lindemann's comments on Paul as an 'aesthete' and a 'sensualist' (*Willa Cather: Queering America*, 34, 36).
4. Blanchard, *Oscar Wilde's America: Counterculture in the Gilded Age*, 3.
5. Oscar Wilde, *Decorative Art in America*, 4.
6. Ibid. 5.
7. Salamensky, 'Re-Presenting Oscar Wilde: Wilde's Trials, "Gross Indecency," and Documentary Spectacle', 575–88: 578.
8. Wilde, *Decorative Art*, 8.
9. Blanchard, *Oscar Wilde's America*, 211.
10. Kaplan, *The Anarchy of Empire*, 98.
11. Rosowski, *The Voyage Perilous: Willa Cather's Romanticism*.
12. Cather, 'Utterly Irrelevant' (16 September 1894).
13. Cather, *The Home Monthly*, 11.
14. Du Maurier, *Trilby*, 42.
15. Cather, 'Utterly Irrelevant' (23 September 1894).
16. Savage, *Teenage: The Creation of Youth Culture*, 35–6.
17. Oscar Wilde, *Dorian Gray*, 175.
18. My argument here is indebted to Simon Joyce's article, 'Sexual Politics and the Aesthetics of Crime: Oscar Wilde in the Nineties', 501–23.
19. Campion's film juxtaposes the male protagonist, Baines, who is the typically visually driven figure I am describing, against Ada McGrath, a mute Scotswoman newly arrived in Victorian New Zealand. Campion, in ways that I think Cather would have immediately registered, carefully syncopates Baines's gazing against Ada's touching in this highly sensory narrative.
20. Fara, *An Entertainment for Angels: Electricity in the Enlightenment*, 15.
21. Simmel, 'Sociology of the Senses: Visual Interaction', 356–61.

22. Mulvey, 'Visual Pleasure and Narrative Cinema', 6–18.
23. See Constance Classen, *Worlds of Sense: Exploring the Senses in History and Across Cultures*, esp. 'The Odour of the Other: Olfactory Codes and Cultural Categories', 79–105. Constance Classen et al., *Aroma: The Cultural History of Smell*, remains the best account of odour in context(s). Classen also reads sensory hierarchies through the prism of gender. See her essay 'Engendering Perception: Gender Ideologies and Sensory Hierarchies in Western History', 1–19.
24. Meyer, 'Contamination, Modernity, Health'.
25. Douglas, *Purity and Danger: An Analysis of Concepts of Pollution and Taboo*, 44.

CHAPTER 4

Pale Shades and Living Colours: Cather's Looks

'Unlike most visual art, which can be experienced in a single gaze, fiction is a matter of subsequent and successive gazes, mimicking chronological time, as it is locked into chronological time.'

Joyce Carol Oates, 'Inspiration and Obsession in Life and Literature'[1]

Contemporary Norwegian author Karl Ove Knausgaard writes about the importance of direct gazing and the ways in which a work of art might be an act of humanistic communion that is close to simply looking at someone: 'What is a work of art if not the gaze of another person?'[2] Knausgaard, a child of the ice and cold of Scandinavia, would appreciate the plethora of looks and gazes in Cather's work, as well as her fierce indifference to indifference, her need to have the human gaze mean something, to establish contact and intimacy in a moment. It is almost impossible not to read the articulation of human connection in Cather's work as if it were not rooted in the emptiness of Homesteader-era Nebraska, the scatteredness of human settlement, the remarkable drama of simply meeting people. For meeting people always represents the drama in Cather's work, the primal seed of narrative. And her deep love of performance and performative spaces (opera houses, theatres, concert halls) must also have emerged from a primary sense of physical isolation. The pleasure of theatre-going was, for Cather, an occasion for being amongst people, watching and observing, and being in a crowd. The oft-noted need for isolation in her middle years, paradoxically, was yet another manifestation of this oscillation between sociability and creative isolation – the famed writer taking pleasure in New York City's theatres and opera houses, but craving a space of her own.

In this chapter I open up a discussion of Cather as what we might term a *polyscopic* writer – an author fascinated by looks and gazing, and of the varied shapes (in terms of dramatic situations and narrative plotlines) that such disparate viewing might then produce. My meditation begins after Cather's death, with her partner Edith Lewis's memory of Cather's own gaze, and then moves on through four stages: an analysis of encounters and looking; an account of gendered looking in fiction; followed by close readings of Cather's scopic writing early in her career (*My Ántonia*) and then during her late writing (*Shadows on the Rock*). Throughout these close readings I show that some of the most fundamental scenarios explored in her fiction (for instance, how a man looks at a woman, or how a white viewer might visually apprehend a black character) are, quite literally, often embodied in a glance or a gaze.

To trace Cather's looks is to think about how a writer's life might be shaped by an early pattern of cultural encounter, but then move into increasing complexity and formalistic sophistication. Cather was a reviewer, to begin with – a tyro journalist in Lincoln, ceaselessly looking at performers. She began as a 'gazer': made money from this, forged her first writing identity in the theatre or opera house, simply looking. The fiction that then unfurled from these first sites of encounter then built narratives out of these initial scopic moments, becoming a form of primal staging that would enable Cather to extend the gaze to encompass women looking at men, colonists viewing their strangely settled and unsettled world, or white immigrants transfixed, paradoxically, by a blind black performer.

Cather's Eyes

Cather's life partner Edith Lewis admired Willa Cather as a person who remembered people in terms of the colours of their personalities. Lewis's *Willa Cather Living* is the best kind of homage, deeply infused and conversant with the author's works – its own syntax and clusters of imagery relentlessly and dialogically engaged with the writer. The memoir is a love poem, thoroughly 'Catheresque' in a sustained attention to the ordinary textures of life; its understated and precise prose, and its unabashed lyricism and romanticism echo Cather's own writing. It also begins, like so many Cather novels, with decisive encounters that turn on spectatorial stagings as one individual meets another. Lewis sees the writer Cather, an intensely visual author, as a figure who sensed people pictorially:

> Perhaps the greatest single indication of her artistic gift was her extraordinary sensitiveness to people – her intense curiosity about them, the depth of her response to them, the way their individuality, their personal traits and behavior, cut deep into her consciousness, so that years afterward she could summon them up, not as pale shades, but with all their living colours, their insistent humanity, to be recreated and given lasting existence through her transforming art.[3]

Lewis's first meeting with Cather is described as a highly scopic scenario and is well worth quoting at length due to its intriguing dialogic engagement with Cather's visual tropes. Lewis, looking at Cather, focuses on her eyes:

> She had curling chestnut-brown hair, done high on her head, a fair skin; but the feature one noticed particularly was her eyes. They were dark blue eyes, with dark lashes; and I know no way of describing them, except to say that they were the eyes of genius. I have never met any very gifted person who did not have extraordinary eyes. Many people's eyes, I have noticed, are half opaque; they conceal, as much as they express, their owner's personality, and thought, feeling, struggle through them like light through a clouded sky. But Willa Cather's eyes were like a direct communication of her spirit. The whole of herself was in her look, in that transparently clear, level, unshrinking gaze that seemed to know everything there was to be known about both herself and you.[4]

This passage was published a few years after Willa Cather died, and was written by the person with whom she shared her life. It is, obliquely but relentlessly, an elegy, and in a way familiar from the narrative strategies of *The Professor's House* or *My Ántonia*, in that it achieves its effects by framing compelled fascination and longing on the part of a rememberer looking back on someone now lost. With a classic Catherian reversal, the feelings of the viewer are transposed on to the object of her or his attention. Jim Burden commemorates Ántonia; Godfrey St Peter commemorates Tom Outland; Edith Lewis commemorates Cather. In each case, the narrative is an act of commitment and mourning, the very fact of its telling an enactment of compelled attention which is also grounded in sensory contact. Lewis's humanistic commitment to rendering Cather recalls one of Cather's earliest comments on the creative process – namely, her 1894 lines about breathing life into one's creations to make them 'living souls'.

> An author is not an artist until he can create characters that we love not for their goodness or their character or their 'cause,' but for themselves. An artist has nothing to do with how much wine we may drink at dinner or how low we may wear our ball dresses. His business is to make men and women and breathe into them until they become living souls.[5]

It is hard to read Lewis's account of Cather and not think continually of the importance of the simple word *living* as a keyword in the two women's lexicon of creativity.

Returning to her comment on Cather, Lewis seems to straddle the two architectures of emotionality and personality: 'But Willa Cather's eyes were like a direct communication of her spirit,' she wrote: 'The whole of herself was in her look, in that transparently clear, level, unshrinking gaze that seemed to know everything there was to be known about both herself and you.'[6] The first part of the description loops back to the classic model of reading character metonymically through the interplay of a holistic self apprehended through each part of a face or figure. Her eyes 'were like a direct communication of her spirit'. Yet this is also a self that knows others, that reaches out, that is in dialogue with others and that is profoundly social – 'everything there was to be known about both herself and you'.

Such writing is, one must acknowledge, also highly privileged, in that it accords the writer, especially the white writer, preternatural gifts of sympathy and understanding. That these gifts are to be read on and through the body gives them even more power: as if Cather's understanding of others, which is, in Lewis's analysis, central to her creative power, was as instinctive as a look itself. This is embodiment read as creative power and cultural capital. And following Lewis's construction of Cather's corporealised talents, it became a trope for later critics to read Cather as a writer with a 'gift for sympathy': hence Edward and Lillian Bloom's 1964 study, *Willa Cather's Gift of Sympathy*.[7] In the readings that follow in this chapter I acknowledge the importance of Lewis's insight, but also see it as more complex in practice – that Cather's work explores, plays out, analyses an embodied world marked by an almost-physicalised sense of sympathy. In this fictional world, as we shall see in *My Ántonia* and *Shadows on the Rock*, a more nuanced and complex rendering of the sympathetic look emerges, as Cather takes that basic instant of human interaction, and creates narratives where such moments focus the gaps between human beings, especially if they come from very different worlds (able-bodied and disabled; male and female; black and white).

As we shall see, Cather steadily opened up, deepened and widened that sense of the initial gaze between one individual and another. She created *dramas* centred on viewing. A prodigal reviewer of performance, Cather then infused narrative with a persistent sense of how the gaze (with its perceptions and misperceptions) sits at the heart of social engagement. This sense of focalisation (quite literally a *focalisation*) then led to passages in her work where queerness, and also a stereotyping of Otherness, came decisively to the fore.

Cather's early writings included quirky examples of art criticism: for instance, vignettes set in art galleries – dramatisations, effectively, of the experience of viewing. Highly idiosyncratic, such pieces looked forward to her fiction's explorations of the social practices and cultural politics of spectatorship. This seems to be the case in Cather's fascinating, teasing account of Henry Scott Tuke's 1898 painting, 'The Diver', which she discussed, writing as Henry Nicklemann, in the 24 November 1901 essay, 'Popular Pictures'. 'When the young art student visits the Carnegie gallery,' Cather writes, 'he is inclined to wonder what pretext the thousands of visitors who are not art students have for going there at all.'

Cather – as Henry Nicklemann – then wanders the gallery, watching the encounters between various viewers and the works. What is important here is not Cather's assuming cultural centrality (as critic and judge of the aesthetic), but her turning of the art gallery into a theatre of appreciation, a place where cultural encounter might literally be witnessed. During this encounter, Cather describes an old gentlemen waiting for his great-nieces to move away, so he might contemplate Tuke's picture. The gentleman smiles wistfully at the image – Cather's attention caught by the viewer viewing.

> I daresay he thought little of the original treatment of the water, or the splendid sunlight, or the painting of the fine, firm young flesh, or the hitch of preparation in the diver's shoulder blades, but he knew why the boy in the rear end of the boat is as radiant with happiness as with sunlight.

Cather then comments of the gazing geezer: 'I accosted him, and we became friends on the strength of old memories of a common and a lost kingship.'[8]

The account is a subtle and coded review of viewing, an account by the female author of the male gaze – that gaze trained on the male nude: the watcher watched. Masquerading as a male writer, Cather recounted an encounter with a male viewer of what might now seem to us a homoerotic painting of young boys in a skiff. Tuke was a British painter (1858–1929) whose late Victorian *plein air* pictures of young men bathing, rowing and sailing were popular in the 1890s; his work fell violently out of fashion for many decades, but has recently been rehabilitated (in fact, Tuke was a central figure in the Tate Britain exhibition, 'Queer British Art 1861–1967'; John Singer Sargent, also admired by Cather, was another figure in that show). The Pittsburgh galleries offered Cather a forum for queer viewing; it is here that we see her imagining a covert bond emerging from a shared appreciation of a coded aesthetic.

The review establishes spectatorship in terms of *mise-en-scène*, a form of dramatic scenario, that echoes in the later fiction. Think about the situation at the start of the story 'A Gold Slipper' (which appeared in *Harper's* in 1917, and then in *Youth and the Bright Medusa*), where the male viewer Marshall McKann, brought on stage to watch Kitty Ayrshire (there are insufficient seats in the main auditorium), will find himself looked down upon by the singer herself:

> In the moment her bright, curious eyes rested upon him, McKann seemed to see himself as if she were holding a mirror up before him. He beheld himself a heavy, solid figure, unsuitably clad for the time and place, with a florid, square face, well-visored with good living and sane opinions — an inexpressive countenance. Not a rock face, exactly, but a kind of pressed-brick-and-cement face, a 'business' face upon which years and feelings had made no mark — in which cocktails might eventually blast out a few hollows. He had never seen himself so distinctly in his shaving-glass as he did in that instant when Kitty Ayrshire's liquid eye held him, when her bright, inquiring glance roamed over his person. (*YBM* 146)

Such a passage demonstrates Cather's highly theatrical sense of viewing, and her sense of how a simple situation might contain a geometry of viewpoints. Stages and mirrors, men being viewed by women: here is Cather's viewing of modern life crisply and powerfully crystallised.

Because 'the everyday' in early Cather texts such as *O Pioneers!* or *My Ántonia* is framed by agricultural labour, pioneer settlement or climatic extremes, the extra-ordinary tends to be ceremonial or performative: moments of being outside the everyday grind. Clothing – and especially the colour that clothing can bring – thus becomes a marker of tonal or narrative change in her works. The reader knows that something significant is about to happen because characters quite literally will start to appear in different, non-quotidian dress. In *O Pioneers!* the landscape descriptions at the start of the novel are of a blank, grey, featureless, relentless prairie world. Colour is vital in Cather's work, often because her characters live in harsh, cold places where colour is a dream for much of the year – four of Cather's novels (*O Pioneers!*, *My Ántonia*, *Shadows on the Rock* and *Lucy Gayheart*) foreground the wintery, monochromatic landscapes of the prairies or Quebec. Colour, as Michael Taussig points out in a discussion of early modern Europe's visual culture, might emerge from a background of monotonous colourlessness, 'Yet it is the very monotony of blackness and colorlessness that makes the momentary spasms of color-lust so revealing'.[9]

Looking at people, especially those who are different (because of clothing, or ethnicity, or performative role), often powers the drama of a Cather vignette. Thus in *O Pioneers!* the murder at the narrative's heart – the slaying of Emil and Maria by Frank Shabata after he finds his wife and lover together – is presaged by an elaborate costume parade, a church processional where Emil wears a Mexican outfit and Marie dresses in peasant Bohemian garb.

> 'Do the men wear clothes like that every day, in the street?' She caught Emil by his sleeve and turned him about. 'Oh, I wish I lived where people wore things like that! Are the buttons silver? Put on the hat, please.' (*OP!* 194)

Frank looks on warily, wary of 'making a fuss over a fellow just because he was dressed like a clown' (*OP!* 196). That is, Cather uses costume in a quite stylised way, as an index of exoticism and desire; Marie's overt fascination with Emil's clothing is a powerful foretaste of what is about to happen. And it is the drama of looking that acts as the motor of the unfolding drama.

'I see you through my affection for you': The Gaze in Cather's Fiction

In *Death Comes for the Archbishop* Father Latour explains the meaning of miracles in terms of sensory refinement:

> 'One might almost say that an apparition is human vision corrected by divine love. I do not see you as you really are, Joseph; I see you through my affection for you. The Miracles of the Church seem to me to rest not so much upon faces or voices or healing power coming suddenly near to us from afar off, but upon our perceptions being made finer, so that for a moment our eyes can see and our ears can hear what is there about us always.' (*DCA* 53–4)

Latour's comment is fascinating on many levels. For instance, as a comment on Catholic doctrine, it suggests that one reason why the Protestant Cather might have been drawn to Catholic subject-matter was because she sensed in Catholicism a more physicalised and bodily devotional practice. (My later chapter on taste, which examines the figure of the sensory recusant Jeanne le Ber in *Shadows on the Rock*, pursues this line of enquiry.) Latour also emphasises a point that underpins many of the moments where Cather fictionalises looking: that the sheer subjectivity of the look is crucial. It is this sense of subjectivism, of a look that is also a filter of sorts, emotionally shaping what we see, that is central to the passages that I now want to place in a form of interpretative collage.

Many Cather novels begin with a moment of looking or gazing, or even with a glance; Cather's work is, in fact, a repository of looks, all explored and dramatised to open up those moments of human connection that were her recurrent subject. Cather is as attentive to the colour of her characters' eyes as any novelist could be, and at the end of her career she even thought of using eye colour in the title of one of her books: one working title for the novel that became *Lucy Gayheart* was *Blue Eyes on the Platte*.[10] Her novels use looking and gazing as a primary code for human sociability. *My Ántonia* codifies all of its initial characters in terms of the colour and emotional cast of their eyes. In the Introduction Jim has 'quick-changing blue eyes', while Jim's grandfather has 'bright blue' eyes ('not at all like those of an old man') (*MA* xi, 11). Mr Shimerda's character, and his eventual suicide, seem almost present in the initial capturing of his face: 'His eyes were melancholy, and were set back deep under his brow. His face was ruggedly formed, but it looked like ashes – like something from which all the warmth and light had died out'(*MA* 24).

There is a constancy to Cather's fascination with eyes, looking and gazing, but there is also multivalency in the ways these looks function, in line with the subjectivism suggested by Latour's comment. When Cather writes about Mr Shimerda, she creates a sense of character that we might call 'Victorian'. Shimerda can be read both holistically and metonymically. Eyes carry mournfulness; a face conveys ashes. A man's fate is written in his countenance. We are not far from a phrenological reading of character, which, as Susan Meyer has shown, certainly percolates through some of Cather's readings/writings of character.[11] On one hand, Shimerda's suicidal fate is written on the face and might be metonymically apprehended in parts of his body. Cather, writing in this fashion, is not far from the kind of commentary that would see the integrity of a man's character as written in the dignity of his forehead. There is a clear narrative arc from Shimerda's face to his death – ironically and fittingly, fashioned from his placing his shotgun into that very face.

But Cather, even as she remains partly rooted in the nineteenth century, also points forward to a more open and modernistic formation of character: character as performative, as dialogic. Here, the ease of metonymic readability is less assured. Bafflement plays its role in social encounters; sensory apprehension of others seems to lead to unexpected affinities or sudden affective closures; social life becomes a complex semiotic game of shifting signifiers; subjectivism works to undermine a look's claim to final authority. In a sense, what Cather is helping us to see is the moment of transition between one emotional order of things and another. Eyes might not convey character metonymically, though it might be that an exchange of glances and the social performance of affect constitute a 'modern' way of imagining selfhood that Cather explored in her fiction.

Cather often begins novels, as Lewis began her memoir, with accounts of eyes and looking. St Peter is said to have 'hawk-like eyes ... there was no evading the searching eyes underneath them; eyes that in a flash could pick out a friend or an unusual stranger from a throng' (*TPH* 13). A fascination with picking out 'the unusual stranger' had been present in Cather's work from the very beginning of her career as a novelist. *Alexander's Bridge* starts with Professor Lucius Wilson spotting an interesting woman on a Boston street:

> He had already fixed his sharp eye upon the house which he reasoned should be his objective point, when he noticed a woman approaching rapidly from the opposite direction. Always an interested observer of women, Wilson would have slackened his pace anywhere to follow this one with his impersonal, appreciative glance. (*AB* 4)

In John Berger's famous analysis of the gaze, it is the male artist who gazes at the female form, and the woman's role is to watch, if you like, themselves being looked at:

> One might simplify this by saying: *men act* and *women appear*. Men look at women. Women watch themselves being looked at. This determines not only most relations between men and women but also the relation of women to themselves. The surveyor of woman in herself is male: the surveyed female. Thus she turns herself into an object – and most particularly an object of vision: a sight.[12]

Cather often reversed this basic paradigm, taking the male face or the male body as the subject for a female gaze. What is perhaps most interesting about the patterns of looking, glancing and gazing in Cather's fiction is how often it is the female spectator who is at the centre of these visual scenarios. Sometimes Cather's narratives simply catch an isolated moment of the female gaze. For example,

> Lena moved without exertion, rather indolently, and her hand often accented the rhythm softly on her partner's shoulder. She smiled if one spoke to her, but seldom answered. The music seemed to put her into a soft, waking dream, and her violet-colored eyes looked sleepily and confidingly at one from under her long lashes. (*MA* 215)

Elsewhere, there is a more concerted and focused look in play. In *The Song of the Lark*, when Doctor Archie meets Thea after many years, her gaze (impromptu but theatrical) seems to penetrate the scarf she is wearing, such is the power of female spectatorship: 'She gave him a piercing, defiant glance through the white scarf that covered her face. Then she lifted her hand and brushed the scarf back from her head. There was still black on her brows and lashes.' As she then says to Archie, 'Let me *look* at you' (*SOL* 455–6).

Thus the viewing at the start of *Alexander's Bridge* is rather untypical of Cather's usual mapping of sight and seeing, which tends to be idiosyncratically configured around gazes and which often takes the male body as its focus. Cather's narratives often imagine a gaze focused on male bodies and faces, a remapping of the expected pattern of the male gaze focused on the female figure, as described by Berger. The Bergerian 'object of vision' at the start of *Sapphira and the Slave Girl*, *My Ántonia*, *Death Comes for the Archbishop* or *The Professor's House* is the male face. Cather seems to play quite consciously with stereotypes of how one considers male physique and physiognomy, invoking and then quietly subverting readerly expectations. *Sapphira and the Slave Girl* introduces Henry Colbert in sentences that quickly define a solid presence and straightforwardness: 'The miller was a solid, powerful figure of a man, in whom height and weight agreed.' But as the paragraph moves on, it is his eyes that mark out a shift in character and sensibility:

> It was only his eyes that were puzzling; dark and grave, set far back under a square, heavy brow. Those eyes, reflective, almost dreamy, seemed out of keeping with the simple vigour of his face. The long lashes would have been a charm in a woman. (*SSG* 8)

And so Cather's prose moves from the all too masculine epithets at the start to the teasing comments at the end – the 'solid' miller with lashes that belong in a woman's face.

The ironic, teasing playfulness of these sentences is not a one-off. Throughout her work, Cather focused her narratives' repeated gaze upon male bodies and faces in such a way as to upset and offset expectations, her ironic tone signalling a wry reversal of Berger's sense of gender and sight. Cather's male characters are quite literally a 'sight'. Compare Colbert's eyelashes to St Peter in his pyjamas:

> The Professor in pyjamas was not an unpleasant sight; for looks, the fewer clothes he had on, the better. Anything that clung to his body showed it to be built upon extremely good bones, with the slender hips and springy shoulders of a tireless swimmer. (*TPH* 13)

In the description that follows, the terrain of the face is again important, and nothing is more significant within that terrain than the eyes. As with so many of Cather's faces, what is then critical is the return of the gaze, as Cather first focuses on the eyes, and then gauges how they look back: 'His wicked-looking eyebrows made his students call him Mephistopheles – and there was no evading the searching eyes underneath them; eyes that in a flash could pick out a friend or an unusual stranger from a throng' (*TPH* 13).

The viewing of St Peter and the viewing of Latour are staged acts where the cultural framing of the body is strikingly foregrounded: we see bodies in certain ways because cultural traditions have taught us to look at the body in certain ways. The brio of these scenes rests in Cather's ironic inhabiting of the typical Western matrix, which places the male view in front of the female nude. Now – and there is almost a nudge and a wink in her prose – the female viewer will have her turn in front of the body.

In Cather's journalistic writings there are fascinating instances of this reversed viewing as she subjects masculine physiology to what is sometimes an exhaustive and neo-scientific accounting. The article 'Training for the Ballet: Making American Dancers', published in *McClure's Magazine* in 1913 (as Cather transitioned into a full-time creative career), is notable for dealing with female *and* male dancers. The article incorporates several photos of Edmund McAuliffe, a boy 'who will be the first American male *premier*'.[13] Cather details the physiologically determined differences between female and male dancers: 'A boy's hip-bones are longer and his hip-joint less elastic. The boy never practises toe-work, which in a male dancer would be effeminate.'[14] Cather's writing about the male ballet dancer is precisely observed, clinical and detailed – and also suggestively embedded in social constructs of gender roles ('toe-work' is 'effeminate').

And yet there is one major exploration made of the traditional male gaze in the Cather *œuvre*: *Lucy Gayheart*. Cather's penultimate novel is a highly sensory text ostensibly focused on music, sound and hearing. But it is also a narrative focused on varieties of visual tragedy that grow from the relentlessness of the male gaze and the misperceptions of that gaze. The first two pages of the novel describe how the townspeople of Haverford gazed on Lucy, and also how their looks failed to capture her vitality, her sheer life-force: 'They still see her as a slight figure always in motion; dancing or skating, or walking swiftly with intense direction, like a bird flying home' (*LG* 5). *Lucy Gayheart* constructs a complex lattice of looks and gazes grouped around the ways the community – and Harry Gordon in particular – envision the protagonist. But Lucy also looks back. Her eyes 'flashed with gold sparks like that Colorado stone we call the tiger-eye' (Cather invoking the 'we' of the community's gaze), even though 'Photographs of Lucy mean nothing to her old friends' (*LG* 6). She seems to have a vitality that exceeds the encompassing gaze, rendering photographs invalid.

The novel traces Harry's and Lucy's sensory entanglements and the patterns of attraction and engagement that structure the ways that they both listen to and look at one another. Cather sets up in the overture, in the ways her novels often organise sensory questions in their opening pages, a question about how Lucy might be looked upon. She captivates and intrigues visually, but a photograph cannot capture that essence. What will it mean to fall for her visual enchantment? Harry falls in love with Lucy, finds his confused attraction unreciprocated, and finally overlooks Lucy at a crucial moment (contributing to her death). Conversely, he is always looking (with fascination and desire) at Lucy. Cather's writing here seems to mime, quite deliberately and directly, a romantic discourse of fascinated gazes and sudden moments of adoration. Harry is smitten:

> She was standing in that crowd of slovenly men, clouds of tobacco smoke drifting about her, slowly turning the combination lock of her father's letter-box . . . She looked so slight, so fine, so reserved – He had turned like a flash and walked rapidly down the street, without going inside to face her. But that glimpse of her, standing in profile with one hand lifted, had been enough. (*LG* 226)

He repeatedly sees Lucy on the street, and will – in Cather's focalised third-person narrative telling – come to read her look, her gaze in his own way: 'It was only when she met Harry Gordon that her eyes lighted up with the present moment, and asked for something. They never looked at him that they did not implore him to be kind' (*LG* 227).

Lucy Gayheart's publication history might be understood as Cather's most ingenious encounter with the literary marketplace and the demands, and opportunities, presented by writing for a large mainstream audience. As David Porter writes, Cather serialised the novel in *Woman's Home Companion*, 'often commenting . . . that she had agreed to place it in a magazine only because of the money she would make' (Porter refers to such admissions made in her correspondence).[15] She then published the novel as a trade edition book, further garnering both financial reward and critical approval, cementing a literary identity that incorporated both elite and middlebrow signals. Reading the novel sensorily, one sees another way that this movement across audiences also had a counterpart in terms of the novel's use of established fictional discourses. As 'Romance', *Lucy Gayheart* proffers itself as a repository of the looks and glances, encounters and chances that we might associate with middlebrow fiction. But Cather explores – 'reads out' might be a better way to put it – the coded implications of that sensory register. Thus Harry Gordon's fate will effectively be that of the male gazer whose gaze failed. Even as he meets Lucy for the last time, Cather describes his look as one of increasing cloudiness: 'Harry's eyes were watery from the cold; he seemed more than ever to look at her through glasses' (*LG* 208). The novel will literally end (in its last sentence) with Harry trapped, seemingly for what will now be a lifetime of gazing, in a ceaseless and automatic viewing of the footsteps Lucy left in the setting concrete: 'he paused mechanically on the sidewalk, as he had done so many thousand times, to look at the three light footprints, running away' (*LG* 242). He keeps the Gayheart house as a kind of locked, privately viewable chamber – Lucy's room is as it was when she was alive, replete with her clothes and a signed picture of Clement Sebastian. All Harry can do is visit, look at her things and privately view them. The sense of fetishism in this scene is palpable: one feels that Cather has created a compelling poetic narrative that addresses the compulsions, and the ultimate failures and tragedies, of male looking.

Viewing in *My Ántonia*

Alberto Manguel writes of the implied presence of a viewer as suggested by a Diego Velázquez portrait:

> Velazquez plays on the fact that a portrait takes for granted the presence of a viewer, a viewer who agrees to a dialogue in which the words are put forward by the subject but in which the meaning must be invented by the viewer.[16]

This is the position the reader–viewer of a Cather character (Nellie Birdseye or Harry Gordon) is in, when they look at the portrait of Myra Henshawe or Lucy Gayheart: 'the meaning must be invented by the viewer', but what if this invention is also a manifestation, an instantiation of power? *Lucy Gayheart* charts Harry's will to power through the gaze; and, in his ultimate neglect of Lucy (which leads to her death), the brutal indifference that might paradoxically underpin such viewing. In *My Ántonia*, which I now want to consider in terms of its structures of viewing, another pattern of visual power (and empowerment) appears.

For Richard Millington, *My Ántonia* is a form of contest informed by oral storytelling and novelistic form. Thus,

> the 'form' of My Ántonia can best be described as a contest between two kinds of narrative – an intergeneric combat, for the possession of Jim Burden and for the allegiance of the reader, between the story and its values and those of the novel.[17]

This understanding of the novel as a form of struggle is pertinent to my account of the senses in Cather. Repeatedly in the narrative we see how Cather represents the way that bodies come together around stories and images centred on cultural communion. Early in the novel, Peter and Pavel's wolf story demonstrates how sociability shapes itself through telling and listening to oral narratives. At this point in the narrative, the new immigrants carry with them the folkloric legacy of their European origins. In this Americanisation novel, cultural practices (a small-town dance, the musical performance of Blind D'Arnault) bring forward new ways for bodies to meet: folktales transplanted, African–American music on the white prairie, dances shared by a diverse migrant population. Listening and looking are vital to all these episodes. The text is thus a form of collage built around episodes centred on the senses.

The sheer ordinariness of much that happens in *My Ántonia* is deceptive. In 'The Hired Girls', above all, Cather explores social interaction and cultural change in ways that foreground the body as the site for new forms of community. Writing about dancing, listening to music and domestic work, Cather here creates a series of vignettes that are differentiated from one another but also threaded together by a narrative idiom based in sensory observations. 'The Hired Girls' focuses on the quotidian world of Black Hawk's young working women, Lena Lingard and Ántonia Shimerda, as well as the worlds of *fin-de-siècle* leisure: a dance, a musical performance. The writing is highly staged and visualised, and reads social interaction in terms of interlaced and cross-cutting forms of viewing. Cather's sense of social engagement, rooted in the nineteenth-century sketchbook and the reviews of performance she had produced voluminously for decades by the time of *My Ántonia*, is of a culture of bodily interaction – a theatre of the everyday.

Although readers, following the novel's title, often focus on Ántonia, Lena Lingard is equally important in many episodes, and here we see Jim's narrative eye literally gazing on her.

> Her yellow hair was burned to a ruddy thatch on her head; but her legs and arms, curiously enough, in spite of constant exposure to the sun, kept a miraculous whiteness which somehow made her seem more undressed than other girls who went scantily clad. (*MA* 160)

A poor woman, Lena's bodily allure is quite literally grounded in the fact that she can barely afford decent clothes, but keeps a 'miraculous whiteness' in spite of working in the fields. In terms of what we would now call intersectionality, Lena is a confounding mixture of embodied poverty and sexual allure, allied to a paradoxical whiteness that scrambles class codes (at one point the narrative notes that the American girls of the town are kept inside during the summer, due to the heat, and also in winter – due to the cold). Characters are continually looking at one another in this novel; and how she looks, and then looks back, forms the basis of Lena's distinctively defiant embodiment.

However, what do we then make of the presentation of Blind D'Arnault, one of Cather's most controversial figures? Blind D'Arnault, a character based on the blind black musicians whom Cather had seen in Red Cloud, seems designed to foreground questions of representation centred on visual cultures. He is blind. And Jim's descriptions might be some of the most objectifying snapshots of the black body in early twentieth-century American writing.

> He was a heavy, bulky mulatto, on short legs, and he came tapping the floor in front of him with his gold-headed cane. His yellow face was lifted

in the light, with a show of white teeth, all grinning, and his shrunken, papery eyelids lay motionless over his blind eyes. (*MA* 178)

As a child, D'Arnault is said to have played piano 'wearing an expression of idiotic rapture' (*MA* 180). His playing is utterly physicalised, sensationalised, a matter of touch and sound: 'It was as if all the agreeable sensations possible to creatures of flesh and blood were heaped up on those black and white keys, and he were gloating over them and trickling them through his yellow fingers' (*MA* 183). There are likely to be few readers not unsettled by this utterly physicalised description of the musician, not least because the objectifying descriptions are also pinned to a repeated emphasis on D'Arnault's African–American identity, a linkage which is in turn tied to a sense of disgust on the viewer's part. He has the 'soft, amiable negro voice . . . He had the negro head, too . . . He would have been repulsive if his face had not been so kindly and happy' (*MA* 178).

To see Blind D'Arnault, then, seems to be an almost parodic process where the white narrative viewer simply constructs primitivist myths around a black figure. Yet the viewing of him then widens out, to encompass not only the pianist, but also the effect his music has on those listening. Again, note the thoroughly embodied nature of the performance, as the pianist is 'vitalized by a sense of rhythm that was stronger than his other physical senses, – that not only filled his dark mind, but worried his body incessantly' (*MA* 183). D'Arnault then hears the sound of dancing feet from the next room – it is the young women, including Lena and Ántonia, dancing to the pianist's tunes. What follows is a dance scene, perhaps the first moment of collective joy and exuberance in the novel, a whirligig of pleasure triggered by the blind black man's performance. And then, triumphant, D'Arnault shows the delighted dancers his gold watch and a 'topaz ring, given him by some Russian nobleman who delighted in negro melodies' (*MA* 186).

One might read the sequencing of this scene, taking the focus from an objectifying gaze upon the black body to a more panoramic or dialogic tableau where we see the impact of African–American performance on white listeners, as emblematic of Cather's complex writings about bodies, difference and performance. One cannot wish away the initial typecasting (reiterative as it insistently is); but what is so striking is Cather's feeling her way toward a dramatisation of black performance that acknowledges the power, influence and cathartic impact of D'Arnault's playing. He creates a turning-point in the narrative: social mingling and sheer hedonism now become possibilities for Cather's characters.

In its movement from racialised gazing to a more dynamic and pluralistic portrayal of sensory exchange or communality, this scene exemplifies Cather's writing of the body in transition. Later passages in the novel capture another sense of transition, this time technological. The novel is one of the first mappings of a new visual culture brought into being with photography. This might seem a strange claim: the material and technological cultures described in the novel hardly seem photographic, but there are at least two moments where cameras and their work play a vital role. After Larry Donovan first seduces then abandons her, Ántonia bears his child. In a tiny but overwhelming detail, she places a photo of her baby daughter in the photographer's shop window. The photographer laughs when he tells Jim how Ántonia would not settle for a cheap frame for the image. 'Another girl would have kept her baby out of sight, but Tony, of course, must have its picture on exhibition at the town photographer's, in a great gilt frame. How like her!' (*MA* 295–6). Ántonia literally places visual testimony to her single motherhood in a public space – a telling marker, in Cather's fashioning of a novel about female autonomy, of her challenge to conventional mores. Ántonia is not only a 'fallen woman', in Victorian terms, but also a defiant visual master of that narrative.

After he writes the manuscript that becomes the novel, Jim had scribbled 'My Ántonia' on the 'pinkish face' of his portfolio as if the male storyteller's words were a literal inscription upon the body (*MA* xiii). But Ántonia remains in control, quite literally, of the imaging of herself and her family. The novel is built around a dialogue between written signs and visual signs, and the control of each. The implied first narrator of the novel (Cather herself?) says that she never wrote her own story of Ántonia: 'My own was never written, but the following narrative is Jim's manuscript, substantially as he brought it to me' (*MA* xiii). This comment has seemed to many readers to cede Ántonia's story to Jim and to male authority (after all, Ántonia's father also uses the possessive form, 'My Ántonia', at one point). And Jim's gazing at the women around him becomes one of the insistent motifs in the novel.

Ántonia contests this sense of control; and Cather creates scopic moments where we see her fashioning her own forms of visualisation. For example, when Jim Burden visits the aged Ántonia on her Nebraska farm, it is she who talks him through the family collection of photos. She is a creator, collector and expositor of images. In an understated and carefully choreographed scene, it is Ántonia who shapes her community's forms of looking, after she brings out 'a big boxful of photographs' (*MA* 338). This micro-narrative is simply quotidian, carefully attentive to patterns of bodily and sensory encounter within a domestic setting:

> the young Cuzaks stood behind her chair, looking over her shoulder with interested faces . . . In the group about Ántonia I was conscious of a kind of physical harmony. They leaned this way and that, and were not afraid to touch each other. (*MA* 338–9)

Margaret Olin has written about the social processes whereby photographs create community, and how they might form the basis of a gestural social process of interaction. For Olin, 'tactile looking' is a way to understand this sensory process: looking at and touching photographs; and being 'touched' in an emotional sense by an image: 'Touch puts people in contact with photographs; but as photographs pass from hand to hand they establish and maintain relationships between people – or try to.'[18] For Olin, photographs foster a gestural communitarianism: 'Gestures turn photographs into presences that populate the world like people and act within it to connect people.' Thus, photographs 'participate in and create relationships and communities . . . communities gather around photographs'.[19] Olin's work suggests a take on the photograph that restores the image to a social context. The photograph is now woven into a social milieu, part of a community's praxis as it shapes connection, exchange and memory. *My Ántonia* becomes a novel where storytelling (think of the oral folktales in the novel, such as that of Peter and Pavel) enters into dialogue with new technologies of image-making, configured along lines suggested by Olin. To think about viewing in the novel is to see how Cather's historical appreciation of the sensorium is vital to her work. The male gaze in the novel might seem to belong to the long continuum of patriarchal seeing diagnosed by John Berger: centuries of looking, of appropriation, the positioning of the female body within matrices of male sight/appropriation. On the other hand, the emergent technology of photography, particularly in the lightweight cameras such as the Brownie (introduced at the start of the century – I imagine that this is the camera Ántonia might have used), offered a technological shift, a form of empowerment. Cather tends not to signal or flag such moments in her work. Glancing details, descriptive shards show us how the world is changing. But in her understated way, Cather adumbrates a very new world then coming into being, configured through sensory change.

The Visual Lexicon of *Shadows on the Rock*

During the mid-1930s, Cather's meditations on visualisation would reach a decisive turning point. In a matter of months, Cather published *Lucy Gayheart*, while *A Lost Lady* would emerge for the second time as a movie in the version directed by Alfred E. Green. Each of these texts, written and filmed, shows the conflicting and complex ways in which the late Victorian Cather now found herself in a world where the body, its dispositions and bodily movement, were being mediated via new forms of technology. The film version of *A Lost Lady* was released in September 1934 and starred the twenty-seven-year-old Barbara Stanwyck (an actress often celebrated for the modernity of her performances).[20] Meanwhile, *Lucy Gayheart* was a highly visual text, tautly edited, and shaped via a series of tableaux and vignettes that seem primed to be remade into a film script.

Ways of looking and forms of visualisation were also central to Cather's 1931 *Shadows on the Rock*. The novel, a form of highly episodic narrative centred on white settlers (here French colonists) and their life in late seventeenth-century Quebec, repeatedly focuses on sensory shifts occasioned by migration and colonisation; the text is a microscopic examination of quotidian sensory life. And looking is central to Cather's sensorised model of history. In fact, the novel opens with Euclide Auclair looking down on the Quebec landscape, watching as the ships leave for France:

> One afternoon late in October of the year 1697, Euclide Auclair, the philosopher apothecary of Quebec, stood on the top of Cap Diamant gazing down the broad, empty river far beneath him ... As long as *La Bonne Espérance* was still in sight, many of Auclair's friends and neighbours had kept him company on the hill-top; but when the last tip of white slid behind the curving shore, they went back to their shops and their kitchens to face the stern realities of life. (*SOR* 7)

Auclair looks down on the settlement of Quebec as a highly visual, scopic colonist: 'His blue eyes were warm and interested, even in reflection, – they often had a kindling gleam as if his thoughts were pictures' (*SOR* 12). Cather links this gaze to his European identity quite explicitly when she shifts the narrative's visual focus to the pine forest beyond the town. 'The forest was suffocation, annihilation; there European man was quickly swallowed up in silence, distance, mould, black mud, and the stinging swarms of insect life that bred in it' (*SOR* 11).[21]

In the opening paragraphs, Cather establishes a fascinated gaze – here partly nostalgic, saturated in melancholy – as a recurrent motif. The novel will play out such moments of rapt looking again and again, as the text explores the resonances of what we might call the 'looks of settlement'. Hence the many domestic objects which seem to offer a sensory plenitude not found in this harsh and strange Northern landscape – for instance, Count Frontenac's tapestries: 'One could study them for hours without seeing all the flowers and figures' (*SOR* 72). Hence the glass fruit that the Count has brought back from a military expedition, a work 'throwing coloured reflections into the mirror and upon the wall above' (*SOR* 71). The landscape itself seems to be an optical trick, both solid as the stone and slate of the town, and as immaterial as the fogs and mists that often roll in – Cather's scene-setting descriptions themselves becoming part of this larger sensory mapping of complex visualisation.

> It was like walking in a dream. One could not see the people one passed, or the river, or one's own house. Not even the winter snows gave one such

a feeling of being cut off from everything and living in a world of twilight and miracles. (*SOR* 74)

For the white settlers, the sensory basis of life has become destabilised, conflicted, paradoxical. The pervasive melancholia of the novel is literally rooted in the body and in the ambiguities of sight. For example, the young Cécile Auclair's dilemma is that she cannot remember an aunt's face – this is highly unusual in a Cather novel, where character is often apprehended facially. 'The face of this aunt Cécile could never remember, though she could see her figure clearly . . . but the face was a blank, just as if the aunt were standing in a doorway with blinding sunlight behind her' (*SOR* 17–18). But this short paragraph is also saturated in clues to the sensory hermeneutics of the novel. There is a lacuna at the centre of her apprehension of her aunt, a human absence rendered literally material. Instead, we have the outline of her form and the aunt's object-world – she is said to be 'like' a piece of furniture and remembered for her rings and handkerchief. Cather is teaching us how to read the situation of the French colonists in terms of human absence and material presence. Faces and flesh disappear as memories of Europe recede; furniture and jewellery remain. At such moments Cather works in a thoroughly modernist way, showing us the cultural predicament of the white settlers. Can human memory and a materialist transplanting compensate for bodily absence? Will the material 'thinginess', if you like, of Cécile's memory be enough to supply a plenitude in place of what is being quite literally represented as bodily absence?

Cather then weaves this sense of visual disturbance or dislocation into her tracking of the community's social life. A second strand within the narrative focuses on looks or gazes that are directed at figures that might repel, shock or disturb us. Let us look at the introduction of Blinker and at the transitions between different forms of sensory appreciation in this section of the novel. Cather uses his physical alterity to validate (through contrast) the beauty and finesse of the Auclair home. But this masculine wounding also sets up a very distinctive Catherian reading of empire and European settlement. Cécile sees a face looking in through the window – 'a terrifying face, but one that she expected' (*SOR* 19). 'The man spoke out of the side of his mouth, as he looked out of the side of his face. He was so terribly crossed-eyed that Cécile had never really looked into his eyes at all, – this was why he was called Blinker' (*SOR* 19). For Cécile, Blinker embodies, quite literally, a cornucopia of forms of sensory disjunction. His face is startling; his gaze is utterly cross-eyed; he finds it difficult to eat due to a damaged jaw. Cather's narrative point of view, sitting somewhere between that of the narrator and that of Cécile herself, articulates a brutal reading of this physiognomy: 'He stood blinking with that incredibly stupid air, blinking out of the side of his face, and Cécile could not be sure that he saw her or anything else' (*SOR* 21).

Cather's sinuous mapping of how the body is performed and perceived allows her to move from the shock of a certain disgust to a more complex representation, where initial distrust ripples out into a sense of the other's alterity and bodily selfhood. A reader can relish and then revel in the aesthetic finesse of Cather's description of St Peter's face, or her tantalisingly complex envisioning of Myra Henshawe and the mirror in *My Mortal Enemy*. But Cather's highly detailed mappings of disfigurement, grotesquerie, disability and ugliness suggest another side to her visualised narrative strategies. This is a significant part of the Cather visual universe: the 'other side' – to adopt her own term for *My Ántonia* – of the aesthete's love of beauty, line and luxury. One thinks of Crazy Ivar, of Blind D'Arnault and of Blinker, the baker's worker that Cather introduces at the start of *Shadows on the Rock*.

Cécile's encounter with Blinker is a fictional representation of what that Bournean way of seeing might look like. Randolph Bourne (as I showed in my first chapter) had suggested, in his 1911 essay 'The Handicapped', ways to frame disability socially and culturally, acknowledging the disabled body as, quite simply, a part of society and culture. At such moments, Cather's writing stages *staring* in complex ways, an opening-up of myriad cultural and social vectors within an encounter (power and shame; enchantment and repugnance). As Lennard Davis notes: 'the disabled body must ... at least tolerate the inquisitive gaze (or the averted glance)'. 'Disability is a specular moment.'[22] Even Blinker's name points to the absolute centrality of viewing to this vignette. Cather's later fiction, in particular, was an extended experiment in thinking through the cultural politics of spectatorship. In *Shadows*, Cather used the child's-eye view (Cécile is twelve) as the basis for an oblique meditation on white settler looking. In *Lucy Gayheart*, Cather made her heroine an ironic focus for male gazing, creating power out of a woman's objectification. And *Sapphira* fashioned a tapestry of looks out of the visual culture of a slave-owning society, culminating in the child Cather captivated by the sight of a freed slave (an episode I discuss in my final chapter).

Cather's *œuvre* is likely to become rich terrain for critical readings based in radical schools such as Whiteness Studies, Food Studies and Disability Studies. As these moments in *Shadows on the Rock* suggest, Cather had started to shape narrative turns around encounters with disabled bodies – corporealised encounters then revealing a movement on from, a transition out of, many centuries' old assumptions of how the disabled body should be represented. Those inherited structures were often, at heart, metonymic or metaphorical: the disabled body standing for, or representing, something that was often bad or corrupted, and at the very least disturbingly other. Cécile's glance, her recoil and then her reflective transition beyond that initial sense of repugnance are important moments in the development of Cather's fiction – a vignette that shows how her deepening understanding of what we might call a sensory ethics of where to look or to listen would become the basis of a more nuanced staging than was seen in her earliest work.

Conclusion: Polyscopic Cather

It is surely no surprise that the putative father of Nancy (in *Sapphira and the Slave Girl*) was a visiting Cuban portrait painter. As with the mirrored scene at the start of *My Mortal Enemy*, Cather folds processes of looking and framing into her work, stitching into her narrative moments where the face is isolated and pictured, often quite literally. *Sapphira* is a particularly fascinating Cather text because it reads identity through social practice and through cultural constructions too. That is, much of the novel charts the quotidian life of ante-bellum slavery (cleaning, cooking, visiting friends and acquaintances, work), but the narrative also limns the cultural world of a slave-owning society. Here, portraits are important. In an early scene, Nancy and Till clean the Colbert parlour.

Then Till cleans the family portraits while Nancy looks on. Nancy 'hoped the painter was really her father, as some folks said. Old Jezebel, her great-grandmother, had whispered to her that was why she had straight black hair with no kink in it' (*SSG* 44).

Cather's decision to make Nancy's father a portrait painter is deliciously and ironically powerful for just these reasons. Although Nancy's father is said to be the painter, she also lives amongst the Colbert men – and they 'had a bad reputation where women were concerned' (*SSG* 68). In a nice encapsulation of my argument about the crossover and meeting between art and life, Nancy is said to be a Colbert bastard because custom and (bad) reputation trump the similitude to the painter. 'That was why, in spite of her resemblance to the portrait painter from Cuba, Nancy was often counted as one of the Colbert bastards. Some people said Guy Colbert was her father, others put it on Jacob' (*SSG* 68). Painting, in other words, is less significant than the community's suspicions about the Colbert men's sexual aggressiveness, impulses which might, in the eyes of 'some people', mean more than the record of kinship suggested by the painting. Art, in other words, counts for less than brutal social assumptions – this is a moment in Cather's fiction (think also about Montoya's attack on the Indian server in *Death Comes for the Archbishop*) when the relatively ordered and safe world of the aesthetic (painting pictures, serving food) is suddenly overcome by brutal human impulses and emotions.

'The conventional portrait stops time and removes the sitter from his or her everyday context,' writes Sally O'Reilly, 'compounding the rarified status of the art object, whereas contemporary artists are generally more interested in the sitter's body as the point at which art and life converge.' And she adds: 'Portraiture, then, has become increasingly mindful of the fact that there is no fixed, sovereign identity, and of the way one's sense of self is formed in relation to the world and to other people – to immediate circumstances as well as to history and socio-political ebbs and flows.'[23] Cather's face-painting prose seems to sit right on the border between an earlier phase of sovereign or fixed portraiture and this new, modern sense of context and of the interplay between life and art. Portraits are reference points in Cather's fiction, objects of beauty to look at, or to serve as the basis for character description, but such portraiture is then inserted into a much more fluid world where art and life converge in the ways that O'Reilly describes.

As a reviewer, Cather was accustomed to fixing her gaze on a stage, a singer, a moment in a play or opera. We sense this scrutinising look in notable moments in her reviewing career (for instance, in the descriptions of Olga Nethersole that I discuss in Chapter 5), and then its reinscription in moments in the fiction, such as Nellie's viewing of Myra at the start of *My Mortal Enemy*. These are crystallised moments that might be adequately summarised as 'the gaze'. But what is fascinating about Cather's narrative inflections, expansions and revisions of this initial scenario is how thoroughly polyscopic her writing then became. She turned the male gaze into the female gaze; read out the racialised gaze into a more complex, dynamic interchange of looks and interactions; and explored how the colonist's surveying vision encountered the resistant materials of a new land. Such narrative processes were, at heart, forms of *narrative* experimentation – ways to conjure more complex shapes out of the simple minimalism of the reviewer's focused looking. But they also then became, in *My Ántonia* or *Shadows on the Rock*, narrative configurations that enabled Cather, in pragmatic but incisive ways, to create innovative fictions of vision.

Notes

1. Oates, 'Inspiration and Obsession in Life and Literature', 80–5: 84.
2. Knausgaard, *My Struggle: Book Two: A Man in Love*, 545.
3. Lewis, *Willa Cather Living: A Personal Record*, 23–4.
4. Ibid. xxvii–xxviii.
5. Cather, 'Utterly Irrelevant' (23 September 1894).
6. Lewis, *Willa Cather Living*, xxviii.
7. Bloom and Bloom, *Willa Cather's Gift of Sympathy*.
8. Cather, 'Popular Pictures'.
9. Taussig, *What Color Is the Sacred?*, 170.
10. Lewis, *Willa Cather Living*, 173–4.
11. Meyer, 'Craniometry, Race, and the Artist in Willa Cather'.
12. Berger, *Ways of Seeing*, 47. The body of work contesting and inflecting Berger's thesis is enormous, and broadly theorises female spectatorship. See Laura Mulvey, *Visual and Other Pleasures*, and bell hooks, 'The Oppositional Gaze: Black Female Spectators', 115–31. Amelia Jones, *The Feminism and Visual Culture Reader*, collects many important articles and essays on this topic.
13. Cather, 'Training for the Ballet: Making American Dancers', 89.

14. Ibid. 89.
15. Porter, 'Chance Meetings in Southern France', 292.
16. Manguel, *Reading Pictures: What We Think About When We Look at Art*, 129.
17. Millington, 'Willa Cather and "The Storyteller"', 689.
18. Olin, *Touching Photographs*, 1.
19. Ibid. 14–15.
20. See Schueth, 'Taking Liberties', for an account of this adaptation (and an overview of Cather's relationship to film).
21. See Michael A. Peterman and Robert Thacker, 'Gazing Down from Cap Diamant', for an account of Cather looking down from the Château Frontenac on to Quebec town. Edith Lewis saw this experience as the imaginative origin of *Shadows on the Rock* (*Willa Cather Living*, 153–4).
22. Davis, *Enforcing Normalcy*, xvi, 11.
23. O'Reilly, *The Body in Contemporary Art*, 33.

CHAPTER 5

Sound Affects: Music, Voice and Silence in *The Song of the Lark*, *My Mortal Enemy* and *Lucy Gayheart*

In the Nethersole trial of 1900, a touchstone for my meditation on Cather and her engagement with late Victorian performance culture, the actress's delivery of her lines was the centrepiece of the prosecution's case. At a crucial moment in the drama, the heroine, Fanny (played by Nethersole), was carried upstairs by her lover, Jean, 'To show the passage of time while the couple was upstairs, as well as to suggest the sexual act ensuing, the curtain rose and fell, according to some accounts, as many as five times.'[1] What made this scene especially inflammatory was Nethersole's delivery of her lines at this climactic moment: according to witnesses at the trial, she intoned 'no', in such a way as to suggest 'yes' (and one of the witnesses, a man, went so far as to imitate Nethersole's delivery of the word, and was then reproved by the judge for his emphatically emotional delivery).[2] 'No' seemed to mean 'yes', but in ways signalling a dangerous female agency that was positively obscene.

In this chapter I explore sound in Cather – not only the voice of the actress, with all its potential for transgressive eroticism, but also the soundscapes produced by Cather's attention to *acoustics* in a broader sense: the sound of the speaking voice, random noise (a bell, a yell) and the quietness of an icy drowning. The grand narrative of Cather's fictions, in terms of how they create plotlines about how an individual might come into and achieve voice so as to accomplish a certain mastery and social distinction, seems straightforward. *The Song of the Lark* traces the arc from mute hopefulness to vocal mastery. *Lucy Gayheart* inverts the pattern, finding emotional desolation in the voice's extinction. However, Cather's novels are remarkable for their exploration of forms of sonic variety, their registering of how utterance takes many forms, and of how power might inhabit a silent moment or a murmured comment just as much as it might the magisterial delivery of an aria.[3]

The Wagnerian Romances: Opera and the American West

For Cather, the settlement of distant places created forms of sensory juncture and transformation. And, often, forms of Aestheticism (appreciating a piece of music, looking at glassware, savouring food) became ways to understand, sensorily, the very new world in which the settler finds themselves. Thus Cather's writing (both fictional and non-fictional) often contains an entwining of sensory immediacy and an awareness of cultural precariousness. That physical immediacy sensed by Rebecca West emerges as a recurrent feature of Cather's writing because the worlds she describe have a form of tentativeness or unformedness about them. Sensory immediacy is proportionally related to what might appear to be a lack of cultural solidity or weight.

Cather explores this dilemma in one of her meditations on musical culture, the Preface to an idiosyncratic work of musical appreciation, Gertrude Hall's *The Wagnerian Romances* (1925) – an essay collected as one of 'Four Prefaces' in *On Writing*. Hall wrote a series of summaries of Wagner's major operas and prose accounts of those musical works (summaries similar to Lamb's *Tales from Shakespeare*, though less accomplished). Cather identified opera as, above all, a hybrid form:

> What Miss Hall does . . . is to reproduce the emotional effect of one art through the medium of another art . . . But opera is a hybrid art, – partly literary to begin with. It happens that in the Wagnerian music-drama the literary part of the work is not trivial, as it is so often in operas, but is truly the mate of the music, done by the same hand. (*OW* 62)

Hall had rewritten Wagner's operas as prose narratives, taking their plots and recasting them as literary fables. She had taken what would normally be a narrative that would be heard and reshaped it into a story to be read. It is easy to see how this sensory remapping appealed to Cather: opera's status as 'hybrid art' was a sensory hybridity too – its plots available to be heard in the theatre and silently read at home. Music critic Philip Kennicott observes the sheer oddity of Cather's argument: 'Wagner's music is rather idiosyncratically linked in Cather's mind to geographies of open space.'[4] This is perhaps because Cather was less interested in Wagner per se than in writing about being a music devotee in rural America and the sensory dimensions of that strangely spatialised musical experience.

The Cather Preface seems conspicuously unconcerned with what would surely be one way to approach Wagner – namely, through the lens of Romantic nationalism. Cather shows relatively little interest in how Hall mediates Wagner's deployment of myth and fable, nor is there any sense of how Wagner became central to the making of German national identity. When Cather does reach for a sense of imagined community, it is not the German nation, represented through opera, but an American community of female listeners and readers, spread across the American West – a setting where Cather situates herself at the start of her essay. She writes:

> I first came upon this book when I was staying in a thinly peopled part of the Southwest, far enough from the Metropolitan Opera House. I have a great many friends who live in distant parts of the country where operas are not given. . . . There are innumerable Women's Clubs, for instance, who take a sort of silent course in music, and conscientiously read the dull books that have been written about operas . . . And persons who have heard the operas sung, and beautifully sung, many times, but who are now living in remote places, will find this book potent in reviving their recollections; the scenes will float before them, as they did before me in the blue air of New Mexico when I first made the acquaintance of these delicately suggestive pages. (*OW* 65–6)

Cather appreciates Hall for giving her readers in remote places a handbook for appreciating culture *sensorily*. One does not need an opera house to appreciate opera, she suggests. Since culture might be remade through hybrid forms, noise becomes silence, the urban environment of opera becomes a remote place, the setting of performance now floats in 'the blue air of New Mexico'. This is as idiosyncratic a paradigm of culture as one might find in the 1920s. Cather writes as a Western American author, placing herself in the Southwest rather than Nebraska – Cather's biographers have regarded Cather's first trip to the Southwest in 1912 as a transitional creative moment (Woodress, O'Brien). She writes as an author ambitiously committed to high culture, to opera, but as a figure rooted in such thinly populated places, problems of cultural transmission become paramount. Cather's solution is improvisational, a form of Frontier cultural experimentalism where she counters a seeming lack of high culture by retelling elite, metropolitan narratives and circulating them via new networks. From the Metropolitan Opera to the Women's Clubs of the Southwest, we see how different Cather's model of culture was to the largely urban forms of high Modernism that were so often deeply suspicious of the 'Masses'. From French classical painting (Breton, Chavannes) to German opera, Cather remained a late nineteenth-century figure in her devotion to high culture, yet she had to find a way of imagining culture within a world of few people, let alone opera houses. In that remodelling of culture, Cather exploited shifts between different sensory modes to forge new cultural formations.

1915: *The Song of the Lark* – The White Singer's Body

Cather came to creative and critical writing even as she first entered into, and then deepened her knowledge of, performance and performers. She began to write theatre criticism at the crest of a cultural wave when actresses were becoming celebrities and central to debates about performance (the word 'diva' migrated into English in the 1880s). As many critics and biographers have noted, her fascination with figures such as Sarah Bernhardt was a major and abiding feature of her life.[5] She wrote about many of the most famous performers of her age to the extent that her works are now becoming vital resources for musicologists such as Alex Ross. And she placed, quite literally, a real-life singer, Helena Modjeska, directly into the narrative of *My Mortal Enemy*.

Cather's fascination with opera and Romanticism, her highly Eurocentric aesthetic, her deployment of Gothic motifs and her complex relationship with literary Aestheticism are all well-known aspects of an 1890s mind shaped by voracious reading and a phenomenal appetite for culture.[6] But Cather had many years of apprenticeship. Her career, in its broadest configuration, was a remarkable experiment where a provincial late Victorian sensibility – shaped by figures such as Henrik Ibsen, Richard Wagner and Chavannes – was then kept *in utero* until a very different time and place: New York City on the very cusp of Modernism.

As a viewer and reviewer of performance and a performer herself, Cather was at the centre of a contested cultural matrix monitoring the metropolitan debates from afar and then, increasingly, entering into the conversation herself. By the time she had established herself as a journalist in 1900 (Cather was still under thirty), she had already mapped out preoccupations she would transpose into her fiction. Thus, performance became central to her fictional representations of social encounter while her fiction often centred on the female artist's body (then viewed, contested and celebrated). In myriad ways, Cather's fiction of the early twentieth century was an elaborate answer to questions posed by the theatrical culture of the late nineteenth century: a thinking-through of debates that had preoccupied critics and writers in the 1880s and 1890s.

Singers and immigrants are linked together in Cather's work because they achieve selfhood through the acquisition of a voice, be it the trained voice of the opera singer or the new language of the migrant. For Ántonia or Thea, the vocational arc for the female character is one which takes the protagonist out of a silence and toward sound: Ántonia learns to speak English, Thea to sing. In both cases, Cather roots self in vocality.

The opening pages of *The Song of the Lark* counterpoint Thea's initial searches for voice (in an artistic sense) with a sense of the precariousness of the migrant's individual voice. Thea will become an artist, a singer, but her journey is framed by her father's difficulty in finding his own voice. The artist's expressive plenitude grows out of the parched soil of migrant life. Peter Kronborg is caught between languages, a preacher who has lost contact with his original Swedish tongue but never really comes into full control of his own expressive idiom. He 'wielded in his Moonstone pulpit a somewhat pompous English vocabulary he had learned out of books at college... The poor man had no natural, spontaneous human speech. If he had his sincere moments, they were perforce inarticulate' (*SOL* 17). His daughter, Thea, is at first equally inarticulate – the family saga is presented as a struggle to escape speechlessness, a struggle to find a voice: the singer's utterance born from the migrant's linguistic struggles. Note how these sentences link articulacy, spontaneity and sincerity. The Cather logic of utterance or writing or song is that one learns to speak, to write and to sing in order to achieve the spontaneous articulation of sincere feeling. Cather is Romantic in her veneration of sincerity and feeling, but a Classicist in her sense that a certain formalism (the formalism of education and training) is necessary to achieve those ideals – her child characters' 'natural' state, frequently being immigrants (Thea, Ántonia), is one of inarticulacy or a potent pre-articulacy that the novels will trace coming into being:

> Thea, who had a rather sensitive ear, until she went to school never spoke at all, except in monosyllables, and her mother was convinced that she was tongue-tied. She was still inept in speech for a child so intelligent. Her ideas were usually clear, but she seldom attempted to explain them, even at school, where she excelled in 'written work' and never did more than mutter a reply. (*SOL* 17)

'As any professional singer will attest,' writes Sarah L. Young, 'singing does not originate in the vocal cords; the voice and its power are born deep within the body and reside on the breath, guided by the respiration of the individual.'[7] *The Song of the Lark*, following this singing logic, becomes a relentlessly bodily text. Cather's development of her characters moves along axes shaped by utterly physical encounters. By taking a singer as her protagonist, Cather represents and explores the female body in ways that would have been unimaginable if Thea had had another career. In Cather's conception of singing, the relentless corporeality of performance occupies centre-stage. Thea moves through stages of bodily development, following a pathway that is more physical than moral. The radicalism of Cather's sense of selfhood is evident in each episode. Thea is a less ethical being or conscious artist than she is a developing body whose maturation attracts attention, fascination and interpretation in ways that can be bracingly innovative for the culture in which they were produced, though also intermittently problematic, which leads to unsettling sentences in Cather's work where characters push right up against (and then break through) social conventions and typical proprieties.

Cather's work is transitional in its sense of the body – at once offering us a neo-Romantic awareness of the body's presence and immediacy, while also registering a certain fracture and disassociation typically associated with Modernism. *The Song of the Lark*, a text poised between Realism and Modernism, tacks between these two readings of the body, even at the level of the individual sentences and paragraphs. At the beginning of the novel, the child Thea is suffering from pneumonia. Intriguingly, Cather fashions a powerful and poignant scenario out of her suffering but finds disassociation and disconnection in the girl's pain:

> He gave her some medicine and went to the kitchen for something he needed. She drowsed and lost the sense of his being there. When she opened her eyes again, he was kneeling before the stove, spreading something dark and sticky on a white cloth, with a big spoon; batter, perhaps. Presently she felt him taking off her nightgown. He wrapped the hot plaster about her chest. There seemed to be straps which he pinned over her shoulders. Then he took out a thread and needle and began to sew her up in it. That, she felt, was too strange; she must be dreaming, anyhow, so she succumbed to her drowsiness. (*SOL* 10)

The Song of the Lark presents a close-up of Thea's sickly body, racked by pneumonia, which we see undressed and almost mummified. Nakedness and the wrapping of the naked form are recurring motifs in Cather's work. As Doctor Archie works to care for Thea, her sense of physical self-separation continues – 'When she was conscious at all, she seemed to be separated from her body' (*SOL* 10) – even as the Doctor's awareness of her physical being is powerfully foregrounded in ways that tremble on the edge of a transgressive, eroticised attentiveness: 'As he lifted and undressed Thea, he thought to himself what a beautiful thing a little girl's body was, – like a flower. It was so neatly and delicately fashioned, so soft, and so milky white' (*SOL* 10). As so often in Cather, the moment of close-up viewing seems to segue fluidly into a different form of sensory appreciation: that of touch. Hands then become important:

> Her hands, so little and hot, so clever too, – he glanced at the open exercise-book on the piano . . . As he pushed back the hair that had fuzzed down over her eyebrows, he felt her head thoughtfully with the tips of his fingers. (*SOL* 11)

At the start of *The Song of the Lark*, the music teacher Wunsch reflects on Thea Kronborg's abilities to apply herself to her musical training. The writing here shows how Cather began to read inherited plotlines (focusing on the development of the artist or the yearning of a provincial aesthete for culture) through an intensely sensory lens. Wunsch's reflections on Thea are sensory, aesthetic and impressionistic – very far from a reading of character grounded in Victorian certainties of moral centredness:

> What was it she reminded him of? A yellow flower, full of sunlight, perhaps. No; a thin glass full of sweet-smelling, sparkling Moselle wine. He seemed to see such a glass before him in the arbor, to watch the bubbles rising and breaking, like the silent discharge of energy in the nerves and brain, the rapid florescence in young blood – Wunsch felt ashamed and dragged his slippers along the path to the kitchen, his eyes on the ground. (*SOL* 33)

In its tracking between the sensory immediacy of the object world and its reading of the body as a repository of 'nerves' and 'energy', this passage demonstrates Cather's embedding of *fin-de-siècle* Aestheticism and Vitalism into the novel of artistic development.

Wunsch's shamed reaction is telling: he 'felt ashamed and dragged his slippers along the path to the kitchen, his eyes on the ground'. Wunsch moves rapidly along a sensory chain from recognising Thea's talents to translating them into a different sense register (a flower, a glass or wine) to a shamed response that recognises the raw immediacy of what he has done. Wunsch is surprised by his own sensory reactions. Moving between forms of micro-sensoriness and micro-social engagement (feeling life on their nerve endings and reacting to others through sense impressions), Cather's characters are often prone to instances of suddenly porous responsiveness. Since Cather's characters often react to one another through sensory immediacy, their responses might be unfeigned, impulsive or unnervingly direct. Such responses might well be awkward, embarrassing or seemingly naïve. Social proprieties might be less significant than a reflexive awareness of Others' physical embodiment.

In the next sections of the novel Cather explores Thea's burgeoning bodily strength – her development as a singer configured in overwhelmingly physical terms as a bodily sequencing where potential is literally embodied, ready for artistic exploitation. In fact, it is remarkable how little is made, by her teachers and mentors, of the cognitive, conscious aspects of becoming an artist. Instead, artistic potential is a highly physical instantiation, felt in sinew and blood. It is also profoundly social – as others respond to and relate to that physical embodiment. What Cather does here is to read out one of the questions raised by late nineteenth-century performance cultures: specifically, how could female power manifest itself in performance? For this is a literal physical power – the ability to project, to fill a theatre with the female voice. As a devotee of female performance, Cather would have been well aware of the sheer physical power needed to project sound into large late Victorian theatres. As Jill Edmonds notes in her account of female performers who took on the role of Hamlet (a roster that included Sarah Bernhardt herself), 'These actresses needed considerable vocal power and projection to fill theatres like Sadler's Wells, the Pavilion in Whitechapel and the 3,000 seater Britannia at Hoxton.'[8]

In *The Song of the Lark*, Cather frames Thea's body, its capabilities and potential and allure, within a sensory matrix where her male mentors and friends view, touch and hear her embodied presence. At the start of the novel, Thea has three such figures grouped around her: the railway man Ray Kennedy; Doctor Archie (first seen tending to a sick Thea); and the music teacher, Wunsch. Wunsch is an alcoholic, and by the end of Part One, 'Childhood Friends', has disappeared to find his future elsewhere. Kennedy is catastrophically injured in a railway accident – Cather, yet again (think of Paul's fate in 'Paul's Case' or the tramp crushed in the threshing machine in *My Ántonia*), choosing to obliterate, brutally, the male body in industrial accidents. And when Thea begins her formal musical education in Chicago, her mentor is the one-eyed Hungarian émigré, Andor Harsanyi (he lost his eye, as a child, in an explosives accident). And so Part One of *The Song of the Lark* charts Thea's growth as an artist, but counterpoints her female physical potential against the quite remarkable bodily dereliction of her male characters. By the end of Part One, Thea is at the start of her career, a career founded on exploitations of her bodily vitality and energy; but as she rises, others decline.

Cather uses these male figures, grouped around the female artist who is the cynosure of the narrative, to create an idiosyncratic remodelling of the courtship novel. Thea is the growing girl and young woman, placed against a gallery of observing males, each of whom is characterised quite distinctively in terms of a bodily presence and a sensory responsiveness to her. In one clear way, the novel's suggestive modernity rests in its transposing of a Rooseveltian 'vigour': *The Song of the Lark* transposes gendered typologies, finding generative vitality in the female body and sickness in male characters. Thea is sick at the very start of the novel, but the narrative charts her awakening into bodily potential and vitality. Meanwhile, male characters sicken and die. By the end, Cather has traced the bodily and sensory curve of an artist's development. Cather's *Künstlerroman*, a novel tracing the artist's growth, has decisively grounded that process in the realisation of a bodily potential that the singer was born with. Fred Ottenburg tells Doctor Archie that 'That color has to be born in a singer, it can't be acquired' (note the term 'color' being applied to a voice). 'The voice simply is the mind and is the heart' (*SOL* 462). And in the final passages of the novel Cather relentlessly figures artistic transcendence in terms of sensory fulfilment:

> While she was on the stage she was conscious that every movement was the right movement, that her body was absolutely the instrument of her idea. Not for nothing had she kept it so severely, kept it filled with such energy and fire. All that deep-rooted vitality flowered in her voice, her face, in her very finger-tips . . . And her voice was as flexible as her body; equal to any demand, capable of every *nuance*. (*SOL* 526)

The promise has been kept: voice now lives up to the body's promise.

My reading of *The Song of the Lark* stresses the novel's fascination with new forms of embodied experience – its exploration of the diva within settings shaped by immigrant and provincial culture, and its remapping of the *Künstlerroman* to make that form an account of sensory development. It is also worth adding that writing this first extended narrative about music gave Cather a way to write about a community of listeners. As a writer preoccupied with music, with singing and listening, she created a number of imagined tableaux where musical communities embodied difference and diversity – and here we see how Cather explored an evolving cultural complexity while remaining drawn to some fairly familiar, even clichéd narrative arcs.

The Song of the Lark is a transitional text when it comes to mining the sensory plenitude of the musical world. As we have seen, Cather's representations of the female body are often exploratory, to an unsettling degree. Her tracing of the diva's development in terms of corporealised maturation is an utterly distinctive and radical contribution to fictions of female vocation. Yet other episodes within the novel reveal a more patchworked representational matrix, and it is often around issues of ethnic and cultural difference that Cather's writing seems most divided, even conflicted. In Chapter X (Part II) Cather creates a scenario around Thea's interactions with the Mexican community, led by Spanish Johnny. This is one of Cather's most intriguing portrayals of informal music exchange – jamming, we might say. Thea and Spanish Johnny exchange musical ideas, adapt a Mexican song together, perform alongside one another. Appreciative exchange and collaboration seem at first to be at the heart of the two figures' artistic meeting. '"Johnny," she said suddenly, "I want you to write down the words of that Mexican serenade you used to sing; you know, *"Rosa de Noche"'* (*SOL* 251). Johnny writes down the verses of the song, and even tells Thea that the song might not be Mexican but might come from Brazil or Venezuela – we seem to be witnessing Cather charting a folkloric, communal imagining of a composite musical tradition. The scenario carries within it a cultural architecture of incorporation – that in Progressive Era American music there might be ways to integrate high and low, European and folkloric forms: the classically trained singer works with the Mexican performer (and Johnny is always associated with his guitar, a defiantly non-elite instrument).

But then, as the scene moves on toward its climax, Cather shifts the dynamics of the interchange between the two figures, now presenting Thea's creativity as somehow released by, liberated by, the Mexican voices. She becomes a vessel for their Otherness: 'Their faces confronted her, open, eager, unprotected. She felt as if all these warm-blooded people débouched into her' (*SOL* 258). Are the Mexicans there to serve Thea, to become enrichers of that utterly embodied creativity I have been tracing? It certainly seems so. For in this sequence we see an enriched Thea achieving an artistic transcendence encoded, quite literally, in the colours of her body and those of her audience. Vocally, she literally creates a sound that will float above – transcend – the communal harmonising she has also been part of.

> Then, at the appointed, at the acute, moment, the soprano voice, like a fountain jet, shot up into the light . . . How it leaped from among those dusky male voices! How it played in and about and around and over them, like a goldfish darting among creek minnows, like a yellow butterfly soaring above a swarm of dark ones. (*SOL* 261)

The soaring voice, the 'dusky' Mexicans, the singer as a 'yellow butterfly' above the 'dark ones': the writing here tracks back toward an overly familiar palette of racialised tropes, while reinscribing a standardised image of musical creativity that belies the complexity and novelty of Cather's explorations of the musical body elsewhere in the novel. This is a writing of the body that is transitional in the sense that the dramatic structure of the scene, and the tropes used to figure musical genius, both track backwards and forwards in terms of how culture and the body are represented. We move forward toward conceptions of musical culture imbued with a radical sense of community and exchange, only then to fall back into a figuring of the singer as embodiment of white transcendence.

1926: *My Mortal Enemy* and the Sensory Epiphany

Cather's narratives about performance focus on listeners, as well as singers and musicians: hence the compelled listeners in Cather's work, including Aunt Georgiana ('A Wagner Matinée') or Marshall McKann ('A Gold Slipper') or Lucy Gayheart listening to Sebastian, or the many men (especially) who listen to Thea Kronborg. In all these stories, the singer has a singular and transformational impact on the listener. What is particularly fascinating about what we might call the 'Cather mode' of voice and character, however, is that she continually extends that sense of performative utterance into her representations of everyday life. Singing and talking often seem to merge in Cather's work, and just as the voice of the singer might shape a new sensibility in the listener, so that the talker's voice might achieve performative affect. In this sense, Cather's celebration of the artist is less a veneration of elite individualism than the promise of a democratic extension of artistry into quotidian life.

My Mortal Enemy twins two speakers/singers: Helena Modjeska and Myra Henshawe, an actual singer and a fictional speaker. Here is how Myra's 'vocative' (Cather uses that term as a noun) works to create heightened intimacy:

> When she but mentioned the name of some one whom she admired, one got an instant impression that the person must be wonderful, her voice invested the name with a sort of grace. When she liked people she always called them by name a great many times in talking to them, and she enunciated the name, no matter how commonplace, in a penetrating way, without hurrying over it or slurring it; and this, accompanied by her singularly direct glance, had a curious effect. (*MME* 54–5)

In an interesting and characteristic movement between sensory registers, Cather then imagines Myra's voice 'speaking to a person deeper down than the blurred, taken-for-granted image of my aunt that I saw every day, and for a moment my aunt became more individual, less matter-of-fact to me' (*MME* 55). The movement between different sensory registers shapes this passage. A voice reaches into a self which is an 'image', but deeper than the quasi-photographic image of selfhood which is said to be the currency of everyday social life. These sentences epitomise a Catherian sensory writing which moves across senses (here, sound and sight), which synthesises a belief in a 'deep' or essential selfhood with a fascination with performative quotidian life, and which deploys modern technology (here, the photographic image) in an often ironic way, to explore how one human being might encounter another.

Perhaps the most difficult aspect of Cather's work for contemporary readers to acknowledge is her openly admitted use of 'real' people as the prototypes for her fictional characters. She not only made that admission, but then gauged the success of her work by comparing such representations to their actual prototypes. For example, in a 1925 interview with Flora Merrill, Cather evaluated her own success in terms of how well she had portrayed the 'real' figure who became Marian Forrester in *A Lost Lady*:

> The question was, by what medium could I present her the most vividly, and that, of course, meant the most truly. There was no fun in it unless I could get her just as I remembered her and produce the effect she had on me and the many others who knew her.[9]

This rooting of fiction in the real or 'actual' figures in made-up or imaginary narratives is a constant feature of her works. It would lead to Cather evaluating her own success as a fiction writer by making claims to her ability to render 'real'-life characters in print; it would lead to the critical arguments around *Death Comes for the Archbishop*, a 'narrative' in Cather's term heavily rooted in historical biography and featuring historical figures such as Kit Carson.[10] Moreover, this process (of positioning the real in the fictional, or building a story upon figures drawn from her own experiences and encounters) has become the focus of much of the scholarship that forms the basis of the Willa Cather Scholarly Edition.[11]

In a discussion of the great film-maker Carl Theodor Dreyer, James Schamus explores what I see as a parallel issue in the work of that artist: the 'quest for a real basis for his own characters'.[12] Schamus argues that Dreyer uses shots that establish the documentary sources of his material (as in the trial transcripts shown at the start of *Joan of Arc*) to establish a 'rhetoric of realism' based on the 'assertion of the film's respect for textual evidence', a realism he then terms 'textual realism'.[13] The parallel in Cather appears to be a form of 'sensory realism', as seen in her comment on *A Lost Lady*: an 'effect' created by a character which echoes 'the effect she had on me' and this 'effect' is primarily rendered in terms of sensory impact, the way a voice or a look might achieve the powerful impact *as rendered in writing*, that such sense-based forms of contact had in real life.

My Mortal Enemy uses encounters with 'real people' to fashion a narrative relentlessly alert to the reality of performance and the performativity of everyday life. *My Mortal Enemy* seamlessly integrates real, historical figures into an imagined narrative. Without a basic knowledge of Cather's turn-of-the-century performance world, a reader might not know, as previously discussed, that Helena Modjeska was an actual historical figure (in contrast, the poet mentioned in the same chapter, Anne Aylward, is purely fictional).

It was within this context (a space framed by questions of performativity and identity) that Cather created her representations of the body in performance. *My Mortal Enemy*, written in 1925 and published in 1926, becomes an act of testimony and remembrance in part focused upon a figure who died some sixteen years earlier. Cather's characters ceaselessly go out to see performance, and within their own homes quotidian experience is woven from an endless flow of sensory moments that make up self-presentation. In Chapter V, Cather deftly fashions an episode which, although 'fiction', is clearly rooted in her early experiences as theatre-goer and drama reviewer. Action is focused through the eyes of Nellie, a proto-Jamesian focaliser in the narrative (as a young person witnessing the complex and ambiguous world of adults), who bears witness to the constant flicker of performed social life.

The tightly focused performativity of these passages precisely frames human interaction as a geometry of glances and moments of listening, as in an Edward Hopper painting. Such a scene seems highly Modernist in its configuration, though, in other ways, the novel looks back to a nineteenth-century world of performance, since opera and theatre remain, for Cather's characters, vital aesthetic–sensory places for interaction. The tight, narrowly focused *mise-en-scène* of the novel is also highly significant. For this is a chamber piece of a novel, not only in that its cast of characters (primarily Myra, Oswald and Nellie) has the neat triadic structure of a chamber drama but also in that we are often quite literally within a chamber: in a drawing room, on a balcony or within a carriage.

My Mortal Enemy forms, with *A Lost Lady*, a diptych of crystalline works that condensed the legacy of Aestheticism, read out the codes of that movement, and thus created transitional narrative. Each novel marked the emergence of a writer decisively attuned to the representational issues framed by Modernism. In *A Lost Lady* (discussed at greater length in Chapter 8) Cather inflected the floriographic discourse that Oscar Wilde had popularised as a foundation for his Aesthetic project. In *My Mortal Enemy* Cather returned to the performative cultures of the 1890s and to her fascination with the diva's body. Her origins as a writer had been forged in encounters with that figure, moments that reverberated in later work such as the 'Three American Singers' essay of 1913. *My Mortal Enemy* brought those encounters directly into fictional narrative, replaying the young Cather's viewing of a real life figure in a hybrid narrative that while 'imagined' also embedded the charisma of an actual singer in fiction. If we return to a passage I quoted earlier (Chapter 2), we now see how Nellie's narration renders charisma as a *sensory* triptych, an amalgamation of sight, sound and touch:

> For many years I associated Mrs. Henshawe with that music, thought of that aria as being mysteriously related to something in her nature that one rarely saw, but nearly always felt; a compelling, passionate, overmastering something for which I had no name, but which was audible, visible in the air that night, as she sat crouching in the shadow. (*MME* 60)

The Modjeska tableau is also an epiphany, an instant of secular transcendence as the viewer experiences a revelation. Cather's deployment of epiphanic moments became increasingly central to her work. Many of my later close readings are at heart explorations of how she used epiphanies, especially as a device to frame the white encounter with Others – a trajectory in her work which would reach its powerful and quite logical climax in the staging of an encounter between an imagined version of the child Cather and the 'slave girl' Nancy in *Sapphira*.

The epiphanic encounter with a performer is a cultural moment, but it is also a moment where *power* is crucial, especially sensory power. The listener, at the moment of the epiphany, is overwhelmingly aware of the singer's vocative strength. Thus Myra's highly physicalised response to Modjeska's voice. We can track the evolution of the epiphany in Cather's work, as she deepened and extended this narrative mode, using it to stage encounters that frequently focused issues of power in the meetings of white characters with Others (native peoples, black characters). From the diva, and the epiphanic encounter with the diva's voice, Cather developed a writing focused on tableaux where sensory encounters might become a way to explore North America's deep historical structures. Thus Father Latour's encounter with Jacinto and the ancient cave in *Death Comes for the Archbishop*, Blind D'Arnault's performance *in My Ántonia*, and the child Cather's meeting with Nancy in *Sapphira*. In all these vignettes utterance is important. The early student fascination with charismatic voice had led her through a series of narrative stagings of utterance, and then into a commitment to what might be termed 'sensory politics'. Thus – in terms of a sensory politics based on sound – think of D'Arnault's piano playing (in *My Ántonia*) or the child Cather's dislike of Nancy's Canadian accent in (*Sapphira*).

In my earlier discussion of the novel I framed the representation of Modjeska as a moment where the circumstances of the singer's life – and the questions of anti-Semitism raised by Modjeska's memoir — were, as it were, shut out by the focus of the epiphanic moment. Steadily, though, Cather used epiphanic moments in a more supple way, using this dramatic crystallisation as a means to focus a hermeneutics based around power, status, and alterity. That is, the initial aestheticised encounter became a vehicle for exploring the deeper structures of North American history, creating a narrative chain that linked Cather's writing over many decades: performative epiphanies steadily becoming represented and read in terms of politics and history.

1935: *Lucy Gayheart*

One pattern shaping the tapestry of Cather's *œuvre* is that of narratives focused on the figure of the *muse*. Repeatedly, over three decades as a full-time creative artist, Cather turned to characters who both embodied and provoked inspiration through their sheer corporeal presence. Think of works such as *My Ántonia*, *The Song of the Lark* and *Lucy Gayheart* as radical revisions of the narrative of 'musedom', especially those *fin-de-siècle* stories of artistry (for example, du Maurier's *Trilby*) that had fascinated the young Cather. Her representations of female muses ground the inspirational power of such figures in a highly sensorised awareness of their agency. Figures such as Ántonia, Thea or Lucy begin their narratives in a state of pre-articulation. Ántonia cannot speak English; Thea is 'inept in speech'; Lucy, to begin with, seems more gazed upon than an articulator of her own selfhood.

Cather roots these female muses in a very specific sensory matrix; it is sound/language that they will eventually achieve a mastery over. And each is a muse-like figure, an inspiration to male figures such as Jim or Harry Gordon, but in each case, the body of the female muse remains a place of sensory aliveness with its own powerful agency. Thus, it seems apposite that when Jim meets Ántonia again after decades, it is her voice that triggers recall and immediately re-associates her with the 'full vigor' of her character, a voice that follows immediately on from the direction of her gaze: 'She was there, in the full vigor or her personality, battered but not diminished, looking at me, speaking to me in the husky, breathy voice I remembered so well' (*MA* 321–2). Muses speak and look back in Cather, and it is the sensory immediacy of this agency that registers forcefully. The final pages might frame Ántonia in ways that repeatedly recall the male gazing implicit in the French paintings that Cather loved so much – such as Breton's 'The Song of the Lark' – yet her sensory vitality breaks out from within that framing. The object of the gaze both looks back and then sensorily reaches out beyond and through the frame (there is a strong correspondence between this paragraph and the introduction of Myra Henshawe in *My Mortal Enemy*).

> Ántonia had always been one to leave images in the mind that did not fade – that grew stronger with time. In my memory there was a succession of such pictures, fixed there like the old woodcuts of one's first primer . . . All the strong things of her heart came out in her body. (*MA* 342)

Lucy Gayheart is one of Cather's most searching and wide-angle novelistic meditations on art and the senses, upon the body and the sheer grounding of art-work within corporealism. Cather creates in *Lucy Gayheart* a form of imagined viewer of Lucy's body. We are continually in the position of a gazer watching the hyperactive Lucy run and skip and dance and skate her way across small town and big city.

Her performativity is captivating to the degree that Cather seems to fashion her narrative around perspectives, tonal touches and verbal inflections that often appear to approach fascination or even desire.

Throughout the novel, Cather orchestrates sensory details to suggest a richly textured world not only of sound but also of smell, touch and sight. As with *Sapphira and the Slave Girl* (whose floral codes I examine in Chapter 8), this narrative is a highly aestheticised storyline filled with blooming flowers. Lucy herself has a vitality that is flower-like: 'She had that singular brightness of young beauty: flower gardens have it for the first few hours after sunrise' (*LG* 7). Sebastian's studio is filled with flowers – including 'a large primrose-tinted vase, full of cream-coloured roses and heavy, drooping sprays of acacia', not to mention mimosas that make the room seem 'like a whole garden from the South' (*LG* 72). And flowers, too, become part of the novel's language of character and selfhood – a singer performing *The Bohemian Girl* phrases the libretto as if the words 'were pressed flowers which might fall apart if roughly handled' (*LG* 191). Lucy herself 'wanted flowers and music and enchantment and love, – all the things she had first known with Sebastian' (*LG* 195).

Cather creates a highly sensory matrix that recalls the 1890s *fin-de-siècle* writing that had shaped some of her earliest reviews and cultural interests. Cather's Chicago is a world of flower-filled studios, impassioned musicians and youthful vitality. It is sound – and voices – that then take centre-ground. *Lucy Gayheart* is, in many ways, Cather's most complex meditation on voice – because it is about achieving mastery through voice, but also about listening and loving sound as well as being captivated by sound. It is also about silence and the loss of voice and musical sound: the novel's three central musicians (Lucy, Sebastian and Mockford) all die. Thus, the narrative begins by following the complexities of being a listener (music and voice), moves into an exploration of what it means to produce sound, but ends with a man (Harry Gordon) who is the one main character unable to turn sensibility into sound. The novel's terrible beauty reaches a climax in Book Three, where we see Harry Gordon moving through a terrain of sonic affect but no music, a world of clocks ticking and phones ringing but no artistic embodiment of the aural.

The novel has charted the disruptive, invasive and compelling power of voice: Lucy was seduced by Sebastian's singing voice in the first place. Sebastian's compelling erotic magnetism is rooted in his voice – a magnetism that brings both Lucy and Mockford into alignment around him. At first, 'a baritone voice didn't seem to be one of the most vehement' of Lucy's wants (*LG* 30), but on hearing him, Lucy is captivated. She 'had never heard anything sung with such elevation of style . . . there was a kind of large enlightenment, like daybreak' (*LG* 32). Lucy – in characteristic Cather-sensory fashion – hears Sebastian in ways that are also haptic, forms of touching: 'The dark beauty of the songs seemed to her a quality in the voice itself, as kindness can be in the touch of a hand' (*LG* 32). Sebastian's voice, in its power and transformational effect, also acts as a kind of prefiguring of Lucy's eventual fate. The novel works by creating a form of sensory lattice of echoes and foreshadowings that work at the sensory level. The epiphanic power of Sebastian's performance suggests 'a discovery about life, a revelation of love as a tragic force . . . of passion that drowns like black water' (*LG* 33).

Presenting us with a central sensory diptych, Cather juxtaposes the vocative power of Sebastian against Harry's vocal limitations. At the instance of her doom, Harry effectively silences Lucy by ignoring her voice; his ability to block out voice, to refuse Lucy's vocalised agency, is indicative of a broader failure, Cather's narrative suggests, of human engagement.

In a way, Lucy's fate reverses the Pygmalion myth. If, in that narrative, the female statue comes to life (and in Shaw's dramatic modification, the commonly spoken Eliza achieves 'life' through being schooled to talk 'properly'), then, in Cather's novel, the vocal and musically expressive Lucy is silenced but achieves a power through her muteness. Lucy never became the artist she promised to be. She accompanied one man (Sebastian) and died because another man ignored her voice. She lingers in the memory because of her bodily reverberation, her trace as a corporeal memory – in death she reverses the typical sensory arc of a Cather heroine, which is to move from body to voice (Ántonia's last scene in *My Ántonia*, when we see her speaking Bohemian, is a good example of this, since her decision to create a bilingual household is emblematic of her autonomy and unconventionality).

Lucy's embodied presence and her silence are ironic takes on stereotypical renderings of femininity, since she remains iconic and powerful, a haunter of Harry. As with the overture to *My Ántonia*, where the first narrator (assumed by most readers to be a version of Cather herself) fails to emerge from silence, *Lucy Gayheart* ironically plays with the silenced or quietened female artist, by then showing how male characters (Jim Burden, Harry Gordon) remain haunted by powerful female agents who have not achieved the artistic autonomy seen in novels such as *The Song of the Lark* but whose bodily presences, even in death, continue to haunt the male protagonist.

Lucy Gayheart is a triptych, divided into three Books (again we see Cather's fascination with quasi-pictorial and panelled ways of creating narrative). The first two Books are full of listening to music, rehearsing, talking about music. Cather has given the everyday intensity and emotionality of being 'in' music, of a life lived within the absorbing culture of performance. After Lucy dies, the final Book – elegiac, spectral – is remarkably silent. Or, to be even more accurate, it has sounds, but rarely the sound of music. Lucy's father has continued to practise his clarinet, though, in summer and in the orchard: a poignant vignette of isolation (*LG* 216). Mr Gayheart is a watchmaker, and the sound of watches ticking is one of the telling details in this sensory mural. Then we are at Mr Gayheart's funeral: prayers are read and 'someone whispered' (*LG* 217). The mourners are reminded of Lucy's death: 'It was like a bird being shot down when it rises in its morning flight toward the sun' (*LG* 217). The narrative then focuses on Harry, quietly going about his business. He remembers playing chess with Mr Gayheart: 'They talked no more than good chess-players usually do' (*LG* 220). He remembers his first glimpse of Lucy – another scene played out as if it were a scenario in a silent movie. The sounds of this last Book are not at all musical: 'Many a time, going home on winter nights, he had heard again that last cry on the wind – "Harry!"' (*LG* 232). Clearly traumatised, Gordon buys cars and travels across the prairies: 'He got into the habit of thinking aloud as he drove; talking, indeed, to his motor engine' (*LG* 232).

From Schubert to talking to oneself in a car: *Lucy Gayheart* deploys Cather's technique of sensory panelling to explore loss and grief.

The final crushing pages of the novel are devoid of music; all that is left is the memory of Lucy's voice, clocks ticking, a man talking to himself in a car. Cather has created a sensory *mise-en-scène*, an auditory mural, where a narrative's resolution takes shape through a series of sounds. Harry remembers Lucy's laugh – a trace of her musical identity: 'her low, rich, contralto laugh that fell softly back upon itself' (*LG* 234). And then there is the sound of the phone, as, in 'the absolute stillness of the night', he hears the 'bank telephone ringing again and again'. 'That would be his wife, calling up to know what had become of him' (*LG* 235) – Harry does not answer. The reader infers marital fracture and Harry's ongoing grief from these carefully separated and arranged details. 'The novel démeublé', then, constructed around the stripping out of sensory detail so that a few spartan auditory features (a clock ticking; a clarinet in a wood; a ringing phone; the memory of a woman's laugh) now contain a whole world of loss and pain.

Conclusion: From Voice to Silence

In a letter of 7 May 1934 to her sister Elsie, Cather wrote of *Lucy Gayheart* that it was 'modern, western, very romantic, non-Catholic' (*SL* 494) (she was clearly aware that her two previous novels had started to create an image of the 'Catholic' novelist). Note the term 'modern'. In its complex narrative shaping of sound affects (music, voice, noise, silence) Cather had indeed addressed acoustic modernity.

As Friedrich Kittler has suggested (see my first chapter), acoustic modernity was shaped by the bodily disassociation brought about by technologies such as the gramophone and the radio: the body no longer needed to be present for it to be the source of human sound. Cather's long and labyrinthine career was a journey through sound – as it mutated through technological change and remarkable shifts in terms of what might constitute an acoustic community. Cather's fictions, over a half-century, engaged with and mapped these sound shifts, and used them to reshape narrative. At first, as a devotee of late Victorian divas, her fiction revolved around the human presence signalled by vocality – but in later works such as *Lucy Gayheart*, 'sound' itself, now increasingly separated from human presence, began to shape her narratives.

Notes

1. Johnson, *Sisters in Sin: Brothel Drama in America, 1900–1920*, 51.
2. Ibid. 51.
3. Richard Giannone's *Music in Willa Cather's Fiction* (first published in 1968, and reprinted in a new edition in 2001) remains the central account of this subject. His tracing of Cather's use of music, her allusions and her deployment of musical structures in the fiction has informed my thinking throughout this chapter. Scholars continue to deepen our understanding of Cather's highly 'musicalised' literary imagination. For recent explorations of Cather and music, see Flannigan, 'Cather's Evolving Ear', and Harbison, 'Cather, Fremstad, and Wagner'.
4. Kennicott, 'Wagner, Place, and the Growth of Pessimism', 191.
5. Funda, '"The Crowning Flight of Egotism": Willa Cather, Sarah Bernhardt, and the Cult of Celebrity'.
6. Rosowski, *The Voyage Perilous: Willa Cather's Romanticism*; Giannone, *Music in Willa Cather's Fiction*. For an account of Cather and late nineteenth-century British writing, including figures such as Wilde and Stevenson, see Reynolds, 'The Transatlantic Virtual Salon: Cather and the British', 349–68.
7. Young, 'The Singer as Artist', 47.
8. Edmonds, 'Princess Hamlet', 72.
9. Skaggs, *After the World Broke in Two: The Later Novels of Willa Cather*, 77.
10. Cather, 'On *Death Comes for the Archbishop*'.
11. The Historical Introductions and Explanatory Notes of several volumes of the Willa Cather Scholarly Edition move into this territory. Hence David Porter's explorations of how Cather deployed 'Nevin-like figures'– that is, fictional characters carrying echoes of the composer and musician, Ethelbert Nevin, who had fascinated Cather (Porter, 'Historical Essay', 264).
12. Schamus, *Carl Theodor Dreyer's 'Gertrude': The Moving Word*, 18.
13. Ibid. 18.

CHAPTER 6

Touch: Haptic Narrative in *The Professor's House, Shadows on the Rock* and *Sapphira and the Slave Girl*

Is touch the most melancholic of the senses? In *The Book of Touch*, Constance Classen discusses bodily loss (through amputation) and how such catastrophe poses very fundamental questions about who we are and what it means to be human:

> What of the self is left, what is refashioned, when our corporeal bundle of sensibilities is reduced through injury, disease, or other causes? What would life be like without a sense of touch? What would life be like with only a sense of touch?[1]

But in Western culture, touch is also profoundly enmeshed with a sense of tactile healing – not only in the Gospels' account of Jesus's healing touch, but in accounts of the power of kings to heal through touch:

> The one kind of magical healing to which official indulgence was liberally extended was the cure by the royal touch. At a special religious service conducted by leading Anglican clergy the monarch laid his hands upon each member of the long queue of sufferers. The patients approached one by one and knelt before the monarch, who lightly touched them on the face, while a chaplain read aloud the verse from St. Mark: 'They shall lay hands on the sick and they shall recover'.[2]

Cather explored touch in her fiction as a way to suggest an unspoken richness of affect. In Cather's 'little towns', touch remains important; there is a modern sense that the bonds between these individuals are no longer straightforwardly those of community or family but also extend to a profound and not always acknowledged eroticism between strangers. This doubleness permeates *Lucy Gayheart*: characters 'in touch' but not always revealing, to others or themselves, what is truly touching them:

> In little towns, lives roll along so close to one another; loves and hates beat about, their wings almost touching. On the sidewalks along which everybody comes and goes, you must, if you walk abroad at all, at some time pass within a few inches of the man who cheated and betrayed you, or the woman you desire more than anything else in the world. Her skirt brushes against you. You say good-morning, and go on. It is a close shave. Out in the world the escapes are not so narrow. (*LG* 175–6)

What a strange delineation of community and the erotics of contact! These lines have a transgressive power, a strange awareness of a contact we would normally not expect to find in the writing of a provincial small town – not least because of the second-person address which implicates the reader. Loves and hates have wings that touch. The sidewalks captivate in their intimacy and potential for seduction. The anonymous figures who brush against us might have cheated on us or might be the object of our desire. The shift in the narrative point of view renders such moments of touch yet more electrifying as the readers themselves are implicated in the emotional exchange with its seductive danger. Instead of a handshake or a glance, the protagonist feels the skirt of the desired one brush against them. For the gender of this 'you' is never clear: male or female, the second person addressed is both curiously anonymous and closely felt, an object to be touched and directly addressed but not fully known. This sense of touch as emotional resonance becomes a dominant motif of *Lucy Gayheart*, a novel profoundly engaged with the musical world and sound, and which none the less deploys tactility to understand yet another level of feeling. Thus, Clement Sebastian's life: 'If you brushed against his life ever so lightly it was like tapping on a deep bell; you felt all that you could not hear' (*LG* 49). And by counterpointing one sense against another, as Cather does in this text, touch becomes a form of compensation for the lack of sensory richness (in the form of flowers) in a frozen Nebraska: 'The thing to do was to make an overcoat of the cold; to feel one's self warm and awake at the heart of it, one's blood coursing unchilled in an air where roses froze instantly' (*LG* 39).

In this chapter, I look at Cather's staging and dramatising of scenes of touch, especially in the later fictions (*The Professor's House, Shadows on the Rock* and *Sapphira and the Slave Girl*). In *The Professor's House*, Cather remaps conventional patterns of affect and emotional bonding into strange and unsettling new configurations; Tom Outland and his male companions on the mesa develop a powerful attraction to a mummified skeleton, which they appositely call 'Mother Eve'. It is the faculty of touch that Cather invokes and explores throughout this work of haptic Modernism. In *Shadows on the Rock*, Cather's reading of the colony is deeply materialistic in the most literal sense: the feel of the objects the colonists surround themselves with is central to a sensory historical fiction. And in the culmination of this thinking through of tactility and its centrality to American cultures, Cather would finally construct in *Sapphira and the Slave Girl* a narrative with a double helix at its imaginative centre: nursing twisted with racist violence, care bound up with sexual predation.

'The Novel Démeublé': Tactility in *The Professor's House*

Discussing the nineteenth-century French theatre director Adolphe Lemoine-Montigny (often simply known as 'Montigny'), John Stokes highlights the importance of furniture (and the rearrangement of furniture) in his experiments with dramatic Realism. 'Little is known about Montigny's exact working methods', Stokes writes, 'but what information there is makes it clear that he stressed above all a character's close relation to things'.[3] Montigny brought furniture into the rehearsal and development of a play, filling the stage to 'force the actors to find their way around these awkward obstacles'. 'He would then reduce the number but, the earlier pattern remaining in their minds, actors would no longer instinctively revert to the straight lines and downstage groupings of neo-classical theatre.'[4]

Montigny's experiments are indicative of the ways in which nineteenth-century theatrical praxis created new ways to think about spatial configurations of realism. Cather was the most theatrical of American fiction writers – ceaselessly alert to theatre and theatrical praxis. As we have seen, reviews of theatre and the theatricality of everyday life formed her first experiments in writing. Thus, when Cather writes about the *mise-en-scène* created by narrative, she reaches for a lexicon that is decidedly theatrical and uses physical staging and the placement of objects as ways to think about narrative. Her essay on narrative form, 'The Novel Démeublé' (1922), is a prime instance of Cather's redeployment of Victorian tropes for modernist purposes. She imagines scenes within fiction as if they were theatrical spaces created by a director such as Montigny.

It is worth reflecting on the contributions of 'The Novel Démeublé' to Cather's theorisation of how the senses related to the praxis of Realism. The essay rejects the over-furnished novel. An attack on accumulation and unnecessary detailing in fiction, it seems fundamentally critical in posture, akin tonally to the other 1920s attacks that Cather fashioned on cultural and literary practice (for instance, 'Nebraska: the End of the First Cycle' in 1923). The essay is often discussed as an account of materialism in fiction, but it is important to note that 'sensations', too, were Cather's focus:

> The novel, for a long while, has been over-furnished . . . There is a popular superstition that 'realism' asserts itself in the cataloguing of a great number of material objects, in explaining mechanical processes, the methods of operating manufactories and trades, and in minutely and unsparingly describing physical sensations.(*OW* 35–7)

In her call for a simplified and selective art, Cather emphasised not only the selection of material objects and settings, but also selection within the world of sensation:

> Literalness, when applied to the presenting of mental reactions and of physical sensations, seems to be no more effective than when it is applied to material things. A novel crowded with physical sensations is no less a catalogue than one crowded with furniture. (*OW* 42)

At the end of the essay, Cather turns from explaining what fiction should not do to an account of what a simplified and selective fiction might achieve. Here, in her famous account of the 'thing not named', Cather envisioned a radical sensoriness – figured in auditory terms:

> Whatever is felt upon the page without being specifically named there – that, one might say, is created. It is the inexplicable presence of the thing not named, of the overtone divined by the ear but not heard by it, the verbal mood, the emotional aura of the fact or the thing or the deed, that gives high quality to the novel or the drama, as well as to poetry itself. (OW 41–2)

'The Novel Démeublé' calls for a radically thinned-down form of Realism, where excess detail is removed and a more shaped and lean form of description emerges. Cather reacted against the excessive accumulation of late nineteenth-century fiction, stuffed with detail (novels as brimming with sheer 'stuff' as the rooms they describe). When an author removes the Balzacian clutter from a scene, the objects that remain take on an augmented significance. Cather created a quasi-theatrical way to think about objects and about how the human body relates to those objects, and these ideas would then shape such works as *My Mortal Enemy* (think about Nellie's first glimpse of Myra, the latter framed in her room), *Shadows on the Rock* (where the objects in sparsely furnished colonists' rooms carry great emotional weight) and, above all, *The Professor's House* (with its sudden shifts between different spatial orders and its isolating of objects within environments constructed as if they were stage sets).

It is easy to see the formalistic impact that this compositional method had on Cather's fiction, not least on the lean neo-minimalism that shaped the early 1920s novellas (*A Lost Lady* and *My Mortal Enemy*). But there are *sensory* implications to Cather's advocacy of the unfurnished novel, too. In a novel shorn of excessive detail, characters react to the object world in telling ways – there is a focus on particularities and very specific features (furniture, objects) within that world. The massive flow or extreme accumulation of late Victorian realism gives way to a world of highly specific sensory encounters. Cather's theorising about furnishing and unfurnishing a novel has a direct relevance to her creation of the sensorium. Almost as if she were creating a highly shaped stage set, the isolation of specific objects is central to the unfurnished novel. Stuff is taken out and characters are pointedly juxtaposed against the stuff remaining. Thus, the sensory feel of 'Tom Outland's Story' is created out of an isolation of objects, the staging of items against a relatively empty landscape. Imagine a more crowded and furnished mesa – the powerful sensory immediacy of Mother Eve's skeleton would be diluted through accumulation. Cather delineates St Peter's psychological response to his environment (he is practically neurasthenic in his responses) by his reactions to domestic features that are carefully isolated and highlighted: 'Certain wobbly stair treads, certain creaky boards in the upstairs hall, had made him wince many times a day for twenty-odd years – and they still creaked and wobbled' (*TPH* 11–12).

The Professor's House: The Hand's Work and the Synchronous Sensorium

One of Willa Cather's first works of fiction was a weird micro-narrative about Ancient Egypt, 'A Tale of the White Pyramid'. Published in a university journal, *The Hesperian*, this 1892 miniature gave Cather one of her first opportunities to write about embodiment, clothing, robing and disrobing, and – notably – mummification.

> Senefrau the first, Lord of the Light and Ruler of the Upper and Lower Kingdoms, was dead and gathered unto his fathers. His body had passed into the hands of the embalmers, and lain for the allotted seventy days in niter, and had been wrapped in gums and spices and white linen and placed in a golden mummy case, and to-day it was to be placed in the stone sarcophagus in the white pyramid, where it was to await its soul.[5]

Hardly what one would expect from the prairie novelist: but instances of mummification form a significant pattern of tropes in Cather's work. In *The Song of the Lark* Dr Archie meticulously wraps the young Thea, ill with pneumonia, in a medicinal binding that practically mummifies her. 'When he had stitched up the flaxseed jacket, he wiped it neatly about the edges, where the paste had worked out on the skin' (*SOL* 11). Then, twelve years later, in *The Professor's House*, Cather produced her most compelling image of the mummified female form in the figure of Mother Eve, the ancient skeleton discovered by Tom Outland and his friends on the Blue Mesa.

Mummies and processes of mummification recur in Cather's fiction, one might suggest, because these artefacts and phenomena are part of an intensely tactile imaginative domain in her work: a creative locus focused on hands and the work of hands. The late fiction especially fashions plotlines, dramatic scenarios, repeated tropes and motifs that centre on what I call 'haptic modernism'. Thus, as a work of haptic modernism, *The Professor's House* is a narrative where the tactile becomes central to a story of sensory dissociation and fragmentation. St Peter's world is one of tactile binaries (touching in an erotic or affectionate way; touching that might suggest pain or repulsion). His abjection is embodied in a sense of super-sensitive and neurotic touch. Again and again, the novel presents bodily forms that are beyond touch, or rebarbatively untouchable, or so strange that characters can barely imagine touching them. St Peter seems almost self-sealed, radically sequestered from the tactile.

Cather constructs the novel around a skein of details grouped tactilely in their various forms. *The Professor's House*, a novel that is often about touch in all its forms, will move from the literal and physical touches of the handicrafts of the opening pages to the emotional touching of the second part of the novel. St Peter is 'touched' by his student Tom Outland, and the Professor will then have his life saved by the 'touching' seamstress, Augusta. Although St Peter is a scholar, he is introduced to us as a man who moves in a relentlessly physical world, a world of carpentry and gardening. Each paragraph in these opening pages recounts one form of handwork or craft, or another. The Professor's daughter, Kathleen, has painted watercolours of him (*TPH* 13). St Peter has created a French garden, a 'tidy half-acre' (*TPH* 14): breaking off a geranium blossom, 'with it still in his hand', he enters his study. The opening chapter of *The Professor's House* becomes a brilliant sensory comedy, as the Professor sits in his study, his dissociation from family and marriage signalled in a relentless series of misunderstandings (of sight, hearing and touch). In the most basic sense, St Peter is failing in his tactile skills – the stairs creak: 'He had a deft hand with tools, he could easily have fixed them, but there were always so many things to fix, and there was not time enough to go round' (*TPH* 12).

Cather presents St Peter as a handworker, marked by affinity with other handworkers: 'He went into the kitchen, where he had carpentered under a succession of cooks' (*TPH* 12). He is an intellectual but also a thoroughly physicalised specimen, a man 'with the slender hips and springy shoulders of a tireless swimmer' (*TPH* 13). Even his head seems hand-crafted: 'The mould of his head on the side was so individual and definite, so far from casual, that it was more like a statue's head than a man's' (*TPH* 14). He is also a gardener, and has created a herb garden, where he planted a rich variety of flowers and 'had got the upper hand' of his land (*TPH* 15).

And then Cather introduces Augusta, the seamstress, and continues with the tactile patterning of her story. She shares the Professor's office at the top of the house, working at her sewing-machine during the day while St Peter occupies the same space by night. Augusta is St Peter's secret sharer, and Cather positions her sensorily alongside the Professor: two very different figures linked by their intensely tactile preoccupations. It is the dressmaker's 'forms' which Cather uses to concretise and embody this sensory connection. The forms – model torsos used for making dresses – suggest a sensual immediacy (Augusta calls one 'the bust'), but also a strange disembodiment (they are, after all, not real but rather representations of the female body), and Cather uses them to frame St Peter's complexly ambivalent relationship to women.

> Though this figure looked so ample and billowy (as if you might lay your head upon its deep-breathing softness and rest safe forever), if you touched it you suffered a severe shock, no matter how many times you had touched it before. (*TPH* 18)

This form has a 'dead, opaque, lumpy solidity ... very disappointing to the tactile sense' (*TPH* 19). St Peter is bizarrely fixated on 'his ladies', preventing Augusta taking them to the new house that the family have moved into.

The novel contextualises a fascination with tactility by constructing idiosyncratic theories about hands, touching and handwork. At one point, members of the family overhear St Peter lecturing – and it is religion and the role of hands that his lecture focuses on. St Peter argues that art evolved out of the ceremonial and ritualistic dimensions of religious experience: 'Every act had some imaginative end. The cutting of the finger nails was a religious observance' (*TPH* 69). Theology then produced craft: 'With the theologians came the cathedral-builders; the sculptors and glassworkers and painters' (*TPH* 69). This is St Peter speaking, and on the next page a similar sentiment is rendered in free indirect discourse: 'The hand, fastidious and bold, which selected and placed – it was that which made the difference. In Nature there is no selection' (*TPH* 75).

Art and the processes of selection which Cather saw as being central to art thus grow out of religion. And it is the hand, the selecting hand of the artist, which then produces painting or builds cathedrals or writes. The novel then becomes an elaborate meditation on 'the hand, fastidious and bold', and focuses on the viability of art in the modern world: a viability produced by the maker's hand. The disappointments of the opening pages signal a radical disintegration of a tactile art world which St Peter celebrates in his lecture. Cather has constructed an intricate narrative lattice which suggests contrasts and similitudes between various forms of tactile experience (sewing, writing, gardening, and then the touch of erotic connection or affective closeness): all these details ultimately shaped into a highly Modernist narrative about cultural disintegration. What Cather is doing here is to incorporate various forms of culture, from religion to crafts, around the foundational sense of touch – presenting tactility as the groundwork of everything from a religious ceremony to the making of clothes or the painting of pictures. In St Peter's reading of cultural dissociation, that integrated tactility has now broken apart. He himself is fated to garden, to write, to swim, to carpenter – but these activities are now hyper-individualised and fragmented; he lives alone, radically alienated from his family. How to reintegrate a life or a culture around touch?

For St Peter – carpenter, homemaker, gardener and writer – lives in a world of radical sensory derangement, where nothing feels quite as it should. The novel is a thoroughly Modernist text, one where the typical 1920s motifs of rupture and dissolution have now been located at the very foundations of human placement in the world, in how we relate on a sensory level to the world around us. St Peter does not think that things have broken in two: he feels on his very fingertips that this has taken place.[6]

If the novel is one of dissociation and rupture, then it locates fragmentation at the level of male sensory encounters with a domestic world coded in terms of the female body and female crafts. For St Peter, a man with his own craft-iness, the world of handwork now seems out of kilter and disrupted. At this point, the narrative imagines Queen Mathilde and her court weaving the Bayeux Tapestry – an image of handwork whose product is a full integration of the personal and the public. St Peter, like many Cather protagonists, glimpses an aesthetic utopia where style and decoration are everything, and where the aesthetic reintegrates fracture and fragmentation. Queen Mathilde might be a royal, and her tapestry a heroic narrative of 'knights and heroes', but the panels are also defiantly quotidian, recording 'little playful' animal stories:

> All the while he had been working so fiercely at his eight big volumes, he was not insensible to the domestic drama that went on beneath him. His mind had played delightedly with all those incidents. Just as, when Queen Mathilde was doing the long tapestry now shown at Bayeux, – working her chronicle of the deeds of knights and heroes, – alongside the big pattern of dramatic action she and her women carried the little playful pattern of birds and beasts that are a story in themselves; so, to him, the most important chapters of his history were interwoven with personal memories. (*TPH* 99–100)

The narrative positions tactile crafts – focused on female hands – as a way to integrate the levels of experience that, in St Peter's world of ruptured male tactility, have simply become dis-integrated. In St Peter's world, the movements between different levels of experience are far more violent and jolting – fragmented and jolting, in fact. St Peter's aesthetic utopia is an Arts and Crafts medievalist idyll where female craft-making brings together human and animal, royalty and commoners. It is a dream of integrated endeavour, of craft become art, a female formalism that stands for possibility in a world where the protagonist experiences fracture.

Touch, above all, creates the sensory 'lead' of these ensembles (thinking of Cather as a writer who creates symphonic narratives out of the five senses). Tactility creates linkages and juxtapositions across the novel: from the estranged tactility of the opening pages of *The Professor's House*, we move to 'Tom Outland's Story', a very different sensorium.

'Tom Outland's Story' marks another point in an evolving sensory narrative. *The Professor's House* is – literally – broken (ruptured) temporally and geographically as Cather takes the reader out of St Peter's suburban professorial existence and back to Tom Outland's working life in the Southwest and his exploration of the Cliff City and the mesa. By placing one narrative within a new narrative space, she also creates a *displacement*, refocusing the flow of the story, abruptly breaking from the tale created in the first Book of the novel – 'The Family' (just about as conventional a title as one might imagine in a bourgeois Realist text). The reader enters another habitus, another kind of sensorium, a world elsewhere mapped through the completely different bodily experiences of Outland in this Southwest setting. In her commentary on the novel (first published in the *News Letter of the College English Association* in 1940, and then in *Willa Cather on Writing*), Cather imagined 'Tom Outland's Story' in deeply sensory (in fact, visual) terms, comparing it to the view through a window in a Dutch painting: 'in most of the interiors, whether drawing-room or kitchen, there was a square window, open, through which one saw the masts of ships, or a stretch of grey sea' (*OW* 31).

Above all, the Cliff City is a place where the tactile achieves centrality to how one literally feels the world, underpinning what Eric Aronoff calls the 'novel's construction of culture as an aesthetic whole'.[7] The lost Indians had a complex material culture built around crafts: they were potters, weavers and builders. Theirs was a culture of the hand. The radical tactile dissociation of St Peter's life is now replaced, in some of Cather's most ecstatic writing, by a plenitude of touch. The initial apprehension of the world through sight (the topographical–exploratory mode signalled by Outland's first gaze at the mesa) is now supplanted by a complex touching of materials. And in Cather's highly sensory representation of craft, it is this touching of materials and making of objects (pottery, clothes) that signals a fusion between the self and the material world, a heightened merging through the sense of touch. 'Tom Outland's Story', an insertion of an earlier narrative into an emergent novel, thus acts in a way that becomes familiar to Cather's readers: a sudden break in the narrative flow, a movement into another sensory space so that when the narrative moves on (or back) to its dominant spaces, readers carry an awareness of how sensory orders might be disrupted or remodelled, and how narrative itself might become a way to chart and understand shifts in the habitus.

Paula Kot reads *The Professor's House* as a fiction growing out of Cather's initial written engagement with the Southwest in a 1916 *Book News Monthly* essay, 'A Visit to the Mesa Verde'.[8] For Kot, Cather had a complex relationship to land speculation, both in the forms it had taken on the Nebraskan prairies and in the case of the Wetherill family's promotion of the mesa (Cather's essay began with an account of Richard Wetherill's discovery of the site). Kot shows how the novel plays out the desire to find a 'pure' engagement with landscape even as the 'tourist gaze' reveals a more acquisitive relationship. Kot reads the novel as acknowledging the 'drama of speculation' – in fact, throughout the novel, processes of speculation (as when Louie speculates on Tom's design for the vacuum engine, or when Fechtig tries to trade the archaeological remains discovered on the mesa) emerge as central.[9]

I would add to Kot's analysis of speculation, discovery and landscape a further gloss: this is a thoroughly sensory discourse in *The Professor's House*. Tom's desire to *see* the mesa jostles against the tourist gaze. But the novel shows us other ways in which the senses and the body itself return one to the sheer material basis of encounters between the male protagonists and the natural and female worlds. St Peter is a curmudgeon, keen to isolate himself from his family and hide away in his office. But the egregiously tactile female forms in that space literally shock him into encounters through touch. At the end of the novel, his semi-willed semi-suicide is averted by seamstress Augusta, a woman who uses her hands – sensory immediacy breaking in again. Outland is very much St Peter's protégé in his Western fascination with systems of knowledge, and his need to look at the mesa (as if ordering it into a system) is very much part of his utterly visualising approach to the world. One way to read the novel is as a sensory contest between St Peter and Outland (a writer and an engineer), their fundamentally visual approach to the world (Western and male), and the tactile and material immediacy of their encounters with the indigenous and female worlds of the mesa and the home.

The novel is famed for its inset narrative, 'Tom Outland's Story', a first-person tale (presumably, Tom's oral narrative as it was spoken to St Peter) about this now dead character's exploration of the mesa lands of the Southwest. Part wilderness story, part Frontier narrative and part exploration fable, 'Tom Outland's Story' presents a lost utopia – the vanished civilisation of the Cliff Dweller people – in contrast to the consumerist and philistine world that the Professor feels he inhabits.

How does the inset narrative relate to the flanking sections of the novel? The parallels with a Puvis de Chavannes mural are quite evident: we are given three panelled sections ('The Family', 'Tom Outland's Story' and 'The Professor') and asked to work out the relationships between them. 'Tom Outland's Story' stands in stark contrast to the other sections, flagrantly breaking apart unities of time and place: we have moved radically backwards in time (to when Tom Outland was alive, before he died in the First World War; and to the pre-Columbus era of indigenous cultures untouched by contact with Europeans) and on to the mesa, with its open vistas and dwelling spaces carved into the rock. Cather deploys juxtaposition, contrast and opposition as the foundation of narrative development. Yet such contrasts serve only to emphasise the main continuity between and across the narrative panels.

The continuity with 'Tom Outland's Story' is built around tactility and hand-based crafts. Tom Outland and his companions move into the mesa armed with tools, and their initial forays into the site are feats of building, excavating and improvised engineering. First, the men get their tools and supplies. They move in, armed with these supplies, and an axe and spade. The encounters with this landscape are visual, then viscerally tactile:

> The court-yard was not choked by vegetation, for there was no soil. It was bare rock, with a few old, flat-topped cedars growing out of the cracks, and a little pale grass. But everything seemed open and clean, and the stones, I remember, were warm to the touch, smooth and pleasant to feel. (*TPH* 206)

Outland shares his mentor St Peter's interest in domestic handicrafts. While St Peter lives alongside the seamstress, Augusta, Outland explores the mesa's hand-worked world, the jars, bowls and mats of the Cliff City. This is archaeological exploration as primarily a matter of handling materials – a thoroughly *embodied* academic discipline. Then Outland's crew also become practical construction workers, rebuilding a road from the Cliff City to the mesa's top. The operation's final stages involve 'three weeks' hard work, and most of our winter's wages' (*TPH* 209). Outland, like St Peter, is devoted to his tactile occupations. After they build their way to the top of the mesa, the men begin to excavate: 'We were now ready for what we called excavating' (*TPH* 210). And in a further narrative synchronicity connecting this part of the novel with the flanking panels of the storyline, Outland discovers a craft-based world which, like Augusta's dressmaking, seems to offer exemplary plenitude to the male onlooker. The Cliff City was built carefully and painstakingly: joists rubbed smooth, the 'door lintels were carefully fitted', and chambers decorated with geometric frescoes and painted borders (*TPH* 211).

And so, when the darker, dystopian underside of the mesa and its world begins to emerge, it is entirely appropriate that it will be touch, of all the senses, that is central to the reshaping of this world. Injury and death undercut the utopia's promise. First, the men come across the mummified figure of the woman they call 'Mother Eve', a figure they think has been murdered – her body carries the mark of assault: 'there was a great wound in her side, the ribs stuck out through the dried flesh' (*TPH* 213). And then Henry is bitten by a snake – it 'struck him square in the forehead . . . He was struck so near the brain that there was nothing to do' (*TPH* 215). These two moments of haptic violence mark the disintegration of Tom's sense of the Cliff City and the mesa as places of utopian tactility. They also point forward to *Sapphira and the*

Slave Girl's mapping of violent touch as a means to understand slavery and racism.

Shadows on the Rock and the 'wretched machinery' of the Body: Touch and Illness

It is very tempting to read an intensely tactile book such as *Shadows on the Rock* – a book focused on touching, healing and sickness – as a displaced creative response to Cather's mother's stroke in 1929. It vividly brought home to her the shattering contrast between will and personality, and the 'wretched machinery' of the now-paralysed body. Note the accounts of how she and her brother tended her (in a letter to Dorothy Canfield Fisher, April or May 1929):

> Mother is completely paralyzed on the right side, and speechless. Yet behind the wretched machinery her mind and strong will, her whole personality is just the same . . . We have excellent nurses, thank God, but a tall, strong woman paralyzed is the most helpless thing in the world. She has to be fed with a spoon like a baby. Constant changes of position give her the only ease she can have . . . Your letter came while I was rubbing her yesterday. I read part of it to her and she remembered you perfectly, and the time she met you at the door. (*SL* 415)

It is the contact of touch that is paramount in Cather's account of her mother: the brother lifting and carrying, Cather herself rubbing. Encounters with her sick mother, such as caring for a paralysed body and learning how to 'read' or 'understand' that body in spite of the loss of speech, must surely have contributed to the works that Cather developed in the 1930s – the care-giving and flesh-tending of *Shadows* and the entwining of lively movement and mortal immobility (the three drownings) of *Lucy Gayheart*. The former is Cather's novel of nursing care while the latter is about a life suddenly shifting from energetic movement to frozen stillness. Both novels read out the dramatic potential implicit in the letter's anguished need to find agency and life force in a seemingly uncommunicative body.

Alongside the biographical evidence that suggests Cather's interest in nursing, touch and bodies, we also have journalistic writing focused on these topics. An early essay for *The Home Monthly*, 'Nursing as a Profession for Women' (1897), created a relentlessly physical sketchbook of what it might mean to be a nurse. Cather focuses nursing on an utterly materialised vision of care, the essay almost reading as if she had simply alighted on this topic in order to get at what would be the real subject: the body itself. She recounts a nurse's 'struggle with one old women': 'First she used alcohol, but it made no impression; then ether, then turpentine; finally she resorted to a stiff scrubbing brush and sapolio.'[10] 'Nursing as a Profession' also gave Cather space to write about violence and injury – 'men who had been torn to pieces by machinery or burned in some tenement fire' – in a foreshadowing of the brutal accidents that run throughout her work like an imaginative wound.[11] In her final sentence, Cather reduced the nurse, quite simply, to being a bodily presence, noting that ' a nurse needs a strong physical personality, the sort of positive and active good health that influences weaker people and acts like a stimulant upon the patient'.[12]

Cather's interest in nursing shaped a number of her fictions and created distinctive contortions in their narrative lines. In *One of Ours* (1922), for instance, the transatlantic crossing of Claude Wheeler and his fellow troops to France occupies a great deal of space. This Book, 'The Voyage of the *Anchises*', is shadowed by the flu: 'a scourge of influenza had broken out on board, of a peculiarly bloody and malignant type'. A footnote – Cather's own – notes: 'The actual outbreak of influenza on transports carrying United States troops is here anticipated by several months' (*OOO* 387). Perhaps redeploying anecdotes and observations derived from her experience of the Spanish flu epidemic of 1918, Cather then turns this section of the novel into an exercise in gender-role revisionism, focusing on how her doughboys care for one another:

> There was almost no ventilation, and the air was fetid with sickness and sweat and vomit. Two of the band boys were working in the stench and dirt, helping the stewards. Claude stayed to lend a hand until it was time to give Fanning his nourishment. He began to see that the wrist watch, which he had hitherto despised as effeminate and had carried in his pocket, might be a very useful article. (*OOO* 395)

Ernest Hemingway infamously attacked the novel, saying Cather had 'Catherized' the war.[13] In a way, he was right: she did 'Catherize' the war, expanding the 'feminised' moments of a war narrative to explore the tactile skills of nursing.

Shadows on the Rock is one of Cather's most tactile fictions, a narrative where tactility, loss and healing are embedded in a story about exile and melancholia. What is it like to be removed from one's homeland in a sensory way? What feelings of loss – of touch, of a hand on a particular material or surface – would the migrant experience? In the opening, remarkably beautiful pages of *Shadows on the Rock*, saturated in migrant sorrow and domestic consolation, Cather creates one of her most detailed and moving portrayals of the body – its needs, its pleasures and its pains. These pages are hardly driven by plot in any conventional sense, but rather by highly physicalised character portraits, which are wedded to retrospective memory shots of recall – flashbacks across time and space. The effect is startling: a sense of the human as a physical–mental hybridity in which physical selfhood exists intensely in the present moment but is ceaselessly framed by memories of earlier physical moments. Cather's sense of consciousness in these pages is highly embodied – it is the moment-by-moment rendering of sensation, or the remembering of sensation, that preoccupies her.

This is writing built around shifts and contrasts between different and competing sensory orders, a central example of Cather's experimental drive to construct a relentlessly physical writing where varying forms of perception and contact are continually foregrounded. The opening sequences of the novel – and they definitely read like sequences, as if connected and threaded together by an inner conceptual logic – are about sight and the colonist's visual mastery of a new landscape. We begin with Euclide Auclair 'gazing down the broad, empty river far beneath him' (*SOR* 7). He and the other Quebecers have watched the last French ship of the year disappear over the horizon. Cather presents Auclair as a visualiser. He looks down on the town, imagining this 'rock-set town' as a Nativity scene: 'cardboard mountains, broken up into cliffs and ledges and hollows' (*SOR* 9). Then Cather uses one of her second-person addresses to further this visual intimacy: 'Divest your mind of Oriental colour, and you saw here very much such a mountain rock' (*SOR* 9) – the reader is literally being asked to look too. Repeatedly, the reader is out in the position of surveyors, colonists or explorers looking down on a terrain, mapping it in our mind's eye: 'The Île d'Orléans, out in the middle of the river, was like a hilly map, with downs and fields and pastures lying in folds above the naked tree-tops' (*SOR* 10–11).

The writing then shifts sensory register, moving from a sense of sight to the touch and feel of this landscape. We are no longer on a rocky promontory, looking down and thinking of maps, able to compare landscapes through visual analogies. The tactile immediacy of the resistant landscape becomes central. Cather's writing registers, quite literally, the ways in which vision distances while touch brings one close. The focus of the descriptions now moves in close to the material world. 'The forest was suffocation, annihilation; there European man was quickly swallowed up in silence, distance, mould, black mud, and the stinging swarms of insect life that bred in it' (*SOR* 11). This is a place where the colonist is smothered or stung, where the tactile becomes oppressive. Intriguingly, Cather's focus then moves out, imagining escape along the river, a place where one 'could travel, taste the sun and open air, feel freedom, join their fellows' (*SOR* 11). 'Taste' and 'feel': a sensory enjoyment which is a midpoint between the visualised distantiation first experienced by Auclair and the too-close tactility of immersion within the suffocating trees of an unexplored continent.

Tacking between sensory extremes is a continual problem for the Cather protagonist. In many ways, the existential question posed for her protagonists is a sensory one: how to reconcile, or at least move gracefully between, the dominance of certain senses? For Auclair, the coloniser's will to visual power comes up against the dangerous tactility of the American landscape – a foundational problem for a Western American who had grown up amongst the highly visualised settlement of the West (through maps, through homesteading, through the literal imposition of an ownership grid on supposedly 'Wild Land'). After the initial overture to the novel, tracing this central dialectic, *Shadows on the Rock* embeds this dynamic between visual mastery and tactile physicality on to the humans that Cather then introduces into her narrative.

The human body in Cather's fiction often takes shape as a matrix that is at the convergence of sight and touch. Bodies are framed in Cather, gazed upon; they are at the centre of performance, seen on stages or in mirrors, or strikingly outlined against vast horizons or within the distinctive *mise-en-scènes* of the modern city. But they are also felt – in all their strangeness or otherness. One of the great and common pleasures of a Cather text is her relentless ability to remind us that nothing is as familiar and as strange as a human hand, or the movement of a human body. In *Shadows on the Rock* the body is both immediate and familiar, but also on the edge of the known: getting to know people might, the pioneer novelist suggests, be a form of sensory pioneering. For this reason, outsider figures always play a key liminal role in her work – not simply because they are socially on the edge of the known, but more intriguingly, because such liminality might place them between sensory orders, fascinating in their sensory interstitiality. Poor women (the hired girls of *My Ántonia*), the seemingly mad (Crazy Ivar in *O Pioneers!*), disaffected and nearly alienated professionals (St Peter in *The Professor's House*), the elderly (Old Mrs Harris), singers and performers (Eden Bower, Kitty Ayrshire, Thea Kronborg), and the disabled or ill will all, in Cather's sensory imaginings, fascinate because they ask questions of how one relates to our fellow beings in the realm of the senses.

The Auclair family live and move in a world of objects (at times the novel reads like a catalogue, an inventory of things). In regard to migrants, their exile takes on a physical embodiment in the form of the objects they have brought from France – things that create what Madame Auclair thinks of as 'this order'. Cécile, their daughter, is further displaced and uprooted by her mother's death, a passing which leaves her and her father yet more sensitive to the meanings the object world might possess. Characteristically, it is the feel and touch of household items that the narrative focuses on: 'Madame had brought out to Canada the fine store of linen that had been her marriage portion, her feather beds and coverlids and down pillows' (*SOR* 30). It is the linen that preoccupies Madame Auclair – the feel of the bedclothes that her husband, soon to be widowed, is sensitive to: 'And he cannot sleep between woollen coverlids, as many people do here; his skin is sensitive. The sheets must be changed every two weeks, but do not try to have them washed in the winter' (*SOR* 31).

In her sentences exploring Sartre's essay on stickiness, Mary Douglas points to the complex interplay between our sense of the aesthetic and our apprehension of the physical world: 'Aesthetic pleasure arises from the perceiving of inarticulate forms' and 'An infant, plunging its hands into a jar of honey, is instantly involved in contemplating the formal properties of solids and liquids and the essential relation between the subjective experiencing self and the experienced world.'[14] At this moment, Cather's writing reflects some of the primary sensory intensity that Douglas points to, a tactility that leads to a keener awareness of the subjective self and the experienced world.

These passages are also focused on the sick and ailing body – and reveal, too, the other side of Cather's sense of the senses: the Eurocentric cast of her representations, the hierarchical placing of European and white forms of sense above those of various Others. In *Shadows on the Rock*, the opening pages typically affiliate tactility with healing and care. As often with Cather, the senses refract through images of tending for disabled, injured or ill bodies. Auclair and his daughter visit Mother Juschereau de Sainte-Ignace, a Reverend Mother who has sprained her ankle. Both Auclair and Juschereau are characterised in terms of finesse and delicacy. Auclair 'began gently to unwind the bandage from her foot' (*SOR* 44); Mother Juschereau's fingers 'were moving rapidly and cleverly, making artificial flowers' (*SOR* 44). Delicacy, precision and care: these are the hallmarks of Cather's tactile Europeans. But Auclair's response to his patient's praise of Indian treatment of injuries ('they bind their leg tightly with deer thongs and keep on the march with their party. And they recover', *SOR* 44) typifies an opposition in Cather's work between such tactile care and a bafflement at the sensory imaginary in which other cultures might operate: 'Dear Mother Juschereau, the idea of such treatment is repugnant to me. We are not barbarians, after all' (*SOR* 44). Importantly, though, Mother Juschereau voices, antiphonally, a question that reads Indian medicine in a more positive fashion: 'But they are flesh and blood; how is it they recover?' (*SOR* 44).

I think Cather's writing became steadily more sensitised to some of these representational cruces where white sensory cultures encounter other worlds. In *Death Comes for the Archbishop*, both

Auclair and Bishop Jean Marie Latour encounter, through the thoughts of interlocutors or through their own reflections, contrary readings of the primitive sensory other. Furthermore, there is the question of whether the care exhibited by the white settlers is itself as care-ful and nurturing as it might at first seem. In *Shadows on the Rock*, a line is drawn between the French settlers and the indigenes in terms of this nursing ideal. But in Cather's last novel, *Sapphira and the Slave Girl*, the reader peers into a world of damaged bodies, both black and white, where the social circuits of care, nurture and nursing seem to be fractured by suspicion and disconnection. The later novel 'answers' a question posed by the earlier novel: is the white settlers' vaunted caring for one another really what it seems?

Sapphira and the Slave Girl: The Habitus of Violence

The sense of an organically developed habitus of violence runs through Cather's last novel; touch is central to the novel's creation of a carefully patterned tapestry or mural made up of violent encounters. In *Sapphira and the Slave Girl*, touch is often the fist or weapon against flesh, or the touch of chains. *The Professor's House* contrasts St Peter's aestheticised sense of touch (writing his books, cooking, and then being saved by a seamstress) against the strangely dissociated tactile world of his home. *Shadows on the Rock* maps tactile environments both resistant and reassuring: the French settlers' domestic world with all its comforting and very touchable materialism in contrast to the strange physicality of the Canadian landscape. And then *Sapphira and the Slave Girl* develops this supple sensory idiom into an even more complex discourse, a way to map and read a habitus through the charting of how imagined characters might touch and feel their way through a created world. This last novel has, if anything, a starker geometric formation than those earlier books, here creating a network of tactile binaries: the healer's hand versus the slave-trader's whip, the knitter's craft and the master's brutal hand, cooking and fighting, sexual assault and nursing.

Cather made one major creative decision in fashioning this novel: she chose to write not about the plantations of the Deep South but about the domestic world of the Upper South. In this place, slavery underpins traditional domestic life rather than the new, quasi-industrial agrarianism of the cotton plantation, which means that Cather can show slaves' lives, especially those of female slaves, as they are lived in absolutely close proximity to whites. The habitus is bi-racial, domestic, largely feminised; it is the domestic world of American slavery, the world of gardeners, cooks and 'body servants' (a phrase Cather uses with exquisite irony). In this world, white and black bodies are continually bound together through sex and violence, even as the 'peculiar institution' of slavery putatively demarcates a colour line. And it is through touch – especially violent touch – that Cather asks us to understand what this actually means, minute by minute, and day by day.

If a cultural anthropologist was asked to construct an imaginary narrative based on what she knew about ante-bellum everyday life, the result might well look like *Sapphira and the Slave Girl*. The narrative often focuses on the ordinary, the everyday and the apparently trivial. What links these glimpsed scenarios and these flecks of detail are narrative chains – typically sensory – that then become a way to understand the deep structures of this world. Touch is one such sensory chain (Chapter 8 explores how this novel uses smell). This sensory chain is one of Cather's major narrative innovations: the linking of threads of a storyline by repeating and inflecting instances of sensory detail, focusing on one sense or another. Thus, in *Sapphira and Slave Girl*, the brutal dynamics of a slave-owning society are shown in two main ways: how characters touch or feel one another and how structures of smell shape social encounters as characters tend gardens, grow flowers, or react against the perceived reek and stench of Others' bodies. In this last novel, Cather redeploys her highly sensory writing to devastating effect as a way to represent, understand and critique her own original society.

Touching in the novel often means hitting, striking or beating another – or the physical and predatory intimacy of a sexual assault (the novel's central scene). At the start of the novel, Sapphira strikes the young slave girl, Nancy, with her hairbrush: 'the red marks of the hairbrush were still on the girl's right arm' (*SSG* 22). With this small detail, and some of the early descriptive–analytical comments at the start of the novel, Cather establishes violent touch as the dominant sensory motif of this society. White society has grown simply to accept the quotidian flare-up of violence, Cather suggests, in a reference to the 'rough mountain boys' and their acceptance of 'the lickings they got at school' (*SSG* 22). Violence has become banal. Throughout the novel one encounters the daily, relentless violent tactility of a slave-owning society, caught by Cather in a chain of grotesque details.

One chapter of the novel is particularly significant for its mapping and recharting of the historical record. 'Old Jezebel' tells us what we would now call the 'back story' of one of the Colbert negroes. As often in a Cather novel, a character from a historical epoch is introduced in a deliberately flattened, understatedly informative manner. The writing here, as Cather takes on the formidably difficult and contentious topic of writing about the Middle Passage (and writing from a white perspective), is stripped down and spare, but telling in its laconic portrayal of routine inhumanity and relentless terror. Jezebel 'saw her father brained and her four brothers cut down as they fought' (*SSG* 92). She is flogged on the slavers' ship, then retaliates – she 'bit through the ball of his thumb' when the mate attempts to throttle her (*SSG* 95). 'Her naked back was seamed with welts and bloody cuts' (*SSG* 95). Later, Henry reflects that he had 'a legal right to manumit any of his wife's negroes' (*SSG* 110), the Latin root of the verb (literally, 'to let go from the hand') only serving to underwrite the novel's fascination with touch and the doings of the hand.

These doings are often violent and pervasive. Cather's white characters wreak violence on the African–Americans; but Cather also shows that their own world is now thoroughly contaminated by arbitrary aggression. We see the Keyser brothers administer a punishment beating to the teenage boy, Casper (*SSG* 129–30). We see Martin Colbert's strange, blue false tooth – the latter a replacement for a tooth he lost in a fight which began with Martin taunting his assailants: 'Come at me with your fists, an' I'll do the best I can, one against two' (*SSG* 162). Martin himself, as his Aunt Sapphira notes, has no calluses on those hands: 'Oh, we have plenty of field-hands – too many!' (*SSG*, 152). Hands and touching are part of a social habitus where fist-fighting is common but slave-owners have little manual labour to perform.

Cather creates a web of connection between different forms of touch in this novel, linking the tactile violence of slavery to healing forms of touch such as nursing and gardening, and asking us to think about how a society can become so de-formed and mal-formed at the most fundamental levels of sensory encounter. The implications of these conjunctions are left in the novel as tableaux and vignettes, with connections waiting to be made between the sensory elements. Cather's late fiction (*Shadows on the Rock, Lucy Gayheart* and *Sapphira and the Slave Girl*) turns the sketchbook sensory potential of the early reviewing and early fiction into the basis of modernist narratives. Each of these three novels focuses unerringly on a major theme in American culture (colony, performance and race), constructing a fictional exploration through detailed attention to the bodily habitus. The result: the banal sophistication of Cather's late trilogy, fictions devoted to the sensory arts of the everyday (cooking or gardening, or simply chatting) that work in an quasi-anthropological way. Look closely, Cather seems to be saying, look very closely at these vignettes, and you will see the deep formations of a culture – even if at times you would rather not be looking.

Conclusion: Tactile Cather

Cather's imaginative journey through modes of tactility – erotic touch, healing touch, and then the violent contact of punishment or abuse – vividly reveal how she understands the narrative potential of a single sense. Plenitude, narrative plenitude, might emerge from the simplest of sensory lexicons. What is particularly fascinating is how she then uses this sensory writing as a means to create historical fictions: the worlds of the Cliff Dwellers, or French colonists, or the slave-owners' South now understood in terms of how their people touched or felt or nursed or hit one another. 'Sense writing' might sound like an inconsequential proposition; but Cather then built complex narrative structures out of episodes focused on this single sense of touch. As we shall see in the next chapter, the experience of *taste* offered another basis on which to grow narrative complexity, and to reach into American pasts, by creating patterns of sensory observation.

Notes

1. Classen, *The Book of Touch*, 305.
2. Thomas, 'Magical Healing: The King's Touch', 354.
3. Stokes, 'Peacocks and Pearls: Oscar Wilde and Sarah Bernhardt', 105.
4. Ibid.
5. Cather, 'The Tale of the White Pyramid', 8.
6. In its attention to domestic space, space-making, craft skills and homely furnishings, the novel is also the most 'Arts and Crafts' work in the Cather *œuvre*. As Constance Classen points out, 'The Arts and Crafts movement emphasized tactile craft skills over depersonalized mass production,' Donald A. Yerxa, 'The Deepest Sense: An Interview with Constance Classen', 27–8: 28.
7. Aronoff, *Composing Cultures*, 74.
8. Though Cather had also used a Southwest setting for an early story, 'The Enchanted Bluff' (1909), a narrative in which a group of young boys talk about a rock in New Mexico, a bluff that had been the home of an isolated Indian village.
9. Kot, 'Speculation, Tourism, and *The Professor's House*', 421.
10. Cather, 'Nursing as a Profession', 4.
11. Ibid.
12. Ibid. 5.
13. Baker, *Ernest Hemingway: Selected Letters 1917–1961*, 105.
14. Douglas, *Purity and Danger: An Analysis of Concepts of Pollution and Taboo*, 47.

CHAPTER 7

Cather, Taste and National Cuisines: *The Professor's House, Death Comes for the Archbishop* and *Shadows on the Rock*

'Is cooking important?' asked Cather in a 1925 interview before providing the answer herself: 'Few things in life are more so! My mind and stomach are one! I think and work with whatever it is that digests.'[1] In this chapter, Cather's fascination with food, taste and national cuisines is tracked reading *Death Comes for the Archbishop* and *Shadows on the Rock* as fictions invested in culinary fieldwork: representations of how food might be placed at the centre of narratives of migration and settlement.

Taste, as fleeting as it might seem (a mouthful of food, a sip of a drink), is the foundation of a powerfully permanent aspect of culture: cuisine. Food is, in many ways, the last part of a culture to change. Only slowly do national food cultures evolve – even as a colonising power or an invader might have changed law, or a state religion, or central aspects of a country's organisation like its educational system. A society's food culture might seem to have a certain nationalist permanence: 'our food'. Even in the current transnational, mutable and postmodern world, one is far more likely to find what might seem (now) a quite old-fashioned deployment of terms such as 'national' when it comes to describing cuisine.

However, change does occur, and food traditions fuse and meld. In *Curry: A Tale of Cooks and Conquerors*, Lizzie Collingham shows how invasion and fusion are the basis of a dish that might at first seem 'authentically' or 'essentially' Indian. Portuguese explorers, the Mughals and British colonists brought different ingredients and techniques to the traditions of Indian cooking (and she sees tea as the most important British contribution to the mix). Collingham's story is one of cultural encounters driving cross-fertilisation and culinary evolution:

> This latest injection of foreign influences continues the process of fusion through the introduction of new culinary techniques and new ingredients that has, over many centuries, given Indian food its vibrancy, and made it one of the world's finest cuisines.[2]

Cather wrote more extensively about food than perhaps any other major American writer; she also wrote about the processes of encounter, contestation and fusion that Collingham explores – she was fascinated, to use Andrew Jewell's term, by 'gastronomical meaning'.[3] In her letters, her journalism and her fiction, Cather returns again and again to the table, to what is brought to the table, and to the socio-cultural codes built around food. In a 1919 essay on America's wartime economising ('Hooverizing'), and then in *The Professor's House*, *Death Comes for the Archbishop* and *Shadows on the Rock*, Cather places food cultures at the centre of fictions inflected by forms of cultural anthropology. In the first, a group of men fashion their own communal world as they make camp in a Southwestern landscape still shaped by the markings of indigenous (and feminised) kitchens. In the second, Cather shows how Europe's missionaries attempt to preserve their food traditions, even as the Southwestern landscape and its people challenge the very basis of what they think of as cuisine. And in *Shadows on the Rock* a different group of white settlers – French colonists in Quebec – find solace in inherited foodways as the colony's political and religious commitments suggest that power (and predation) are very much part of a society's culinary culture.

These texts form the basis for this chapter's exploration of Cather and taste. Such an exploration runs counter to one important critique of Cather – namely, that her interest in cooking and cuisine was trivial. It was Lionel Trilling, writing in the *New Republic* in 1937, who condemned her for having a 'mystical concern with pots and pans' before linking such interests to the 'gaudy domesticity of bourgeois accumulation' championed by the *Woman's Home Companion*.[4] For Trilling, 'pots and pans' and 'domesticity' were central to his analysis of Cather's failure. But to read Cather closely – within a framework suggested by recent work on food, culture and society – is to see that Cather used domestic narrative (and pots and pans) as a way to open up powerful reimaginings of the diverse foodscapes of the Americas. Such studies as Jennifer Jensen Wallach's *How America Eats*, Sidney Mintz's *Sweetness and Power* and Carole Counihan's *Food in the USA* establish the foundation for innovative work focused on the complexities of American food cultures, the significance of immigration in the history of cuisine, and the role of race in food production and consumption. Now, Cather's work appears within a rich intellectual framework that bears witness to the range and depth of her writing about culinary cultures.

Food and War: 'Roll Call on the Prairies'

Even before Cather worked on the major novels that show the depth and range of her thinking about taste, food and the cultural politics of food, she had written about these topics in intriguing ways.

Cather's 1919 essay, 'Roll Call on the Prairies', written for *The Red Cross Magazine* about food production during World War One, addresses the practical impact of the US Food Administration and its impact on the daily lives of Americans following the nation's entry into the conflict in 1917. Under the leadership of Herbert Hoover, this organisation worked in a quasi-philanthropic way, urging Americans to preserve food so that vital supplies could be shipped to American troops and allies in Europe. This policy quickly gave rise to its own verb – 'to Hooverize' – and Cather charted its impacts in an essay which sheds important light on her understanding of food's cultural and political significance.

Travelling west, Cather saw the impact of national policies on small-town life and on the domestic world. 'The women were "in the war" even more than the men,' she wrote. 'Not only in their thoughts, because they had sons and brothers in France, but in almost every detail of their daily lives.'[5] Although Cather had, by this time, lived in New York for over a dozen years, she still turned back to the West in order to find examples of cultural adaptation and innovation that fascinated her. Her interest in local cultures and her antipathy to standardised production meant that the sheer convenience presented by a Manhattan bakery was less interesting than the very vivid demonstration of creativity presented to her in the Western states. Thus, these everyday sensory shifts – tasting a new bread as ingredients became unavailable and new 'breadstuffs' were used – were signs of a creativity that could be literally tasted on the tongue.

Cather's extended comments about cooking depict an America that takes on an improvisatory relationship to food: in place of mass-produced food, innovation; instead of continental food chains, the importance of the local. 'In the first place, diet and cookery, the foundation of life, were revolutionized (city people could never realize what this means in the country and in little towns),' Cather writes. 'All the neighbor women began to tell me how to make bread without white flour, cakes without eggs, cakes out of oatmeal, how to sweeten ice cream and puddings with honey or molasses.'[6] This provincial innovation contrasts with the city's convenience:

> All winter long they had experimented with breadstuffs. In New York we merely took a new kind of bread from the baker — hoping it wouldn't be worse than the last — and grumbled at the grocer because he wouldn't give us more sugar.

Thus: 'But in the little towns, Hooverizing was creative and a test of character as well.'[7]

Wartime cooking in the American provinces becomes a form of collective innovation and 'a test of character'. Here, food is localised and highly gendered in terms of production and culture, formed out of a complex interaction between traditional dishes (we are still in a world of bread, cakes and ice cream) and new ways of making do. *The Professor's House*, *Death Comes for the Archbishop* and *Shadows on the Rock* took this basic template (food and the local, food and gender, food as improvised reconfiguration of tradition) as the basis for many of Cather's most memorable scenarios.

Cookouts: Men and Cuisine in *The Professor's House*

The culinary world of *The Professor's House* represents one of Cather's obliquely powerful interventions into American cultural history. Here, in 'Tom Outland's Story' (the inset narrative at the heart of the novel), Cather journeys to the Southwest's mesas, and in a story about young men exploring America's ancient Pueblo cultures, shows us how Trilling's 'mystic concern with pots and pans' was, in fact, a way to reflect on gender, culture and power.

Katharina Vester notes, in *A Taste of Power: Food and American Identities*, that at the end of the nineteenth century, American culinary culture was a place of gendered arguments about food and its preparation. She explores Progressive Era 'Narratives of "manly cooking"'. Faced with 'the erosion of social differences between the sexes and the decline of male privilege', writers stressed the adventuresome, the exotic and the celebratory within male cooking – a manly art.[8] Theodore Roosevelt and Ernest Hemingway (both figures who were part of Cather's literary and cultural milieu) especially concern Vester. She argues that their veneration of campfire cooking and wilderness cuisine was part of a larger *gendered* cultural struggle. The 'tradition' of campfire cooking was at heart an invention; in nineteenth-century cookbooks, 'Campfire cooking was not an experience to strengthen the spirit, but an onerous chore best left to others.'[9] Thus, Theodore Roosevelt's *Hunting Trips of a Ranchman* (1885) was one place where this outdoors identity emerged, establishing male identity in terms of a highly individualised and violent new Western self.

Vester also focuses on Hemingway, who published an article, 'Camping Out', in the *Toronto Star* in 1920. In the Nick Adams stories that began his fiction career, he performed powerful cultural work by resetting configurations of cooking, the natural world and the masculine self along lines initially set out by Roosevelt. 'Big Two-Hearted River', the central story in *In Our Time* (1925), focuses on Nick Adams as a post-World War One figure seeking to establish control over self and environment through cooking. 'Nick "salvages"', in Vester's words, 'cooking from its connotation with feminine expertise by making it dirty and dangerous and by taking it out of the kitchen: men's cooking is connected to smoking fire and sputtering fat and slowly rolling lava.'[10] With his primitivist cooking and defiant self-reliance, Roosevelt's late Victorian outdoors male achieves a further cultural centrality through Hemingway's writing, becoming an embodied response to both the Great War and the waves of cultural change that destabilised traditional gender oppositions from the decadent 1890s (and the New Woman) to the 1920s (and the Flappers). Note in the story how utterly isolated Nick is, how the landscape he moves through is burned and devastated, and how his cooking is absolutely primitive. Nick finds a masculine plenitude in wilderness cooking, as Vester suggests, but the very extremity of his position (a Melvillean *isolato* foraging in the Midwestern woods) points to the sheer fragility (even madness?) of this cultural project. A reader might concur that D. H. Lawrence's famous identification of the American literary hero as stoic and isolated (the basic premise of *Studies in Classic American Literature*, published in the United States in 1923) was justified.

That is, until we look again at how Cather conceives taste cultures at this time. As a prominent female journalist, a writer for magazines such as *Home Monthly*, Cather spent much of her early professional career in the milieu that shaped – effectively acted as a gatekeeper for – America's food cultures (a process visible in the advertisements for culinary ware and recipes that filled these magazines alongside writing created and edited by Cather). Cather's 1920s and early 1930s writing seems particularly attuned to food cultures: vignettes or tableaux featuring the preparation and consumption of food pepper the fictions from this time. Often, there is also a deeply *gendered* dimension to these narratives: frequently and provocatively Cather writes about the man in the kitchen, or the man by the campfire (taking the Rooseveltian or Hemingwayesque figure), then displacing or modifying some of the cultural vectors they fashioned. *The Professor's House* exemplifies three significant areas where Cather remodelled the emergent standard of a masculinised food culture that had become, in the works of Roosevelt especially, part of a project for national revitalisation: geographical displacement, communal work, and families and food.

Geographical Displacement

Cather's world of cooking is more a case of *worlds* of cooking. At times, she might appear to have a conception of domestic cultures more in line with the contemporary, highly comparative models we are now familiar with (as in Collingham's *Curry*). If Roosevelt and Hemingway work within an American foodspace that is thoroughly nationalistic and often focus quite deliberately on what would become known as the Heartland (Nick Adams moves through the Michigan woods; Roosevelt was a ranch hand in the Dakotas), then Cather creates a much more pan-American, hemispheric series of representations, turning her and the readers' attention to the Hispanic and French traditions, as seen in the Southwest and French Canada.

This 'food trilogy', as we might know it, places different configurations of male protagonists in three contrasting American foodspaces. First, in 'Tom Outland's Story', the inset narrative that forms the centrepiece of *The Professor's House*, Cather imagines the Pueblo kitchens of the Cliff Dweller communities that had once dotted the mesa lands of the Southwest. In the later 1920s, *Death Comes for the Archbishop* signals a further opening-up of this approach as Cather places her French priests (Latour and Vaillant) in Southwestern/Mexican landscapes where the high European table, with its roasted meats and fine wines, seems a distant memory. In episodes such as that detailing the slaying of the cleric Friar Baltazar, Cather creates parables of culinary encounter – Baltazar's ferocious monitoring of table manners triggers a brutal meeting of a missionary priest and an indigene servant. In *Shadows on the Rock*, Cather then shifts her attention to French Canada, to the domestic world of Quebec, and to the hunting, preserving and preparation of foods – French in origin but now, increasingly, fashioned from local ingredients. This food triptych takes us (quite literally) from one end of North America to the other and suggests a great and eclectic diversity of ingredients and preparation.

Communal Work

Eating and cooking together, food gathering, preparation: Cather writes about kitchens, shared culinary spaces and communal work. The notion of a Cather character eating alone seems bizarre (St Peter is one of the few characters to do this, a clear index of his self-imposed masculine marginality in the home).

In 1916, Cather published an essay about her explorations of Mesa Verde – one of the Southwestern places that triggered her fascination with the region. Published in *The Denver Times*, it is a quixotic travel essay that establishes the context for her work's interest in the domestic arts of 'The Ancient People' (Part IV of *The Song of the Lark*). Travelling to the Mesa, Cather finds an environmental–cultural enclave that is highly sensory, ritualistic and structured around food. The landscape is a feast for the eye and the nose – she tells how she could always smell the 'sweet clover' when staying there. At the centre of this culture are ancient versions of that 'mystic concern with pots and pans' decried by Lionel Trilling. The original white explorer of Mesa Verde, Richard Wetherill, found 'their pottery, linen cloth, feather cloth, sandals, stone and bone tools, dried pumpkins, corn and onions'.[11] In this well-ordered primitive utopia (the sense of space and arrangement in the Cliff Dweller site is a 'reproach to the messiness in which we live'), food is paramount: 'Their lives were so full of ritual and symbolism that all their common actions were ceremonial – planting, harvesting, hunting, feasting, fasting.'[12] That is, their 'common actions' were essentially culinary; the world of Cather's 'vanishing American' structured around rituals of taste.[13]

Cather's cultural example of remodelling here is one of what might be called 'radical conservationism': of a community woven deeply into its environmental setting and then harmonised around ritual. Cuisine is central; food is what makes for community in Cather's reading of the pre-colonial Americas. This observation becomes amplified and deepened in the fiction, and Cather extends her reading of how the Cliff Dwellers had built community around food into her representations of contemporary American domestic culture. Thus, even in the wilderness narrative that is 'Tom Outland's Story', an impromptu, rather homo-social family evolves to share kitchen duties. Outland meets Henry Atkins, a genial old Englishman who accompanies him (and Roddy Blake) during their mesa adventure. Blake, a former hospital orderly, maintains domestic duties and cooks for the other two, but he is also a frail figure, frightened of storms and too damaged to herd cattle. Cather's male community is interdependent, made up of the lost and the damaged. Cooking, in this community, is less a Hemingway-esque ritual of wilderness survival than shared consolation: Cather replaces the campfire ranchman with the communal cook. Atkins was 'a wonderful cook and a good housekeeper' (*TPH* 195). Food on the mesa is communal and domestic – not only for this quirky ad hoc male family, but also in regard to the Indians who once lived there.

Outland discovers the remnants of a kitchen. There are jars, grinding-stones, ovens, the remnants of meals, a roof made sooty by cooking:

> It was evidently a kind of common kitchen, where they roasted and baked and probably gossiped. There were corncobs everywhere, and ears of corn with the kernels still on them – little, like popcorn. We found dried beans, too, and strings of pumpkin seeds, and plum seeds, and a cupboard full of little implements made of turkey bones. (*TPH* 208)

Families and Food

The Professor's House juxtaposes the mesa's intense communality and sensory richness against the corporeal derangements of St Peter's life: he is a connoisseur and a gourmet who eats alone. The novel's sense of psychological breakdown is literally *embodied*, shown in apparently trivial (and odd) verbal exchanges which illuminate just how far St Peter is from the sensory plenitude he discovered on the mesa. Book Three of the novel even includes St Peter's visit to the Doctor, and a discussion of his eating habits. St Peter tells Dr Dudley that he eats '"In every sense of the word, well. I am my own *chef*"' (*TPH* 268). The doctor tells him he is a gourmet, and confesses that he would like a dinner invitation to the Professor's house (the reader will probably think this is an unlikely prospect). Such moments mark Cather's wry and understated interventions into cultural politics: for Hemingway and Roosevelt, dining alone might incarnate steadfast male self-sufficiency, but in Cather's novel, the practice simply seems rather odd. Cather creates a careful culinary matrix here, positioning the implicitly melancholic vision of St Peter alone against the bustle of the mesa kitchens, with their gossip and sharing.

The Death of Baltazar:
Food in *Death Comes for the Archbishop*

Rebecca Earle, in *The Body of the Conquistador* (a study of food and early modern Spanish America), explores food, colonialism and the body. For the Spanish, 'Food helped make them who they were in terms of both their character and their very corporeality, and it was food, more than anything else, that made European bodies different from Amerindian bodies.'[14] Earle's careful charting of the projects (and perils) of Spanish American food culture (how to cultivate food, how to avoid sickness, how to remain 'European', even as one consumed Amerindian foodstuffs) is pertinent to my commentary on Cather and food. Cather's priests privilege and attempt to preserve their own traditional culinary practices. They also move within cultures and environments where such maintained tradition is always in jeopardy – not only because the cultivation of food might be complex and difficult, but also because the *culture* of food no longer has a shared basis. Earle shows how Spanish colonists created elaborate practices to maintain a national identity embodied in food and its consumption. Cather's priests, Latour and Vaillant, face a more precarious pathway.

One reason for this is that they are French, not Spanish. Cather's choice of material and protagonists – French priests moving within a Hispanic terrain – already disrupts the patterns of Spanish American foodways. Cather's French priests have to learn Spanish and the ways of the natives, but they also remain loyal to their own cuisine, even if producing a French meal is difficult in this land of beans. In a sense, Cather 'de-naturalises' the association between Spanish America and Spanish food. One sees how food cultures might be read in terms of relativism and hybridity, how 'Europe' might actually mean making distinctions between French and Spanish cuisines. Power and prestige are also part of the ways that Cather constructs food as a social and cultural practice.

In a testy 1938 letter to her publisher, Alfred A. Knopf, Cather expressed her disappointment with Marguerite Yourcenar's French translation of *Death Comes for the Archbishop*. She felt that Yourcenar had no feel for the landscapes of the Southwest, no cultural understanding.

> She has not informed herself about its people or customs . . . In so far as that country and people are concerned, her mind is an utter blank . . . You will notice she speaks of these passages as descriptions of 'American landscapes'; as you know, it is Mexican landscape, not 'American'. (*SL* 546–7)

Yourcenar, in Cather's reading, had 'Americanised' a landscape and culture that she herself felt to be radically different.

The novel deployed a panelled, tapestry-like narrative shaped around vignettes focused on sensory difference – particularly an alterity grounded in the sense of taste. So we come to the tale of Fray Baltazar, which bears comparison with the Aztec narrative in 'Coming, Aphrodite!' – both have a certain orientalist violence, a lurid primitivist melodrama. In this story, set at the start of the early eighteenth century, an early priest, Baltazar, lives a missionary existence amongst his indigenous flock in a remote part of Spanish America. Baltazar is a gourmet, a chef, a connoisseur of taste. His power is embedded in exploiting the natives for the food they produce. 'He took the best of their corn and beans and squashes for his table, and selected the choicest portions when they slaughtered a sheep, chose their best hides to carpet his dwelling' (*DCA* 110). He has a fine garden, watered by local women, 'despite the fact that it was not proper that a woman should ever enter the cloister at all' (*DCA* 110). His journeys are also culinary, trips to find peach seeds or grape cuttings. 'The early churchmen did a great business in carrying seeds about, though the Indians and Mexicans were satisfied with beans and squashes and chili, asking nothing more' (*DCA* 111).

In the novel's cautionary tale of consumption, Baltazar's care for his flock has been undermined by a relentless gustatory excess, a sensuality of the table and garden. In this novel, a character's fate might literally depend on what he eats and how. Baltazar Montoya is a priest, an epicure, and a thoroughly Western figure in his table manners and rituals. It is this epicurean vanity that finally undoes him. He plans a dinner party to show off his garden and kitchen.

> In that great kitchen, with its multiplicity of spits, small enough to roast a lark and large enough to roast a boar, the Friar had learned a thing or two about sauces, and in his lonely years at Ácoma he had bettered his instruction by a natural aptitude for the art. (*DCA* 115)

When a servant, an Indian, spills sauce over one of his guests, Friar Baltazar furiously throws his pewter mug at the young man, killing him; the community ceremonially takes its revenge by leading the quiescent Montoya to a cliff, from where he is hurled off to his fate. The final vengeance is thoroughly embodied in the physical landscape that Baltazar created. The women abandon the garden, and 'took pleasure in watching the garden pine and waste away from thirst, and ventured into the cloisters to laugh and chatter at the whitening foliage of the peach trees, and the green grapes shrivelling on the vines' (*DCA* 121).

Death Comes for the Archbishop presents indigenous domestic cultures seemingly 'outside' the aestheticised European order of things. Many of Cather's vignettes in the novel focus on priests meeting other tastes, other smells and other sights before trying to assimilate (or not) their sensory Otherness. It is Catholic practice, understood in Cather's distinctively sensual and sensory manner, that functions as a prism, refracting sensory experience through Catholic ceremony and hermeneutics to create a thoroughly embodied representation of cross-cultural encounter. Cather alchemises Catholic experience and history, stripping out details about church institutions, for example, and concentrating instead, with her highly physicalised and minimalist prose, on the two men's corporealised experiences of a new world. Cather sets up the teleological drive of the church mission at the start of the novel (Latour's brief is to re-establish church authority and then extend papal power into the newly annexed United States territories), but then pays little attention to the back story of the exposition of such processes (which she compresses into paragraph-length, 'backgrounding' overviews).

The novel reads as the examination of a bodily problem posed by a distinctive social, cultural or environmental context. Taken as a whole, Cather's career can be thought of using this interpretative question. *My Ántonia* and *O Pioneers!* centre on the European body and the embodiment of European culture (primarily, the performative European culture represented by opera, theatre and religious ceremony), once transplanted to the American Frontier. The early novels pose these questions in terms of straightforward juxtapositions of self and society. But as her writing develops, Cather moves narrative toward more conceptually complex staging of her basic paradigm. Thus, *The Professor's House* presents a man who has spent a life working with highly mediated representations of reality (he is a historian) but now exists in a hyperbolically materialist world of tactility. *Lucy Gayheart* takes the vitality of the performer's body (Lucy is always dancing, skating or running) and asks us to think about whether such embodied vitality resonates after death (all the novel's performers perish but persist in memory). *Sapphira and the Slave Girl* asks us to look at juxtapositions of bodies (black and white, able-bodied and disabled, the punished and the powerful) within the ante-bellum South.

Shadows on the Rock: Food and Form

Cather's formalist aesthetic is distinctive. Her letters, essays and lectures on narrative and novel-writing often focus on questions of formal arrangement or on the architectural decisions that arrange a narrative shape. The making of fiction, in the Catherian commentaries, is typically a highly formalistic process: the insertion of the 'nouvelle', 'Tom Outland's Story', into *The Professor's House*; or the yoking of two discrete narratives ('Alexandra' and 'The White Mulberry Tree') to form *O Pioneers!* Questions of definition are also important to Cather: hence the letter to the *Commonweal* magazine that declared *Death Comes for the Archbishop* to be a 'narrative' and not a novel.

The decisions Cather made regarding this formalistic question related to her body-pictures and her representation of embodied experience. As we have seen in the case of *The Professor's House*, 'Tom Outland's Story' brought the skeletalised form of a Native

American (Mother Eve) into the narrative. The joining of 'The White Mulberry Tree', a melodramatic tale of a violent and all too corporeal tragedy to the feminised pastoral, 'Alexandra', decisively foregrounds and expands the *physicalised* palette of *O Pioneers!* Cather's compositional process repeatedly creates new patterns in narrative: conjunctions and juxtapositions that highlight the bodily themes of these novels. Thinking again of what Cather had learned from Puvis de Chavannes, the overall effect is one of panelling (movement of the reader's eye between two panels). These movements, across juxtaposed or contrasting narrative micro-narratives, bring the body into decisive focus.

Cather created three formalistically experimental novels at the height of her career and then wrote short explanations for their radical shape: *The Professor's House* (*nouvelle* inserted into narrative), *Death Comes for the Archbishop* (a 'narrative', not a novel) and *Shadows on the Rock*, for which she uses the Greek rhetorical term, *anacoluthon*. That term means 'discontinuity' (literally, 'not following'), and therefore also carries the meaning of an inconsistency or incoherence (typically, the word is used to describe sentence structure or syntax). Her use of the term occurs in a letter to the Governor of Connecticut, Wilbur Cross, a former Yale English professor who had written a glowing review of *Shadows*. Cather described the novel in terms of the feeling that Quebec had aroused: 'It is hard to state that feeling in language; it was more like an old song, incomplete but uncorrupted, than like a legend. The text was mainly anacoluthon, so to speak, but the meaning was clear' (*OW* 15).

Here we see Cather at her most idiosyncratic and experimental as she claims to have built a novel around a certain discontinuity. We can then use 'anacoluthon' as a term to guide our reading of the book, allowing it to suggest ways to interpret the narrative. For the effect of a privileging of discontinuity is to place renewed emphasis on the discreet elements (chapters, vignettes, micro-narratives) within the text, while also drawing attention to the process of how that text might be 'made whole'. Lacking evident coherence, we fall back on the episodes within the novel, the very admission of incoherence demanding that we think of how integration might take place, which leads to the creation of a *slow* reader: it is not really possible to read for the plot, to read swiftly, or to be borne along by the full tide of narrative when it comes to *Shadows on the Rock*. The discontinuities and lack of integration – this anacoluthon – break the narrative: literally, we are given pause. We can even put a number on such breaks: *Shadows* is made up of six Books, and the number of short chapters within those Books adds up to thirty-one, followed by an Epilogue. Within those chapters, there are further breaks, as the novel consists of many anecdotes or reported stories, all of which have frames built around them. These sub-headings create a formal structure very different from the architecture of a single narrative comprising thirty or so chapters. The effect is a formal dis-integration, a deliberate breaking of narrative linearity into something that appears more like a collection of short stories, especially because the narrative moves backwards and forwards in time, collating anecdotes, vignettes and sketches that go beyond the focused concentration on the individuals – Cécile and Auclair in their home in Quebec. We become *slow readers* because Cather leaves us to make sense of this assemblage or montage. What are the connections between the subordinate elements within anacoluthonic narrative? Is this simply, as the term implies, incoherence? Meditating on Cather's comment on the book and then slowly working one's way through the novel, the reader recognises Cather's audacity. In a sense, she presents the reader with a riddle – the anacoluthonic riddle of trying to create meaningful patterns within a plethora of narratives.

One pattern focuses on the significance of French domestic culture and its fate in the austere New World of Quebec. And within that depiction of domestic culture, food plays a major role. The world of *Shadows* is profoundly shaped by a sense of enclavedness: being in a tightly defined space (the rocky promontory on which Quebec City is built; the linguistic enclave which is French-language culture within an increasingly Anglophonic continent). Within that enclave, Cather creates questions of adaptation and permanence, continuity and transformation. Food itself is central to Cather's mapping of these concerns. Cather's French settlers continually face two central questions: how to preserve and pass on the food cultures they have inherited; and how to adapt and transform the raw (and often strangely Other) materials of Quebec into something new, something that might remind them of 'home', but is instead a new form of cuisine.

As stated, the reader of late Cather must become a slow reader, one who savours episodes, anecdotes and vignettes. Such a reader is also, by necessity, a cultural anthropologist, an interpreter of the culturescapes that Cather creates. The closing pages of *Shadows on the Rock* share with the concluding pages of *Sapphira and the Slave Girl* a certain 'late Cather' virtuosity that suggests the patterns of cultural power that sit within and below quotidian life. 'The Dying Count' thus becomes an assemblage of fascinating shards (anecdotes, glimpses of quotidian life, domestic tableaux) that build toward a complex representation of power in the colony.

In this world of apparent abundance – also a world shaped by exploitation and violence – the Auclair household has a powerful and understated modesty. This communality provides the basis for Cather's extensive depiction of family life in *Shadows on the Rock*. The widowed apothecary, Euclide Auclair, and his daughter, Cécile, construct a domestic world after the death of their wife and mother that is largely built around food rituals: awaiting shipments from France; getting supplies from local hunters; preserving foods; preparing and sharing meals. In this narrative, family life seems to be nothing other than cooking and eating. Medicine would be the other main activity, but since Auclair is an apothecary, his skills often take the form of the preparation of cures in ways that might seem quasi-culinary.

Shadows on the Rock places Cécile in the fascinating position of someone learning about food cultures. Not only do we see her preparing and enjoying food (or being repelled by it, as when she hears about Pierre Charron's wilderness diet), but also we watch her become a quasi-ethnographic interpreter of culinary meanings. The famous crystal bowl of glass fruits – a decorative object that Count Frontenac has brought with him to New France – is the first example of such processes. The Count interprets the glass fruit for Cécile, telling her how they were a present from a Turkish prisoner he was holding on the isle of Crete. The glass was 'made by the Saracens . . . . Here in Canada it reminds one of the South' (*SOR* 71). The glass fruit travels between and across cultures (it is also, as a gift stemming from conflict, a stark reminder of how power inflects even the domestic world). The genius of this symbol is that the glass fruit will not decay or rot – these objects are permanent reminders of how food works semiotically (the dried mushrooms in *My Ántonia* fulfil a similar purpose, carrying with them cultural meanings from their origin in Bohemia). As Terence Martin has noted, this is a 'novel of preservation'.[15]

Later, Cécile and her father reach different conclusions about ground human bones. Cécile has heard a story about how an English sailor converted to Catholicism after being fed a 'tiny morsel of bone from Father Brébeuf's skull' mixed into gruel (*SOR* 146). Auclair takes a materialist line on this story: 'I consider human bones a very poor medicine for any purpose' (*SOR* 147). Cécile remains fascinated by the miraculous conversion of the sailor; her father remains a proto-Enlightenment figure. The episode is significant for its sense of competing visions of the body, and its mapping of taste as primarily a material and not a quasi-transcendental process. Again, Cather works with that opposition outlined in my first chapter between Mary Baker Eddy's transcendental negation of the body and Randolph Bourne's trenchant reinstatiation of corporealism. In Joshua Dolezal's words, Auclair is a figure who 'believes in standards of competency and holds himself to those standards while maintaining a refined aesthetic sensibility'.[16] He is a highly empirical practitioner, suspicious of the wilder beliefs of folk healing (hence, too, his rejection of medicines made from lizards or serpents).

The white settlers live in a paradoxical food world. Their inherited cultures might be deeply infused with a valorisation of the national cuisine – this is certainly the case with the French settlers Cather focused on in *Death Comes for the Archbishop* and *Shadows on the Rock* – but the new worlds they have colonised offer meagre resources when it comes to creating, say, a delicious dish of lamb *saignant*. Hence the anxiety, the cultural angst and then the delighted pleasure with which Latour and Auclair approach the kitchen and the plate. Becoming a settler requires a loss of one's identity that comes from inheriting, knowing intimately and then venerating one's 'own' cuisine. On the other hand, what might be more of an 'estrangement' than putting alien food into one's mouth? Cather takes this fundamental moment of cultural estrangement (who has not worried about eating the food in a foreign country?) and deploys it as the axis of plot.

Jeanne Le Ber and Pierre Charron: A Bodily Diptych

One major episode in *Shadows*, the story of Jeanne Le Ber, is a parable about the body, its needs and appetites, the abjuring of corporealism, and then the re-emergence (or reinstantiation) of the body through language. Jeanne Le Ber is a hermit, a religious zealot who, at a very young age, decides to retreat from the world. We already see, in the imagined world that Cather develops in *Shadows on the Rock*, Quebec's intense sensoriness; it might be on the edge of the known, Western world, but it is connected to that world through a network of sensory connections. How food and material culture connect colony to the metropole, and how domestic culture links the settlers to their homeland: these are Cather's subjects. However, Jeanne Le Ber gives this up, becoming quite literally immured, a mystical idealist whose route to spiritual growth lies in the narrowing and shrinking of the physical world. While Auclair and Cécile move through a colonial settlement that, while small, still contains strong physical contrasts, Le Ber lives in a confined, uniform space. Everything about her world suggests austerity and monotonic sameness. Auclair and Cécile prepare and savour a range of foods, but Le Ber lives spartanly on frugal fare. Sensorily, she works toward her self-erasure: barely seen, not heard, far from the French culinary world or the touch of human beings. Tellingly, and as if to point up the sensory significance of the tale, when her story is told it reverses its import, becoming a fable of sensory plenitude. Her story 'brought pleasure, as if the recluse herself had sent to all those families whom she did not know some living beauty, – a blooming rose-tree, or a shapely fruit-tree in fruit'. Her name 'again gave out fragrance' (*SOR* 159).

Terence Martin suggests that *Shadows on the Rock* offers little 'explicit criticism of extreme asceticism'.[17] However, the panelling effect of the novel, the use of an anacoluthonic technique and the referencing of tapestries suggest a different way to approach Le Ber's asceticism. Certainly, there is little 'explicit criticism', but the juxtaposing of tableaux and the movement across vignettes suggest a contextualisation of Le Ber's abjuration of the senses. Specifically, we see that Le Ber's renunciations contrast sharply and critically with the domestic comforts and the sheer immersion in sensory pleasure that offer solace to Cécile and her father.

In one of Cather's telling pairings, we later discover that Le Ber was loved by Pierre Charron, a hunter and fur trader. Charron lives the type of sensory life that Le Ber renounces. He is fully immersed in the world's physicality, so the pairing of Le Ber and Charron takes on that juxtaposed and contrasting significance we see so often in Cather's work.

Cather's bodily pictorialism is especially powerful in this pairing. The detailing of the portraits is low-key and understated, but once we step back from what is a diptych, we see how Cather deploys these two characters emblematically, suggesting the opposed ways that white settlement might work. Jeanne Le Ber pursues purity and sequestration – a religious idealism leading to a narrowing of bodily possibility (and gustatory pleasure). The colony becomes a form of a sensorily deprived prison into which the settler immures herself. On the other hand, Charron is a hunter–trapper, and as with Cather's portrait of Kit Carson in *Death Comes for the Archbishop*, he moves through a more syncretistic world fashioned from variegated food and material cultures.

The Le Ber/Charron pairing is one of several diptychs in Cather's late fiction – juxtaposed pairings that place sensory contrast at the centre of bodily narrative. In *Lucy Gayheart*, the protagonist's exuberant sensuousness (immersed in music, performing, skipping, dancing and skating) contrasts with Harry Gordon's stolidly confined world of bourgeois respectability. Again, at the end of the novel, after Harry locks Lucy's room with commemorative items from her life and then sees her frozen footsteps in the concrete sidewalk, Cather asks us to look at a world of frozen, stilled or immured corporealism. *Sapphira and the Slave Girl*'s central diptych is the married couple, Martin and Sapphira Colbert: she, confined to her room for the most part, a jealous guardian of space and personal encounter; he, a figure who moves more comfortably across and over cultural boundaries. As we shall see in the next chapter, Martin's ability to share in the floral and botanical cultures of the slaves is one sign that he is not confined to his own sensory world, but also able to appreciate that of Others.

In *Shadows on the Rock*, Cather creates a gustatory diptych by placing Jeanne Le Ber in juxtaposition to Pierre Charron. The former is a figure of abnegation and austerity, the latter immersed in the tastes of this world. An exuberant character, the 'hero of the fur trade' (*SOR* 195) is always exploring, fishing, hunting, trapping – and drinking. He is a hybrid with 'the good manners of the Old World, the dash and daring of the New' (*SOR* 198). Disappointed in love after Jeanne immures herself at the age of fifteen, Charron goes into the woods – where he 'learned the Indian languages as a child' (*SOR* 199). Charron is recognisably a Cather version of James Fenimore Cooper's hero, Natty Bumppo: the white settler who moves amongst the Indians, creating an idealised colonial identity both civilised and 'savage'.

He is also a wilderness cook, of the type celebrated by Hemingway and Roosevelt. Cather then inserts a sly, understated allegory about men, cooking and wilderness into her narrative. Cécile wants to travel downriver to the Île d'Orléans – a short canoe trip beyond Quebec City. Charron takes Cécile along on this little expedition and the whole excursion becomes structured by Charron's and Cécile's experiences of food. Cécile worries for her father – he has just bought provisions for her to cook – but she sets off with the trapper–hunter. But he also amuses and horrifies Cécile with tales of outrageous primitive cooking: 'When you can go to an Indian feast and eat dogs boiled with blueberries, you can eat anything' (*SOR* 216). The trip to the island parodies wilderness masculinism – Charron tells how he once had to eat boiled moss and roasted bear skin (*SOR* 216–17) – and a quiet celebration of Cécile's love of her own home comforts. She is horrified by the dirty bed she has to sleep in when they stay with the Harnois family on the island. For Cécile, home remains associated with her mother's memory: 'She thought a great deal about her mother, too, that night; how her mother had always made everything at home beautiful, just as here everything about cooking, eating, sleeping, living, seemed repulsive' (*SOR* 221). This section of the novel ends with one of Cather's sensory summations in a concluding statement that is both a character's internalised thinking and a narrator's commentary:

> These coppers, big and little, these brooms and clouts and brushes, were tools; and with them one made, not shoes or cabinet-work, but life

itself. One made a climate within a climate; one made the days, – the complexion, the special flavour, the special happiness of each day as it passed; one made life. (*SOR* 227)

These sentences might well lie behind Lionel Trilling's 1937 attack on Cather. Trilling misses the psychological aptness of such writing – Cécile's love of these tools is a physicalised embodiment of her sense of loss (of her mother). Attention to the warm female domestic world also offers an alternative to what Cather has presented as the hyperbolic wilderness world of the otherwise sympathetic Charron. This 'life itself' is, furthermore, counterpointed against Jeanne Le Ber's abstinence and abjuration. The result is a complex sensory frieze that places food and domesticity at the heart of a reimagining of the other side of colonial history.

Food and Power

It is possible to read Cather's works as a debate with forms of culinary imperialism. In *Death Comes for the Archbishop* it is a character (Latour) who offers a thoroughly Western defence of the historical significance of soup: 'It is the result of a constantly refined tradition. There are nearly a thousand years of history in this soup' (*DCA* 41). In the case of *Shadows on the Rock*, Cather's narrative voice links conquest with food: 'a new society begins with the salad dressing more than with the destruction of Indian villages' (*OW* 16). The vignettes and parables that make up these two collage-like novels themselves create more complex, layered models for how one might consider food and power. In fact, one might think of these statements as if they were ideological claims then subjected to forms of extended fictional debate, as Cather's staged tableaux reveal the weaknesses and contested significance of such apparent culinary Eurocentrism.

Cather's reading of power centres on food cultures, on how a colony is created to extract raw materials, on how a market might be created, and on how the colonists' domestic lives work. In *Shadows*, Count Frontenac recounts the story of his second audience with the French King at Fontainebleau. The King invites the Count to accompany him as he feeds the carp: 'Those at Fontainebleau are probably the largest and fiercest in France':

The carp there are monsters, really. They came grunting and snorting like a thousand pigs. They piled up on each other in hills as high as the rim of the basin, with all their muzzles out; they caught a loaf and devoured it before it could touch the water. Not long before that, a care-taker's little girl fell into the pond, and the carp tore her to pieces while her father was running to the spot. Some of them are very old and have an individual renown. One cold creature, red and rusty down to his belly, they call the Cardinal. (*SOR* 277)

This is one of Cather's obliquely symbolic, parable-like micro-narratives: working as a key to this section of the novel, it offers a strange little tale of the apparent plenitude of the natural world, as well as the dangers of that world. Ironic references to the human world (the old carp named the Cardinal) alert the reader to themes of predation and potential danger. It is a miniaturised narrative, a tiny sliver of an anecdote that contains the clues to how we might read this last section of the novel. For 'The Dying Count' then offers the reader a series of illustrations of both bounty and danger, of a world ready to be corralled and exploited, but also a world of potential threat. Frontenac, like the King, is a figure embedded in systems of power and authority – offering Auclair some money to make a fresh start outside of Quebec, he looks at the apothecary with 'contempt and kindness' when his offer is refused (*SOR* 279). Frontenac is a cynic in many ways and his power expresses itself in the exploitation of resources. Bishop Saint-Villier voices his displeasure with Frontenac for his 'worldly' way of using brandy to create a foothold in the fur trade dominated by the Dutch and the English traders. The Bishop denounces the brandy trade 'openly from the pulpit', while the Apothecary was present. Auclair makes a compromise with Frontenac's worldly policy:

> since the English and Dutch traders give them all the brandy they want, and better prices for their skins as well, we must lose the fur trade altogether if we deny them brandy. And our colony exists by the fur trade alone. (*SOR* 295)

Conclusion: The Cultural Politics of Food

On first reading, Cather's 1919 essay on Hoover's World War One food policies seems to be a slight and ephemeral journalistic work, typical of her utterly professionalised 'woman of letters' relationship to the literary marketplace. But like so many of the essays she wrote or the interviews she gave, this short account acts as a key to a number of Cather's major works. Hoover, a future US President, made his name as a philanthropist and bureaucrat organising food production. Cather's fiction also reads food in terms of national cultures and larger structures of power: *The Professor's House*, the male chef, the body and communal cuisines; *Death Comes for the Archbishop*, the colonial body and indigenous/hybrid food; *Shadows on the Rock*, Europe's food legacy and the sensory inheritance of the colonists; *Sapphira and the Slave Girl*, the ante-bellum South, slavery and the layered power structures of a racist society. Constructed this way, as a skein of investigations that repeatedly circled around taste and food, Cather's works look less a case of Trilling's 'mystic concern with pots and pans' than a searching and remapping of the culturescapes of a diverse America.

Notes

1. Tittle, 'Glimpses of Interesting Americans', 312.
2. Collingham, *Curry: A Tale of Cooks and Conquerors*, 255.
3. Jewell, 'Chocolate, Cannibalism and Gastronomical Meaning'. For accounts of Cather and food see: Dixon, 'Willa Cather's Immigrants'; Romines, 'The Double Bind of Southern Food'; Welsch and Welsch, *Cather's Kitchens*; Tsank, 'Under the White Mulberry Tree'.
4. Trilling, 'Willa Cather', 10–13.
5. Cather, 'Roll Call on the Prairies', 27.
6. Ibid.
7. Ibid.
8. Vester, *A Taste of Power: Food and American Identities*, 67.
9. Ibid. 79.
10. Ibid. 88.
11. Cather, 'Mesa Verde Wonderland', 7.
12. Ibid.
13. Walter Benn Michaels, 'The Vanishing American'. Michaels's article remains the classic analysis of Cather's exploitation of myths of vanishing native cultures.

My own readings, as in this chapter, suggest that Cather also deployed such 'primitivism' to critique aspects of her own culture.
14. Earle, *The Body of the Conquistador: Food, Race and the Colonial Experience in Spanish America, 1492–1700*, 2.
15. Martin, '"Grande [sic] Communications avec Dieu": The Surrounding Power of *Shadows on the Rock*', 33.
16. Dolezal, 'Cather's Medical Icon: Euclide Auclair, Healing Art, and the Cultivated Physician', 235.
17. Martin, '"Grande Communications avec Dieu"', 45.

CHAPTER 8

Cather's Smellscapes: Perfumes and Flowers, Disgust and Seduction

> When McKann had been in Paris, Kitty Ayrshire was singing at the Comique, and he wouldn't go to hear her – even there, where one found so little that was better to do. She was too much talked about, too much advertised; always being thrust in an American's face as if she were something to be proud of. Perfumes and petticoats and cutlets were named for her.
>
> Willa Cather, 'A Gold Slipper' (YBM 141)

A major thesis – perhaps, the major thesis – underpinning the cultural history of aroma is that there has been, within modernity and within Western culture, a steady denigration of the sense of smell, while other senses (notably, sight) have steadily risen to top what might be seen as a sensory hierarchy. In other cultures, and in pre-modern cultures, smell has had a much greater significance. Now, if smell signifies, it tends to be in negative ways – the smell of foulness, decay or dirt – while the positive connotations of smell are associated with the bland uniformity of our largely deodorised cultures. Odour underpins cultural classificatory systems where others smell bad. Furthermore, as Brian Moeran argues, smell has been underestimated by philosophers and psychoanalysts, linked more to pleasure than cognition:

> Because it was seen to lie at the junction between the 'distant' – and thus 'noble' and 'intellectual' – senses of sight and hearing, on the one hand, and 'near' or proximate – and thus more 'animal' and 'sensual' – senses of

taste and touch, on the other, smell has occupied an ambivalent position which, because it also does not lend itself to mental abstraction, has made philosophers regard it as a 'primitive' sense that is more important to sensory pleasure than to intellectual cognition. What is highly developed as a (sexual) sense among animals should not be examined too closely among humans.[1]

In this chapter, I use a term coined by geographer J. Douglas Porteous – 'smellscapes' – to examine Cather's rendering of cultures of odour, scent and perfume. In *A Lost Lady*, in her fictionalisations of the ancient cultures of the Southwest (*The Song of the Lark*, *Death Comes for the Archbishop* and *The Professor's House*), and finally in *Sapphira and the Slave Girl*, Cather uses the sense of smell as a form of diagnostic cultural tool, a way to prise open the lid of America's lost historical cultures, to disinter the frontier of Hispanic America in the middle of the nineteenth century or the ante-bellum environments of Virginia. Porteous notes that 'in the humanistic study of smellscapes . . . the insider:outsider antinomy is a crucial one'.[2] In all these novels a central antinomy (materialist/aesthete, colonist/indigene, slave/master) is identified, embodied and then, in Cather's intricate sensory writing, explored through reconstructions of historical smellscapes.

'Paul's Case', *A Lost Lady* and Floriographic Writing

Cather was always alive to the significance of flowers, and deployed floriographic discourses throughout her writing, from 'Paul's Case' at the start of her career to *Sapphira and the Slave Girl*. Cather perhaps came as close to any writer (certainly a twentieth-century novelist) to creating a fictional ethnography of flowers akin to the work of anthropologist Jack Goody in *The Culture of Flowers*.[3] Flowers, that is, are a delightful part of the natural world (thus, Cather wrote memorably of wildflowers in *My Ántonia*), but also form part of cultural systems related to medicine, desire, mourning and luxury. In 'Paul's Case', she inflects the European language of flowers by placing her young aesthete in the Gilded Age metropolis of Pittsburgh. In *A Lost Lady* she revisits the nineteenth-century novel of adultery by using flowers to emblematise power, corruption and lies. The smellscape of the mesa and its cultural significances are central to the 'Ancient People' episode of *The Song of the Lark*, while the disturbing smell of a geological feature becomes the key to a major episode in *Death Comes for the Archbishop*. A late novel such as *Shadows on the Rock*, as Christina Giorcelli notes, features live flowers (for instance, the lilacs in Bishop Laval's garden) alongside the dried flowers in apothecary Auclair's shop, while Mother Juschereau makes artificial flowers from scraps of material and paper.[4] This extensive creative exploration established a platform for Cather's flower-writing in *Sapphira and the Slave Girl* – a novel where she focuses on the South's beauty and terror.

Cather's relationship to nineteenth-century floral poetics evolved from a certain resistance in her early writing to the endorsement and exploration of floriographic discourse in the later fiction. In an 1894 student article, as well as alluding to an 1890 anthology (*Pastels in Prose*) that included major European writers of the language of flowers such as Huysmans and Baudelaire, Cather chastises those who described daisies, and then called for a more 'human' realism.

> It may be well enough to describe a daisy in an inimitable phrase, but daisies play such a small part in the real life of the world. Word artists have had their day of greatness and are rapidly on the decline. We want men who can paint with emotion, not with words.[5]

So how did Cather move from a refutation of floriographic discourse to some of the most extended usages of this mode in American fiction? The answer, I think, is akin to the creative evolution I traced in Chapter 3's observations about Wilde: Cather pushing back against and seemingly rejecting figures who undoubtedly engaged her, only to acknowledge these influences more fully late in her career. The Cather of the 1890s was, in a sense, discursively 'closeted' – still refuting, or at the very least clouding, her relationship to the queered cultural discourses of the *fin de siècle*. But just as the 1932 Introduction to *The Song of the Lark* finally reveals her discipleship to Wilde, so the novels (especially *A Lost Lady* and *Sapphira and the Slave Girl*) mine the floriography that she had at first seemed to reject. Ironically, her fiction creates an extended

American echo of the French literary–cultural world described by Suzanne Braswell:

> All of this indicates a vibrant floral culture in France, whose popular origins impacted the thought of poets and artists of the period, inciting them to explore the hidden depths of the language of flowers while stretching the bounds of its traditional expression and milieu.[6]

Cather's late Victorian and *fin-de-siècle* cultural origins are very clear in her apparent familiarity with the language of flowers. The language of flowers was an aestheticised semiotic series of signs that served, in a highly formalistic and in many ways repressed society, as a literal language capable of conveying a range of emotions. Oscar Wilde's radicalism rested in his subversion of Victorian sexual and moral codes – 'earnestness' in its multiple guises. But within his *fin-de-siècle* moment, Wilde's rewriting of the language of flowers became a synecdoche for this whole strategy: decoupling the usual association between the flower X and the emotion Y, Wilde undercut a whole edifice of cultural assumptions.

'Paul's Case' demonstrated Cather's familiarity with Wilde's remodelling of this Victorian cultural discourse, exemplifying her willingness to Americanise European aesthetic codes. From the very first paragraphs, Paul's sense of aestheticised difference and willed otherness reveals itself through his choice of flowers. His flamboyant opposition to his local culture embodies itself in an assertive deployment of carnations and roses (and, of course, his highly industrialised death is 'de-flowered' in the starkest way as he is crushed by a train).

The basic plotline of the story is built upon Paul's relationship with flowers. Paul wears a red carnation in his buttonhole: 'This latter adornment the faculty somehow felt was not properly significant of the contrite spirit befitting a boy under the ban of suspension' (*PC* 74). His pupils are swollen 'as though he were addicted to belladonna, but there was a glassy glitter about them which that drug does not produce': the narrator claiming a knowledge of druggy plants that one imagines was not a typical part of a Red Cloud education. For his teachers, the insubordinate Paul's 'whole attitude was symbolized by his shrug and his flippantly red carnation flower' (*PC* 74). Paul is an aesthete, appalled by the lower middle-class provincialism of industrial Pittsburgh. Flowers come to symbolise his sense of otherness and his yearning for escape into beauty:

> After each of these orgies of living, he experienced all the physical depression which follows a debauch; the loathing of respectable beds, of common food, of a house penetrated by kitchen odors; a shuddering repulsion for the flavorless, colorless mass of every-day existence; a morbid desire for cool things and soft lights and fresh flowers. (*PC* 76)

Thus the story's very *fin-de-siècle* fascination with temperamental pathologies is directly tied to his love of the floral.

Paul's escape will be an imaginative and a sensory one as he seeks 'the indescribable thrill that made his imagination master of his senses' (*PC* 79). Stealing money, he leaves Pittsburgh, the Carnegie Hall and the actors he adores (Paul sends the performers flowers), and then heads to New York. Immediately, he buys flowers, sets out his violets and jonquils, and then, freshly bathed, finally relaxes. He is 'Lulled by the sound of the wind, the warm air, and the cool fragrance of the flowers' (*PC* 80): escape from provincial life as a flight into floral odours. And then the story reaches its dénouement. The city is thrillingly artificial in its deployment of flowers; Paul sees flowers under glass in local shops: 'violets, roses, carnations, lilies of the valley, somehow vastly more lovely and alluring that they blossomed thus unnaturally in the snow' (*PC* 81). He spends his days enjoying his flowers until news of his crime travels east, and his father sets out to find him. Wearing his badge, the red carnations, Paul heads into the country for his floral suicide:

> It occurred to him that all the flowers he had seen in the glass cases that first night must have gone the same way, long before this. It was only one splendid breath they had, in spite of their brave mockery at the winter outside the glass, and it was a losing game in the end, it seemed, this revolt against the homilies by which the world is run. Paul took one of the blossoms carefully from his coat and scooped a little hole in the snow, where he covered it up. (*PC* 83)

And then, weakened, he dies accidentally–suicidally as a train crushes him.

'Paul's Case', published before Cather was thirty-two, demonstrates her interest in reading out, extending and deepening nineteenth-century discourses. In the story's obsessive attention to floriography, it looks to Wilde and Aestheticism. However, Cather decisively Americanises this most European of fictional codes, using floriography to create a counternarrative that could be placed in a mainstream magazine but map the cultural and sexual margin.

Two decades after 'Paul's Case', Cather uses floriography extensively in her ironic recapitulation of the nineteenth-century novel of adultery: *A Lost Lady*. This might seem a slight, pellucid novel (or novella) – a precise work, but one miniaturised in setting and scope. A modernist version of the novel of the adultery, Cather's text is also an oblique pioneer novel, taking as it does the story of Captain and Mrs Forrester (and their settling of the West) as its subject. On one level, the novel serves as a very shrewd reading of the early 1920s literary marketplace as Cather so deftly fuses an array of established narrative patterns to create a new hybrid form: the novel of adultery; the novel of Western settlement; the drawing-room novel of manners; and the post-Jamesian novel of surface and social etiquette. It is as if the Cather of *Alexander's Bridge* revisits that first novel but decisively recentres her focus from the East Coast to the Great Plains, again trying to create the vital bridge between her Aestheticist loyalties and the imaginative 'homecoming' she describes in her 1931 essay for *The Colophon*, 'My First Novels (There Were Two)' (*OW* 91–7).

A Lost Lady decisively looks back to the Aestheticism of the late Victorian era and then remodels its tropes in intriguingly proto-Modernist ways. In particular, the novel takes one sense – smell – to construct a narrative chain out of the language of flowers. The young Niel, the focalised centre through whose consciousness we see Marian Forrester, reads her dalliance with Frank Ellinger as an aesthetic betrayal: 'This day saw the end of that admiration and loyalty that had been like a bloom on his existence. He could never recapture it. It was gone, like the morning freshness of the flowers.' And then Niel speaks the following lines to himself. '"Lilies that fester," he muttered, "*lilies that fester smell far worse than weeds*"'

(*ALL* 82). He continues to reflect that 'it was not a moral scruple she had outraged, but an aesthetic ideal' (*ALL* 83). *A Lost Lady* picks up the amoral baton originally proffered by Wilde and Kate Chopin: the reading of human actions as aesthetic as much as (a)moral. It is certainly possible to encounter readers disturbed by the novel's careful sidestepping of conventional Victorian judgementalism: Marian Forrester is a fallen woman who seems not to have to pay for her sins. The novel seems 'modern', not least for its lack of characters occupying conservative positions. Moral judgements are translated – in a very Wildean way – into aestheticised comments, such as Niel's reflection about festering lilies.

As narrative, *A Lost Lady* deploys flowers as part of a symbolic chain that threads through the novel. The force of Niel's reflection about the festering lilies thus derives from their part within a novel-length system where flowers, their fragrances and their visual beauty, are repeatedly used to suggest the aesthetic plenitude of the Forresters' lives. 'The windows were open, and the perfume of the mock-orange and of June roses was blowing in from the garden' (*ALL* 84), Cather writes in one of a series of suggestive floral details. Niel figures his moods using the language of flowers: 'Would that chilling doubt always lie in wait for him, down there in the mud, where he had thrown his roses one morning?' (*ALL* 95) Mrs Forrester's skin is figured florally: 'In the brilliant sun of the afternoon one saw that her skin was no longer like white lilacs, – it had the ivory tint of gardenias that have just begun to fade' (*ALL* 106). The short chapter about the Captain's funeral (Chapter VI) is basically about the decorative arrangements surrounding the ceremony: the 'great armful of yellow roses' brought by Adolph Blum (*ALL* 138), Mrs Forrester's pledge to plant rose bushes next to her dead husband's sun dial, and then the 'creaking of the big cottonwoods' (*ALL* 139) signalling seasonal change.

The novel's final two chapters have the imagistic complexity, the sense of ambiguous resolution, that one might associate with a great Modernist poem. Mrs Forrester still captivates – wearing her 'short black velvet cape, fastened at the neck with a bunch of violets' (*ALL* 150). She hosts a meal for Niel, Ivy and the locals. Ivy remains the philistine, scoffing at the others' interest in clothes. The meal is not a success (Cather using food socio-culturally, as ever); Mrs

Forrester's desire for an aesthetic is lost on the utilitarian people of Sweet Water. In the last chapter, Cather ties Mrs Forrester's fate to that of the pioneers, but unlike the pioneers, she 'was not willing to immolate herself, like the widow of all these great men, and die with the pioneer period to which she belonged' (*ALL* 161). One evening, Niel stops by her property to 'look at the honeysuckle' (*ALL* 161) and sees Ivy Peters embracing Marian Forrester. And so Niel turns away from her, at last. But in the last paragraphs, Marian's emblematic power emerges again, a woman with a sense of ardour: 'She had always the power of suggesting things much lovelier than herself, as the perfume of a single flower may call up the whole sweetness of spring' (*ALL* 163). The apparently transitory beauty of flowers finally achieves a form of permanence – through memory – that overcomes the cultural passing of the pioneers and what, to a conventional moralist, would seem the trashiness of Mrs Forrester's flightily indiscreet life.

Finally, Mrs Forrester passes. She sends money to put flowers on the Captain's grave for Decoration Day (the forerunner of Memorial Day), and after her death, her new spouse, Henry Collins, sends money 'for the future care of Captain Forrester's grave, "in memory of my late wife, Marian Forrester Collins"' (*ALL* 166). The aesthetic moment, in other words, marks the final point of rest.

One might think of the language of flowers as a fixed and codified semiotic system. A flower corresponds to a certain signification, and typically takes its place within a context (social, ceremonial) where its meaning is both stable and transparent. Whereas lilies, for instance, were typically associated in the nineteenth century with death and mourning, Wilde's deployment of them as a decorative flower, displayed for aesthetic pleasure, unmoored them from their usual setting. Cather is a post-Wildean writer in that she displays flowers, and takes pleasure in writing about flowers, in ways that tend to disconnect them from a particular pattern of meaning. Often, Cather simply lists flowers as if revelling in their plenitude. But since her settings are usually the barely 'settled' prairies of the Great Plains or the remote mesas of the Southwest, the 'language' of such flowers remains *in utero*, awaiting its decoding. Thus in *My Ántonia*, in a rush of colour, Cather lists a number of plants and flowers native to the prairie: cone-flowers, rose mallow, gaillardia.

The writing has the precision and attentiveness of nature writing, but it also eschews symbolic readings in favour of simple observation: 'Across the wire fence, in the long grass, I saw a clump of flaming orange colored milkweed, rare in that part of the State' (*MA* 225). Such native wildflowers are 'new', if you like, to the language of flowers. They await the signifying process, the decisive insertion into the taxonomies of symbolic association that the Victorian era had produced in abundance. This sense of the sheer difference of certain flowers – the awareness that they lay outside the received European world of floriography – then became an important motif in Cather's writing, especially in the Southwestern novels, where the Otherness of certain smells became part of her fictional mapping of cultural encounters.

The Southwest's Olfactory World

Smell is, overwhelmingly, the sense that Cather associates with the Southwest and Mexico. 'The Ancient People' section of *The Song of the Lark*, 'Tom Outland's Story' in *The Professor's House*, and *Death Comes for the Archbishop* feature extended imaginative reflections on smell and scent. In all three of these narratives, smell becomes a central sensory dynamic in the story, integral to Cather's mapping of self and culture. As I noted earlier, smell tends to be ranked lower, in what is effectively a sensory hierarchy, than sight. As cultural historians suggest, smell is often inserted into an orientalised system: all too often, we find strange foods, stranger cities to be 'smelly'. Cather is a deeply interesting figure because one can see in these novels a certain exploration and then contestation of these ideas. Moreover, we see her writing become both more complex and culturally attuned as she moved through those years, from the mid-teens to the late 1920s.

Biographers have often credited Cather's trip to the Southwest in 1912 with radically reorienting her creativity, catalysing her into a new phase of her career, and with helping her shift from her career as journalist and editor to being a full-time creative writer. Typically, scholars either stress the distinctive landscapes of Arizona and New Mexico that Cather encountered during her trips to the Southwest or they highlight the people Cather met there – notably the rancher and amateur archaeologist, Richard Wetherill.[7] But the 1912 trip was also a sensory reorientation: an induction into a different culture of smell to the ones she had encountered on the Great Plains or in Pittsburgh or New York City. The travel article 'Mesa Verde Wonderland Is Easy to Reach', which Cather published in 1916 (marking out her new geographical focus), ended with 'aromatic pinon smoke' curling into the air above the mesa.[8]

In writing about the Southwest, Cather enters into a very different olfactory culture to that of the Great Plains: different in terms of the human and natural orders she encounters. The Southwest's Hispanic and Native cultures encompass different olfactory worlds to those Cather knew in Nebraska, while the distinctive topographies of canyon and mesa also contain a completely different eco-system of vegetation. Cather makes a great deal of use of this new sensorium in *The Song of the Lark*, *The Professor's House* and *Death Comes for the Archbishop*. There is, then, effectively a creative tension in much of Cather's presentation of the odiferous Southwest. One might say that her sense of the overwhelming smelliness of the Southwest conforms to that cultural hierarchising of the senses mentioned by anthropologists. On the other hand, since Cather's characters move into spaces where there are few associations between native odours and European–American culture, such figures might appreciate the smell of flowers in ways that can be provocatively open to cultural difference.

To begin with, in *The Song of the Lark*, Cather associates the Southwest and the Pueblo Indian culture (her version of the 'vanishing American' trope) with forms of white cultural renewal. Her white protagonists find creative, spiritual and emotional rebirth against a background shaped by Southwestern native cultures, which are both culturally rich and, happily for white America, denuded of actual presence. In 'The Ancient People', Native American presence is spectral, a form of benign haunting of the white self.

Cather's protagonist, Thea Kronborg, is a singer whose bodily growth and development form the central plotline of this radical re-envisioning of the *Bildungsroman*. Thea arrives exhausted in Flagstaff, northern Arizona: 'The personality of which she was so tired seemed to let go of her' (*SOL* 326). She is on the verge of artistic failure, but then enters into a form of bodily renewal through immersion in a Southwestern sensorium. Sight is not as important as the other senses: 'The faculty of observation was never highly developed in Thea Kronborg' (*SOL* 331). Thea seems to edge out of her Western identity, moving away from language toward a form of enriched sensory primitivism. Her thinking appears pre-linguistic – her 'incomplete conceptions . . . had something to do with fragrance and color and sound, but almost nothing to do with words' (*SOL* 330). A song is now 'much more like a sensation than like an idea, or an act of remembering', *SOL* 330). Music becomes a 'sensuous form'. And finally, in this ecstatically utopian paragraph, Thea becomes pure sensoriness itself: 'She could become a mere receptacle for heat, or become a color, like the bright lizards that darted about on the hot stones outside her door; or she could become a continuous repetition of sound, like the cicadas' (*SOL* 330).

Thea's renewal is, therefore, utterly embodied. In 'The Ancient People', Cather develops sensory narrative into an imagined space to explore representations of the female body, of place and of the creative self. The result is a profoundly singular piece of writing, as 'Modernist' in its own ways as the early works of William Carlos Williams or William Faulkner. Yet this is also a fictionalised environment where such transformations, or rediscoveries, are very much facilitated by native landscapes, at once sensorily enriching and comfortingly empty. Has Cather projected a white enrichment of the senses via a deliberate sidestepping of indigenous presence?

Certainly, smell is vital in this part of the novel: the smell of piñon trees, the distinctive aromas of cooking or the plentiful flora. When she arrives, 'the chokecherry bushes were in blossom, and the scent of them was almost sickeningly sweet after a shower' (*SOL* 329). Thea then bathes in a pool amongst this rich flora. She becomes flower-like herself: 'But when she thought of the moonflowers that grew over Mrs. Tellamantez's door, it was as if she had been that vine and had opened up in white flowers every night' (*SOL* 331). She learns to appreciate the olfactory richness of Panther Canyon in an archaeological way – at one point she dislodges carbon flakes from her lodge's roof – 'the cooking-smoke of the Ancient People. They were that near!' (*SOL* 332). The irony here is that smell can seem so immediate and yet so intangible –

the 'cooking-smoke' makes the Pueblo cultures both present and yet also dematerialised. Smell, in other words, becomes a form of symbol for the white encounter with the indigenous world, being both captivatingly and restoratively present, even while the literal agents who created those odours have now vanished. In later rhapsodic sentences the construction of the sensory landscape as one that is, at heart, of service to the white self becomes quite explicit. What seems to link Thea's revitalised awareness of her creativity to this landscape is, quite directly, the nostril: 'In singing, one made a vessel of one's throat and nostrils and held it on one's breath, caught the stream in a scale of natural intervals' (*SOL* 335). That is, the narrative has folded back a reading of sensory alterity into a fable about Thea's creative renewal: the smells of the Southwest are, finally, instrumental – of use to the white body.

If Cather had stopped writing about the odours of the Southwest with *The Song of the Lark*, her sense writing of place might now appear an expansion and yet reinscription of familiar tropes. But her later work created more complex and challenging representations of smell and alterity in this terrain. Smells are everywhere in Cather's historical fiction about 'old' Mexico, *Death Comes for the Archbishop*: the smells of pines on the hillsides, the smells of varied cuisines, and the smell (as we shall see) of the crack in the ground where Father Latour and Jacinto stretch themselves out. Intriguingly, Jacinto means 'hyacinth' in Spanish. *Death Comes for the Archbishop*'s olfactory world marks a significant advance, in terms of representations of cultural complexity and encounter, on the Southwest landscapes of *The Song of the Lark*. In the 1927 narrative the smells of indigenous cultures and those of European cultures emerge primarily through flowers, cooking and the odours of landscape itself. In all three ways, Cather shows an increasing sensitivity to the way culture might be read through the nose. Beautiful fragrance and repellent odour both play their roles in narratives focused on the meetings of the explorer–priests, Latour and Vaillant, and the indigenous peoples. Cather's understanding of what we might categorise as a 'softened' or progressive settler culture takes shape through the priests' fascination with gardening and flowers – expressions and embodiments of Western culture, of course, but also capable, in the novel's readings of exchange and hybridity, of being appropriated and remade by the agency of Indians and Mexicans.

In one vignette, drawn from the early sixteenth-century history of the church, a neophyte named Juan Diego fills his *tilma* with roses: 'The *tilma* was a mantle worn only by the very poor, – a wretched garment loosely woven of coarse vegetable fibre and sewn down the middle.' Juan tells Bishop Zumarraga that the roses have been sent as a sign. 'At this he held up one end of his *tilma* and let the roses fall in profusion to the floor. To his astonishment, Bishop Zumarraga and his Vicar instantly fell upon their knees among the flowers' (*DCA* 51–2). Flowers, and a knowledge of flowers, and symbolic deployments of flowers, play important roles in the novel's tracing of how the native peoples might surprise the European priests. Eusabio, a Navajo, is a figure whose deployment of flowers signifies a cultural power that immediately impresses. He shows Latour a 'bunch of crimson flowers', notes that in the native language they are called the 'rainbow flower', and observes that they have bloomed early (*DCA* 245–6) – the flowers are actually penstemons. Such incidents might seem trivial or insignificant, but they trace a form of sensory micro-politics in the narrative, a chain of vignettes that shows local contestations of power, moments when the European field of knowledge is radically expanded by the corporealised knowledge of local peoples.

Death Comes for the Archbishop features one episode ('Stone Lips') that also acknowledges the limits of cross-cultural understanding, and does so by grounding that blocked encounter in sensory terms. Travelling through the mountains in winter with his Indian guide, Jacinto, Father Latour seeks shelter. He finds himself in a forbidding landscape, sometimes only able to see the 'red blankets on the shoulders of the Indian boy' (*DCA* 133). The two men take shelter in a cave; Latour is struck by an 'extreme distaste' – 'he detected at once a fetid odour, not very strong but highly disagreeable' (*DCA* 134). Latour feels sickened by the place, and odour underpins his disgust. But Jacinto then encourages him to make a fire, tells him the cave is a ceremonial spot, essentially insists on him taking the place on its own cultural–sensory terms. Eventually, the 'fragrance of the burning logs' banishes the odour (*DCA* 136), and then in a further sensory turn, Latour listens to a vibration seemingly coming from the earth itself – in fact, it is an underground river.

Reflecting on the episode, Latour remembers the cavern 'with horror' (*DCA* 141). But he also notes that 'neither the white men nor the Mexicans in Santa Fé understood anything about Indian beliefs or the workings of the Indian mind' (*DCA* 141). Such a comment comes after a scenario based on sensory disjunctions and misconceptions; it is an acknowledgement, modest but telling, of gaps in cultural understanding, misprisions and a recognition of alterity. 'Stone Lips' is one of Cather's dramatic panels where we see her using her increasingly complex sensory writing to dramatise encounters across cultural lines, acknowledging, in ways that would become more frequent in her late fiction, that sensory narrative might reveal the limits of European–American understandings of other ways of being, other forms of embodiment.

Sapphira and the Slave Girl: Embodiment and Odour

Cather's last novel forcefully demonstrates her continued fascination with historical fiction and with rewriting the codes of literary realism. The novel asks a central question: how can a historical novel capture the lost sensory past? Cather said of *My Ántonia* that she had attempted to write the 'other side' of the rug – the alter-narrative, if you like, of conventional storytelling: '*My Ántonia*, for instance, is just the other side of the rug, the pattern that is supposed not to count in a story.'[9] *Sapphira* is a novel about the 'other side' of history: the domestic and everyday experiences within or to one side of the 'grand narrative' of the ante-bellum South. Ann Romines's notes for the Scholarly Edition compellingly illustrate the sheer range and depth of the historical research thus involved in the composition of this text. This fictional world is a relentlessly embodied one, in terms of both Cather's fascinating accounts of human bodies, and her mapping of how bodies interact when framed and shaped by that 'peculiar institution' of slavery.

Sapphira reads as if it were an ultra-precise, rigorously encoded novel of manners. Here are the domestic rituals and everyday ceremonies of the ante-bellum South, carefully and exhaustively assembled into a series of tableaux. What Cather employs is the historical novelist's techniques to shape a form of fictionalised analytical discourse which then *shows* the micro-cultures of slavery. Recording the looks and smells and the sounds and tastes of Virginia before the Civil War, Cather captures the sensory dimensions of quotidian life within a slave-owning society. In its embracing of the apparently banal, *Sapphira* becomes a remarkable novel as it creates sensory tableaux focused on the 'other side' of slavery (which is to say, its daily actualities rather than the exculpatory narratives that putatively justified that peculiar institution). This is microscopic delineation of a culturescape. What is it like to own people, but then to live alongside them as they live, grow old, become ill and die? Where is the boundary between proprietorial ownership and paternalistic 'care'? Writing largely, though not exclusively, through a third-person narrative focalised through her white characters, Cather presents these questions as embodied moments in focalised time.

Sapphira is the most foully odiferous and the most fragrant of Cather's novels, to adopt Alain Corbin's phrase.[10] Its detailed, highly textured representation of the ante-bellum South focuses specifically – and to significant dramatic effect – on the flowers, foods and bodily smells of that lost world. One way to read the novel might be as an extended, quasi-Proustian recapturing of family memory via smell: Cather returns to the Virginian world she had left and recalls it through a sense that the French writer had established as the foundation of (involuntary) memory.

Another interpretative approach is to see *Sapphira* as a radical experimental novel that reconfigures historical narrative in terms of the everyday sensory textures of a community's culture (how it smelled, how it produced smell), and that read 'smell culture' (especially) in terms of power. It is in the uses, the *embodied* uses, of a sense of place that *Sapphira* emerges as a quite remarkable experiment in historical imagining. It is the most dramatic and suspenseful of Cather's novels; her characters forge a criss-crossing web of sexual predation, mutual suspicion and idealistic empathy. Within that matrix (dramatic, even melodramatic), a sense of smell becomes integral to Cather's articulation of the emotional vectors that finally converge on the figure of Nancy, the slave girl.

Cather's Virginia is 'naturally' beautiful, even as it presents slavery as 'natural' too. Indeed, the lush and beautiful settings force us to think about what is natural, what makes for nature, and how the artifice of social constructions (notably, slavery) then might become naturalised.

Sapphira Colbert is a guardian of Anglo inheritance and cultural tradition; her carriage even carries the family crest. This is a conservative society, mindful of its roots in immigration from Britain, of the key social differences between churches (notably, Baptists and Episcopalians) and of the patterns of land ownership and inheritance. In her novels of white settler culture, especially the trilogy she fashioned around the colonial cultures of Quebec, the Southwest and Virginia, Cather extends and deepens the imaginative reach of the historical novel to create highly detailed imaginary mappings of New World societies, all of which focus especially on the sensory and embody formations of culture within those enclaves. Within a broad historical framing, Cather details the minutiae of social ritual: tea time, dinners, cooking, and social visits with other households. *Death Comes for the Archbishop*, *Shadows on the Rock* and *Sapphira and the Slave Girl* form a white settler trilogy whose long narrative become a narrative mural, if you like, made up of myriad tableaux and vignettes focusing on how white colonists of many Americas created their embodied cultural worlds.

For Cather's white settlers, smell culture defines what they have and where they come from, while it is also the epicentre of their encounters with Otherness. *Sapphira* presents the odour of the other in the most brutal way possible: through the stench of the slave imprisoned on the ship, the *Albert Horn*. Cather's terse, historically grounded description makes clear the crowded, brutal conditions under-decks: 'As there was no drainage of any sort, the slaves' quarters, and the creatures in them, got very foul overnight. Every morning the "tween decks" and its inmates were cleaned off with streams of sea water from the hose' (*SSG* 94). The Captain – 'not a brutal man' (*SSG* 94) – fumigates the decks. 'Himself, he never went near the slave deck; he couldn't stand the smell' (*SSG* 95). The slaves' liminal position – human but also animalised (creatures) – is embodied in the white response to their smell: they are repugnant but also occasionally cleaned. Cather's lapidary noting of this dynamic (cleansing and odour, the white policing of black lives) is a powerful rendering of 'offensive bodies' and how culture constructs systems around such corporeality. Alterity registers through the nose. Cather shows European–Americans, such as the captain of the slave ship or Father Latour in *Archbishop*, recoiling at the smell of the Africans or at the indigenous places they now encounter. These vignettes directly engage with that odoured difference that sense historians see as integral to the hierarchical encounter between the rest and the West.[11]

Sapphira is a novel as alert to the fragrant and foul as *Death Comes for the Archbishop* was. Much of the action takes place either in the lush bowers, gardens and pastures of Virginia, or in kitchens, smokehouses and Henry Colbert's mill. Even if odours are not directly being referred to, we are amongst the foods and flowers that suggest smell. The novel also captures the ways that a society uses odour codes for cultural purposes. In one particularly poignant vignette, Cather uses the outsider figure (readers will remember the tramp in *The Song of the Lark* or Crazy Ivar in *O Pioneers!* occupying a similar position in the sensory schema of those novels) to point to the deeper structures of the sensorium of Virginia. 'Tansy Dave' is named for tansy, a herb known for its pungent scent (*SSG* 203, 498). Sampson, Nancy's father (and a 'yellow man', or mulatto: Cather monitors the coding of skin colour), calls Tansy Dave over. Then the miller remembers when Dave, 'that half-witted ghost of a man, was one of the happiest boys on the place' (*SSG* 204). Dave fell in love with a 'coloured maid', Susanna, brought to the area by a certain Mrs Morrison, from Baltimore:

> Dave always escorted her home. Lizzie told the Mistress that every night after supper Dave changed his shirt and went down the creek to court Susanna, and before he started he rolled over and over in the tansy bed, 'to make hisself smell sweet.' The nickname 'Tansy Dave' had stuck to him long after he ceased to go a-courting, and after he no longer tried to make hisself smell sweet. (*SSG* 204–5)

But Susanna's mistress, who disapproves of slave-owning, will not allow Sapphira to buy Susanna (so as to further the relationship with Dave). Dave falls apart, becoming a wild man and a wanderer.

Dressed in rags, trading clothes for whisky, he becomes a marginal figure, foul rather than fragrant.

Note the subtlety of Cather's narrative shaping. Dave, smitten by desire, uses the tansy's pungency to make 'hisself sweet'; Martin Colbert lets 'an intoxicating fragrance' pull him toward his assault. The parallels and juxtapositions are clear: Cather uses odour both to bind the two figures together and to juxtapose them. Martin's odorous encounter has few consequences for him. Dave's scented failure leads to destitution. Cather uses narrative patternings of contrast and similitude, centred on a shared sense, to allow us to see how slavery charts very different fates for black and white.

Sapphira is a novel filled with the flora and fauna of the Shenandoah Valley, a fragrant backdrop that Cather uses to create the *mise-en-scène* for Martin Colbert's attempted seduction of Nancy. Rachel Blake (Sapphira's daughter) takes Nancy flower-picking in a luxuriant stretch of the turnpike called the Hollow, a classically Catherian setting for floral richness, microscopically rendered and implicitly sexualised: 'The ground beneath them was covered with bright green moss and flat mats of wintergreen full of red berries. Out of the damp moss between the exposed tree roots, where the shade was deep, the maidenhair fern grew directly' (*SSG* 169). Through this intensely sensory environment, Martin Colbert moves as a predator.

In the next chapter, following the panelling effect we have seen so often in her fiction, Cather adjusts the perspective – this time to shift the focus from the visual to the odiferous. We are now in the homely world of the smokehouse. Nancy enters: 'All day long, through spring and summer, the smoke from hickory chunks went up to cure and season the rows of hams and bacon hanging from the rafters of the roof' (*SSG* 176). What follows forms an apparently simple but (in fact) complex scene which shows Cather using her embodied writing to imagine the seduction of the 'slave girl'. Cather presents Nancy, brutally, as having absorbed the slave-owner's ways of thinking about her black self. Cather's sentence mimes an internal dialogue that Nancy has with herself, infused with what seems to be a thoroughly 'colonised' mindset: 'Someway no troubles followed a body up there; nothing but the foolish, dreamy, nigger side of her nature climbed the tree with her' (*SSG*

176–7). As throughout this novel, the idiomatic term 'body' seems to have a particular force and ironic resonance: Nancy is, in many ways, nothing but a 'body'. Then, in one of the abrupt moments of physical terror that punctuate Cather's fiction, Martin Colbert makes his move:

> The instant her head was turned Martin stepped lightly on the chair, caught her bare ankles, and drew her two legs about his cheeks like a frame. Nancy dropped her basket and almost fell out of the tree herself. She caught at the branch above her and clung to it. (SSG 179)

The sexual invasiveness is plain enough, the physical detailing of the encounter precise and resonant: her bare ankles, the legs wrapped around Colbert's face. But in order to tie this moment to the other skeins of meaning she is tracing, Cather underlines the scented nature of the contact:

> Martin framed his face closer and shut his eyes. 'Pretty soon. – This is just nice. – Something smells sweet – like May apples.' He seemed murmuring to himself, not to her, but all the time his face came closer. Her throat felt tight shut, but she knew she must scream, and she did.
> 'Pappy! Oh, Pappy! Come quick!' (SSG 180)

And so her father, Old Jeff, comes running from the smokehouse. What is interesting about this episode is Cather's poetic patterning of narrative around terms that focus on the senses. Martin 'frames' his face between Nancy's leg, as if literally embodying the power of the visual that has been so much a part of how Cather develops her sense of the Colbert family's culture. But it is her smell, her odoured otherness, that becomes seductive for Martin – we almost hear him grasping for an analogy that will explain her scent. In her microcosmic detailing, Cather explores how slavery is literally written on the body: 'He knew she must be pursued carelessly and taken at the right moment, off her guard. He was vexed that he had let a pleasant contact, an intoxicating fragrance, run away with him' (SSG 181).[12]

The young Colbert seeks to seduce by immersing his quarry in a heady, luxurious world of coolness and scent: the floral glade of a nearby wood. Cather's highly dramatised and behaviourist sense of psychology in this novel means that Colbert's cunning is revealed through action – his manipulations evident in the core of essentially *setting up* Nancy within this very specific space, dangerously Edenic as it is. In this heady environment, Colbert plans to sweep Nancy away and intoxicate her into submission. Cather's mapping of the senses shows us acute and relentless awareness of how embodiment shapes culture, and how that culture becomes bound into systems of power.

Cather's delineation of Colbert and Nancy in the wood plays with many cultural assumptions and inheritances one might have about the sense of smell. Smell is 'primitive', lower down the hierarchy of senses, inferior in particular to sight. It is also, typically, associated with women and racial others, with the natives and the colonised. But in Cather's sensorium, odiferous encounter unsettles these oppositions. *The Fragrant and the Foul*, Alain Corbin's great study of odour within French culture, captures smell's radical doubleness and its deconstructive sensory power.

This liminalisation initially focuses on smell, then becomes the dominant way in which Cather's narrative adopts or mimes the white view of blackness. There is a certain tenderness in Sapphira's caring for the elderly Jezebel, but the latter is also positioned as a creature:

> She had wasted since Sapphira saw her last. As she lay curled up in bed, she looked very like a lean old grey monkey. (She had been a tall, strapping woman.) Her grizzled wool was twisted up in bits of rag. She was toothless, and her black skin had taken on a greyish cast. Jezebel thought she was about ninety-five. She knew she was eighteen when she was captured and sold to a British slaver, but she was not sure how many years passed before she learned English and began to keep account of time. (*SSG* 88)

Time and the body: Jezebel, uprooted and enslaved, drops out of time with only an approximate age. In this novel, it is the white settlers who live in highly precise historical time. Cather uses historical time in an almost fetishistic way in *Sapphira*, as if to demonstrate that within this white ante-bellum world there is continual and ultra-specific timekeeping: the situating of the self moment by moment in a chronology. Hence the novel's opening page. 'The Breakfast Table, 1856' announces the opening of Book One, and what then follows is a meticulous and precisely detailed monitoring of Henry Colbert as he exists and acts with a detailed chronology.

> Henry Colbert, the miller, always breakfasted with his wife – beyond that he appeared irregularly at the family table. At noon, the dinner hour, he was often detained down at the mill . . . . On this morning in March 1856, he walked into the dining-room at eight o'clock, – came up from the mill, where he had been stirring about for two hours or more. (SSG 7)

Cather takes the practical necessities of historical narrative – that one has to situate a story in time, give details of history and establish a timeline – and uses and expands those requirements to suggest a more complex point: that the white settlers and their descendants, and the slaves, live in very different chronological worlds.

The remarkable ending of the novel is often read in terms of both Nancy and Cather herself (as a young girl) entering the narrative: Nancy returns to Virginia after twenty-five years, and Cather imagines herself encountering, as a child, her own fictionalised character. What is also significant about this epilogue is the sense that historical time, earlier seen as very much owned by the white characters, is now ordered and shaped by the African–American ones, with the Cather child figure as witness to a reordering of narrative mastery.

Conclusion: The 'lovely emotions' of Bodies

In her 1925 interview with Flora Merrill, Cather based her sense of the novel's success on how she managed to render the human immediacy of the prototype behind the invented figure – claiming that readers who knew the original Mrs Forrester (in *A Lost Lady*) recognised her fictional rendering. Cather is open in acknowledging that an actual figure lies behind an invented character, and then goes further to suggest that the very strength of narrative lies in such transmission. Cather argues that the novel's power derives from such imaginative alchemy. Given that Cather's comments emerged in 1925, it is remarkable how unconcerned she was with advancing any conceptual opposition to the biographical or 'real' roots of literary art. While Joyce was idealising an author 'refined out of existence', or Eliot exploring an aesthetic 'objective correlative' that served to mask the biographical context of literary production, Cather foregrounded the artist's personal connection with a living person as the foundation of literary creativity. And while the persona or mask had become another way for writers to expand their creative field, Cather continued to deploy unadulterated contact between the author–protagonist and an Other as the basis for storytelling. This was fundamentally a form of bodily rendering.

> The type of writer we have been talking about has a brain like Limbo, full of ghosts, for which he has always tried to find bodies . . . All the lovely emotions that one has had some day appear with bodies, and it isn't as if one found ideas suddenly.

Such bodily rendering was also a profoundly sensory process, as Cather indicated in a further refinement of this idea: 'Before this the memories of these experiences and emotions have been like perfumes. It is the difference between a remembered face and having that friend one day come in through the door.'[13] Think of Cather's fiction as built around a triad: sensory impression; the memory of bodies; and the capacity of narrative to create forms of corporeal recall that would retrieve those impressions and memories. As we shall see in my next chapter, Cather would finally deploy that triad to excavate the legacy of slavery.

Notes

1. Brian Moeran, 'Marketing Scents and the Anthropology of Smell', 153–68. Freud notoriously argued, in a footnote in *Civilization and its Discontents* (1929), that *Homo sapiens* began to walk upright to distance himself from the ground. This exposed the genitals, and so sight – not smell – became the prime vehicle of sexual excitation.
2. Porteous, 'Smellscape', 358.
3. Jack Goody's study, with its sense of the transactional, symbolic and artistic significances of flowers, has informed my readings of Cather's floriography.

Once spotted, flowers seem to constitute a major discourse in her work, both producing culture and acting as a form of commentary on culture.
4. Giorcelli, 'Writing and/as Weaving: *Shadows on the Rock* and *La Dame à la licorne*', 268–9.
5. Cather, 'Utterly Irrelevant' (28 October 1894), 13.
6. Braswell, 'Mallarmé, Huysmans, and the Poetics of Hothouse Blooms', 84.
7. O'Brien, *Willa Cather – The Emerging Voice*, 403–20, is perhaps the major account of this creative renewal and imaginative opening-up.
8. Cather, 'Mesa Verde Wonderland Is Easy To Reach', 7.
9. Merrill, 'A Short Story Course'.
10. Corbin, *The Foul and the Fragrant*.
11. Hyde, 'Offensive Bodies', 53–8. See also, in that same collection, Gale Largey and Rod Watson, 'The Sociology of Odors', 29–40, which discusses 'odorphobia' and (im)purity. See also Constance Classen, 'The Odour of the Other: Olfactory Codes and Cultural Categories', in *Worlds of Sense*, 79–105. 'It is evident in most such cases that the stench ascribed to the other is far less a response to an actual perception of the odour of the other than a potent metaphor for the social decay it is feared the other, often simply by virtue of its being "other", will cause in the established order' (80).
12. The overwhelming intensity and 'whole-body' sense of smell experienced by Cather's characters is not, I think, merely fictional imagining. Anthropologists have noted the ways that odour can become embodied and felt in ways that transcend a single sense. Kathryn Linn Geurts observes that, in West Africa, 'many Anlo-speaking people' would affirm 'that smell was definitely two senses and that the nose was by no means the only part of the body affected by odor'. Geurts, *Culture and the Senses*, 67.
13. Merrill, 'A Short Story Course'.

CHAPTER 9

Conclusion: The Body of the Author

In this concluding chapter I look at how Cather's own self-presentation, through photography, both furthered her fiction's fascination with the senses and with embodiment, and provided clues to how we might read her creative work. I examine the final stages of Cather's career, from the late 1920s through to the 1930s and on to the beginning of the next decade – a period that saw a summation of a career's investigation into embodiment, and further developments in her imagining of the corporeal. In *Sapphira and the Slave Girl*, especially, Cather brought her sensory orchestration of narrative to a compelling culmination, reimagining the domestic spaces and quotidian encounters of the ante-bellum South. The end of that novel featured Cather inserting herself, imagined as a young child, into the narrative. In this chapter I link that narrative *démarche* to her fascination with writers' bodies and their physical presence.

Cather's Hands

Cather's career intersected in intriguing ways with a number of artists who, in their own ways, mapped new bodily modalities, from her first viewing of the divas of the 1890s. One such intersection occurred in 1927, when *Vanity Fair* published Edward Steichen's photographic portrait of Cather. Steichen's photo has become an important part of the story of Cather's creation of her own image, but the picture was also part of his own narrative – a

1920s movement between a number of important female bodies and faces. Steichen was a visual poet of the face and a mapper of the clothed body. The radical informality of his portraits enabled him to frame women's bodies and faces in ways that now seem presciently contemporary.

A posed tensile immediacy marks Steichen's female icons. His 1924 portrait of the actress Katharine Cornell sees the actress gripping the front of her low-cut blouse. Is she about to part the shirt? Is her grip (we see the veins and muscles of her hands) defiant, or embarrassed and tense in the face of Steichen's camera? His image of Therese Duncan, Isadora Duncan's adopted daughter, was taken in Greece in 1921, and reshapes classical posture into a thrillingly powerful image. 'Wind Fire – Therese Duncan on the Acropolis' dissolves classical stasis into movement – even the grass by her feet seems alive. This is the point where the statue seems to break into movement.

Hands play a central part in Steichen's iconic images of 1920s women, suggesting power, resistance, and a tensile strength which invites the viewer's scrutiny and theatrically displays autonomy. Cornell's hands grip her blouse; Duncan's hands curve around her head, creating a frame within a frame, pastiching the process of being pictorialised by the male viewer. Hands also play a coded role in Steichen's image of Greta Garbo and then in the earlier 1927 portrait of Cather. In 1928, just a year after his *Vanity Fair* portrait of Cather, Steichen took his famous pictures of Greta Garbo. Here, Garbo's hands and hair seem to be caught mid-movement: it is as if we are looking at a second-long snapshot or still caught amongst a series of movements. Energy and movement are implicit, even with the moment of stillness. In the sequence of Garbo images, Steichen uses her hands to imply nervous energy and restlessness. And Garbo's hands are the most active aspect of the composition: running through her hair, propping up her face, or elegantly and intriguingly touching fingertip to fingertip. Garbo's idiosyncratic elegance is a blend of composed refinement and implicit energy; her hands act metonymically in these images, suggesting a broader bodily vitality. The Garbo portraits take the camera far in toward the gaze, breaking down respectful distance between viewer and viewed. But the animation of Garbo's face, and the stylised gestures, make this into an interrogative and dialectic process. That which is gazed upon exerts its own captivating power.

And so Steichen's famous 1927 *Vanity Fair* image of Cather took its place in the context of his explorations of how the female face and body might be photographically remodelled within an informal, utterly modernistic visual lexicon. As Michael Schueth notes, *Vanity Fair* was founded in 1914 to rival Mencken's *Smart Set*. By the 1920s the magazine had 'captured the spirit of the postwar era – witty, playful, experimental, and rich'; and by 1923 Steichen was working for *Vanity Fair* and *Vogue* as a commercial artist.[1] In his image, Cather is posed, but not over-posed; one might imagine a series of flanking images around this one shot. Her body is relaxed, composed but not rigid. Her clothing embodies a certain Western informality: her shirt is loose-fitting, cuffs rolled-up, and her Middy tie smart but relaxed. Cather is professional and casual; there is a strong suggestion, too, of workmanlike immediacy in the creased blouse and the open-necked collar (with its echo of Whitman's white shirts). Cather is sitting down – a typical pose we might associate with an earlier phase of largely domestic photography of women. But while a sitting posture might imply demure passivity, in Cather's posture there is a feel of implicit but powerful agency, not least because the image is so resolutely stripped of softening (and imprisoning?) domestic paraphernalia.

The semiotics of the clothing are suggestive. But it is the self-confidence of Cather's gaze and the unadorned strength of her face that exert the greatest power. Cather's wryly smiling face is creased and clearly ageing. Her face is open, welcoming; she is *au naturel*, and as many of my students point out, almost looks like a favourite aunt. But the rolled sleeves and tie convey, too, a form of workaday readiness. She might just have stepped out of the editorial office. There is something both friendly and dependable, casual but determined, about the bearing of face and body. And Cather's gaze directly pulls us toward her, meets the viewer's gaze.

Titled 'An American Pioneer – Willa Cather', the *Vanity Fair* portrait plays up Cather's identity as a Western writer, deploying sartorial informality as a way to place her within the American literary pantheon.

Cather's image in the Steichen photograph corresponds to an image of Cather as a western writer, yet the picture showcases her in other critical ways as well . . . Cather visually communicates a sense of her 'forthright' style. Cather, this photograph suggests, is not regal like Edith Wharton, nor is she so stylish and 'fast' as the younger Jazz Age writers such as F. Scott Fitzgerald'.[2]

The text underneath socialises the individualism of the gaze. This text, which scholars tend to think was written by Cather herself, situates the Whitmanian author in a definite social context. Cather is the daughter of Western pioneers. Cather now positions herself as a 'daughter', and within a geographical and cultural context. The text now frames the proudly independent figure within the portrait. Cather narrativises her own self and gaze.

The year 1927 was perhaps the juncture in the formation of Cather's public image as a writer with regional, national and transatlantic identities. By now the number of Western Cather novels was significant (the pioneer novels and *The Professor's House* with its Midwestern college town setting and Southwestern locations, not to mention *Death Comes for the Archbishop* and even *My Mortal Enemy* with its West Coast finale). The photograph and the extensive caption represent a high-water mark for the creation of Cather as a distinctive Western American icon, an image furthered in 1930 by the award of the second Howells medal (a prize given for the best American fiction of the previous half-decade) to *Death Comes for the Archbishop*. The early promise signalled by *O Pioneers!* and *My Ántonia* had evolved into a conclusive identity. The broader publishing and advertising networks thus synthesised a distinctive figure incorporating regional and national personae.

The Physicality of Influence:
Madame Grout, Sarah Orne Jewett and Katherine Mansfield

Cather fashioned her own bodily image. And as a literary critic, she was obsessively interested in other writers' physical identity. Across her letters and literary essays, a repeated trope is that of the physical encounter with the literary creator, or (even more intriguingly) an utterly physicalised encounter with the effects or the image or the reputation of a writer. The impact of a writer is, quite literally, felt on the body in these accounts of an author who might exert what we might call, in a partial echo of Harold Bloom, the physicality of influence.

Cather's letters and non-fiction writings feature a number of episodes where she described the embodied presence of her fellow-writers: not the author's textual embodiment but a quite literal physicality. A number of these essays appeared in the 1936 collection, *Not Under Forty* – Cather described them as 'scrupulously truthful accounts of accidental meetings with very interesting people' (*SL* 526). Her first published work was her 1891 student essay on Thomas Carlyle, a piece that imagined Carlyle striding across the Scottish landscape.[3] In 1900, she published an account of her meeting with Stephen Crane (in Lincoln, 1895), a brilliant vignette that compared Crane's thin hands to those of the English aesthete and illustrator, Aubrey Beardsley (Crane appears as a kind of cousin of Cather's Paul).[4] And in 1902 she visited A. E. Housman in London, an episode that provided Ford Maddox Ford with the materials for an anecdote in his 1932 memoir, *Return to Yesterday*. In a 1945 letter, Cather said she would write an accurate account of that meeting (in fact, she never did so) (*SL* 649).

Cather entitled her essay about a meeting with Flaubert's niece 'A Chance Meeting', and in a way all these meetings were chance encounters, almost as if Cather's life was fated to return again and again to a primal scene of a random meeting between strangers of the sort seen repeatedly in the novels. To write about other writers was usually to write about the body, as Cather's correspondence and occasional essays attest. This is particularly evident in the accounts of Cather's relationship with Sarah Orne Jewett, a friendship frequently cited by biographers and critics as integral to her evolution as an artist. For Sharon O'Brien, for example, the twentieth-century artist, Cather, grew toward artistic self-definition through a creative dialogue with her late Victorian mentor.[5] Cather's encounter with Jewett took place at that pivotal moment as she moved toward consolidating her career as a journalist and literary businesswoman, and edged closer to becoming a full-time author. The highly confessional letter to Jewett (19 December 1908) frenziedly casts Cather's transitional career in terms of relentless embodiment. She compares herself to a trapeze artist: 'My mind is off doing trapeze work all day long and only comes back to me when it is dog tired and wants to creep into my body and sleep' (*SL* 118). And: 'I feel diluted and weakened by it all the time – relaxed, as if I had lived in a tepid bath until I shrink from either heat or cold' (*SL* 118). Even though she is in her mid- thirties, 'when it comes to writing I'm a new-born baby every time – always come into it naked and shivery and without any bones' (*SL* 118). Cather figures the excitement of work for McClure in terms of electricity:

> I do think that kind of excitement does to my brain exactly what I have seen alcohol do to men's. It seems to spread one's very brain cells apart so that they don't touch. Everything leaks out as the power does in a broken circuit. (*SL* 119)

In many ways, this is a glorious *pot-pourri*. One cannot imagine Cather the editor tolerating such a mishmash of analogies: she would – surely – have edited down, reduced and made consistent some of the chaotic rhetorical patterning within this letter. But that *unedited* excess is perhaps the point of the writing here: the body and its ailments, and their link to creative dysfunction, simply overflowing from and breaking out of a typical late Victorian lexicon. That bodily language is almost comic in its frenzied reaching-out toward a variety of bodily states. She imagines herself as a performer, a baby, an animal. If there was just one trope in play, the letter might seem relatively conventional; but the impression is that of a writer trying on a plethora of bodily styles.

Cather reads out and extends the physicality which is, intriguingly, very much part of Jewett's fictional world. For scholars have recovered *The Country of the Pointed Firs* as a subversive text that created representations of the female body beyond the codes of late nineteenth-century or sentimentalised Romance. For George Smith, Jewett's novel is a radical regionalist text notable for its representations of 'an autonomous female body in terms of abortion and lesbianism'.[6] This reading of Jewett, combined with attention to the rhetorical shaping of the letter (now possible after the publication of that correspondence), throws new light on the relationship between the two authors, who can be seen sharing a genealogy of the body, a fascination with new representations of female corporealism. We see, in this rhetorical and narrative patterning, the movement from Victorian to modern, the emergence of a more liberated body.

The 1933 essay, 'A Chance Meeting', tells of a meeting with Flaubert's niece, Madame Grout, in a spa hotel in Aix-les-Bains in 1930. This is an elegantly provocative take on the Jamesian international theme: a series of crystalline vignettes where cultural and linguistic meetings are also *bodily* encounters. Cather meets an elderly Frenchwoman whose name she does not know at first, and then discovers that this is one of the great author's surviving relatives; through her new friend, she meditates on male European icons such as Turgenev, on Flaubert's legacy and on changing fashions in music. This seems at first to be a traditional travel sketch: tableaux set within European hotels, a world of leisured taste, the transatlantic literary elite. 'A Chance Meeting' might seem to give plenty of ammunition to critics such as Granville Hicks (who decried Cather's alienation from *engagé* fiction and the literature of political commitment).[7] But read as if it were 'the other side of the rug', the essay becomes a micro-narrative that tellingly brings together major themes of Cather's late career: literary inheritance, generational passing and cultural (inter)nationalism. As in 'Old Mrs. Harris' and *Sapphira and the Slave Girl*, these preoccupations are then focused on to the body of an ageing woman: a literal *corporealisation* of abstract themes.

Cather is, in fact, more aware of Madame Grout as physical presence than as named person:

> Her name, I thought, would mean very little; she was what she was. No one could fail to recognize her distinction and authority; it was in the carriage of her head, in her fine hands, in her voice, in every word she uttered in any language, in her brilliant, very piercing eyes.[8]

The elderly Grout defies age but embodies its power (she is a vital link to Flaubert and to French nineteenth-century culture, a walking form of cultural capital). She is one of late Cather's ageing matriarchs, a still-powerful figure even as she nears death:

> As I watched her entering and leaving the dining-room I observed that she was slightly lame, and that she utterly disregarded it – walked with a quick, short step and great impatience, holding her shoulders well back. One saw that she was contemptuously intolerant of the limitations of old age.[9]

Cather presents this defiant vigour as the product of cultural engagement.

> It was interesting to observe Madame Grout at the opera that night, to watch the changes that went over her face as she listened with an attention that never wandered, looking younger and stronger than she ever did by day, as if the music were some very potent stimulant.[10]

Michael Ondaatje has written of his compositional process: 'What the novel should allow, with all its time, space and language, is the opportunity to enter another life, or to invent something small and distinct, or to make indelible a stranger lost to history.'[11] For Cather, the process of making a stranger indelible was clearly a feature of her narrative art and fed into her occasional writings, such as this essay. That 'indelibility' was also a bodily permanence. The essay folds together a sense of vanishing and a sense of presence: the great writers are no longer with us, but their artistic legacy still finds physical embodiment in a survivor, a descendant. It is almost as if the disappearance of the originating author is counterpointed against the continued embodiment of the literary legacy in another figure (there are decided Gothic undercurrents – a sense of haunting – in this essay). So, when Cather returns to the original Flaubert texts, they now have a bodily and familial intimacy: 'The five hundred pages of that book were now peopled for me with familiar figures, like the chronicles of a family I myself had known.'[12]

Cather deployed narrative arcs focused on issues such as cultural permanence and transmission, or the processes of memory within a society; and bodily encounters remained central to those arcs. Meeting Madame Grout in a hotel effectively allows Cather the chance to imagine encounters and re-encounters; Cather turns public social space into an arena where you get to know others through bodily-social meetings. From the Lincoln theatre to the

European hotel: each is a social space where strangers become known. A hotel is a place of comings and goings, entrances and exits, a place where a series of meetings with a stranger might become the foundation for friendship. The arc back to Cather's early theatre reviewing is quite evident: there, too, the foyer is the place of encounter, where strangers might become familiars. In Cather's writing of modern life, the quintessential modern places are the hotel and the theatre, sites for spectacle and performance, and for encounters that turn strangers into friends. But even in this world of taste and privilege, there remains a certain contemporary edginess, a sense of drama and difference, of implicit otherness even in the most comfortable of meetings.

As an American meeting Europe's complex literary heritage, Cather presented herself primarily as a bodily encounterer, a writer who *meets* other writers. As noted earlier, her writing looks back to a *belle-lettriste* tradition shaped by De Quincey's highly personalised and scandalous essays on the Lakeland Poets. But Cather then extended dramas of encounter toward writers' bodies that might have seemed marginal: older, disabled and ageing figures. Within this process she used corporeal encounter as the grounding for empathy and sympathy.

Cather's writings about the body of the writer are notable for their counterpointing of intimacy and obliquity: we 'feel' the author in terms of imaginative closeness (the impress of her words on our imagination) and corporeal distance. In her essay on Katherine Mansfield, also published in *Not Under Forty* and then reprinted in *On Writing*, Cather praised the New Zealand author in sensory terms. She described the 'first-rate writer' as a figure with 'the thing that is his very own, his timbre, this cannot be defined or explained any more than the quality of a beautiful speaking voice can be' (*OW* 107–8). In this crucial late exploration of writing's relationship to lived experience, Cather focused on the apparent triviality of Mansfield's work, arguing that 'She chose a small reflector to throw a luminous streak out into the shadowy realm of personal relationships' (*OW* 108). Cather read Mansfield as a chronicler of family life shaped by covert, 'shadowy' emotional structures, where individuals pursued their lives beneath the quotidian flow of group existence, and she figured this dynamic in visual and auditory terms: 'the real life that stamps the faces and gives character to the voices of our friends' (*OW* 109). Cather then reused the image that she had first deployed in 'The Novel Démeublé' – that of 'the overtone':

> It is this overtone, which is too fine for the printing press and comes through without it, that makes one know that this writer had something of the gift which is one of the rarest things in writing, and quite the most precious. (*OW* 110–11)

There is thus a sensory logic to the final years of Cather's career: a trajectory toward a writing that would bring the writer's body, the writer's sensory presence, directly into narrative itself. The 'chance encounter' would, finally, involve Cather herself, imagined as a child, encountering one of her own characters: and that crystallisation would occur at the very end of her last novel, *Sapphira and the Slave Girl*.

Sapphira and the Slave Girl: 'That old darky song'

Edith Lewis's memoir, *Willa Cather Living*, begins with a remarkable anecdote where Cather vocalises blackface, greeting a visitor as follows: '"I'se a dang'ous nigger, I is!"'[13] Whether this is a true story or not is simply beyond knowing now – what is significant is that Lewis (by then Cather's literary executor and symbolic guardian of her cultural reputation) placed the anecdote early on in her memoir, as if signalling the importance of race, identity and voice to Cather's life and work.

The historical research for her novel had brought Cather into contact with emergent scholarship centred on African–American history and culture. Ann Romines, in the Historical Essay for the Scholarly Edition of the novel, explores Cather's research in the New York Society Library, an institution located near her apartment. Romines notes that 'Cather's most apparent use of her Society Library research was in the story of Jezebel's capture in Africa in the late eighteenth century and her transportation, via the Middle Passage, to the Baltimore slave market.'[14] Cather had, for instance, checked out from the library John R. Spears's *The American*

Slave Trade: An Account of Its Origin, Growth and Suppression (1900). Romines's work also highlights Cather's developing sensitivity to the representation of her black characters. For instance, there is an extremely important textual crux which she discusses. In the final published version of the novel Cather describes the African-American character Jezebel as being 'tall, straight, muscular, long in the legs'. The Drew typescript (an earlier manuscript version of the novel, produced before the final revisions) has sentences that make an argument for her 'well-shaped' physique being unusual amongst African women. Romines later writes (in one of her Explanatory Notes to the text):

> The Drew typescript of *Sapphira* makes it clear that Jezebel's 'well-shaped' physique is exceptional among the African women: 'She had none of the usual bodily characteristics of the African female; the hanging belly heavy thighs and (*excise* squat legs) the over-developed breasts' . . . This derogatory passage does not appear in the published novel. (*SSG* 461)

Cather was clearly still drawn to the stereotyped annotations of the black body which had marked and scarred her earlier writing (as in the picture of Blind D'Arnault in *My Ántonia*). She was also, textual evidence suggests, revising and deleting such character sketches. For some readers, this manœuvre would still constitute a partial apologia – the initial phrasing too strong, too racist, to be obviated by later textual emendations.

Certainly, there are readers who find the novel ultimately to be a historical rendering of slavery continually shaped by Cather's *white* authorial identity. For Toni Morrison, in 1992's *Playing in the Dark*, the novel 'turns at the end into a kind of memoir, the author's recollection of herself as a child witnessing the return, the reconciliation, and an imposed "all rightness" in untenable, outrageous circumstances'. Cather's own entry into the text, when she imagines herself as a child, constitutes 'delayed gratification for the pleasure of a (white) child'. This text is thus a *'safe* participation in loss, in love, in chaos, in justice'.[15]

The novel has, to other readers, seemed to engage with the nation's racist historical legacy, but also to deflect that attention. Critics have read the book as a historical testimony that is remarkably full and direct, but also oblique in its representations of ante-bellum society. Cynthia Griffin Wolff's essay on the novel cites Lewis's comment and asks: 'How can we understand the complete meaning of this eruption? What untellable story does it intimate?' Cather's exclamation is a comment 'rich with intimation but bereft of full disclosure'.[16] The suggestion that the novel is somehow cagey or indirect or not fully open is an interesting one, and worth pursuing – especially given that, in many ways, it seems *explicit* in its depictions of violence (as I showed in my discussion of tactility in the novel in Chapter 6). Other scholars place the text in a tradition of white writing about the ante-bellum South, reading *Sapphira* as a text that abjures abiding nostalgia to create a complex reckoning with slavery's horrors. For John Jacobs, while Cather 'represents that stereotypical world, she reveals beneath its surface the irreducible human identity of masters and slaves'.[17]

In this final section I extend Jacobs's observation by looking at how the novel's representation of the body, and the body in culture (for instance, in paintings, or via the gossip of parlour talk), make for a complexly critical, anti-nostalgic narrative. But I also try to take on the implications of Wolff's observation about the 'untellable story' it addresses. To resolve this paradox, a reader has to see how the complex architecture of this superficially simple tale imagines the deep structures of a slave-owning society (and its aftermath) through a narrative tapestry centred on the sensorium.

'The housekeeper had taught her that the shuffling foot was the mark of an inferior race' (*SSG* 43): *Sapphira and the Slave Girl* is a novel where understated observation of bodies within a domestic system reveals slavery's encoded dynamics. An overt ideological struggle plays out amongst the white family members, who have very different understandings of slavery, given their religious affiliations (the cast includes Episcopalians, Quakers and Baptists – each sect with a different view of slavery and abolition). But it is in mapping the micro-level of bodily interaction that Cather's writing uncovers the cultural codes underpinning slavery. At first, the superficial gestural codes of *Sapphira and the Slave Girl* seem fixed, not least because of the illnesses of the characters, or the work routines which keep them confined to specific rooms and houses. Sapphira Colbert is lame, housebound and chairbound.

Her husband has retreated to the mill, where he spends his time annotating the Bible. The African-Americans work within a highly choreographed world of precise social etiquette. Cather seems to be rendering ante-bellum society in terms of frozen social praxis: a place of literal embeddedness and fixity, where all know their place. Her world is less glamorous than that of Mitchell's *Gone with the Wind*, but equally hypostatised. Yet social and cultural dislocations take place at the Catherian micro-narrative level, in a look or glimpse, or a sudden random collision of bodies – it is this other side of a social system that becomes the space where body narrative unfolds.

In this Epilogue, distinctive social–cultural stories are always written on the body. For instance, when a local 'Rebel boy' returns from the war, a leg shattered in combat, 'the Hayfield people, regardless of political differences, came in relays . . . they carried cold water from the springhouse and with a tin cup poured it steadily over his leg for hours at a time' (*SSG* 268). Thus 'Nancy's Return' begins with anecdotes about forms of white reconciliation, episodes that suggest postwar emotional reconstruction through the work of white nursing or through shared farming on the poor soil of the Shenandoah Valley. Cather positions this bodily culture of reconciliation quite precisely in historical time: 'The day of Confederate reunions and veterans' dinners was then far distant' (*SSG* 270). This is, then, a time of bodily flux, of a disrupted habitus, a moment when enmity gives way to the staging of white reconciliation and white reconstruction (celebrated in social ceremonies).

Cather situates historical fiction at moments when embodied knowledge is in decisive flux, where the habitus of everyday life is unsettled. And this had always been the case in her work: the tales of European migrants in *O Pioneers!* and *My Ántonia*, corporeal adoption and adaptation, and the emergence of new physical cultures such as the small-town dance or African–American performance; *Death Comes for the Archbishop*, the pivot when 'Old Mexico' transitions to 'New Mexico', and when European food cultures encounter the indigenous diet; *Shadows on the Rock*, the white settler transition from being 'French' to 'Canadian', with all the physical disorientations that entails. And now, in this Epilogue, Cather chooses to look at a very fluid decade, the 1870s: the era of Reconstruction, the moment after the Civil War but before Jim Crow and the rowing back of pre-1877 developments. In these novels of the historical moment, cultural and societal changes are literally felt on the body, registered in the microcosmic world of gesture, physical disposition and the emergence of a new sensorium.

In the last section of the novel, Nancy returns from Canada (she had fled there to escape Virginia and the Colberts). Charismatically, she holds the young Cather's attention. She is already known in stories, celebrated, and her arrival orchestrated. 'The actual scene of the meeting had been arranged for my benefit' (*SSG* 275). Cather then patterns 'Nancy's Return' around a fluid interplay of the senses: sight, sound, touch – all play particular roles as characters look at these long-separated individuals, observe clothing, listen attentively, embrace one another. Nancy is strange and familiar, culturally and bodily. 'When Nancy laid aside her long black coat, I saw with astonishment that it was lined with grey fur, from top to toe! We had no coats like that on Back Creek' (*SSG* 276). Nancy, a 'gold-skinned woman' or 'gold-coloured' figure (*SSG* 276–7), now possesses class distinctiveness. The young Cather listens to Nancy's Canadian accent, which she dislikes (*SSG* 277). She notes the social, tribal almost, differences between her people and the now-foreign Nancy. Nancy's mother feels that her daughter's way of speaking marks her out as someone of a higher class (*SSG* 279). There is a sense that a new, very different society has emerged. Nancy's husband, who works for the same family that she does, 'was half Scotch and half Indian'(*SSG* 278) – he has a hybrid identity that is explicit (rather than implicit, as was the case in the miscegenated prewar world).

Nowadays, we would say that Cather's portrayal of Nancy, and the encounters between her and the Cather family, are embedded in 'intersectionality': the writing moves ceaselessly between descriptive annotations that signal race, class and national identity. Nancy speaks Canadian English; remains the 'gold-skinned woman' of her bi-racial origins; now wears clothes that denote urban sophistication. The scene's detailing allows these features of Nancy's new life to sit in the narrative, awaiting the close readerly decoding that Cather has helped to foster in her making of an anthropological reader alert to corporeal semiotics of dress, speech and manner.

Practically every paragraph of these last pages contains a line or phrase that suggests the complex intermixing of lives that is the emergent culture of post-Civil War North America.

This is a culture of continual verbal exchange, of anecdote and storytelling. The family servants 'told stories until they went to bed' (*SSG* 280). Max Gluckman's 1963 essay, 'Gossip and Scandal', recovered gossip as a social practice worthy of study. For Gluckman, gossip has a highly functionalist significance within communities, acting to solidify group identities: 'The important things about gossip and scandal are that generally these are enjoyed by people about others with whom they are in a close social relationship.' And: 'That is, the right to gossip about certain people is a privilege which is only extended to a person when he or she is accepted as a member of a group or set. It is a hallmark of membership.'[18] Within the world glimpsed in 'Nancy's Return', gossip is now a place where the African–American characters have become a central part of 'a group or set', and as storytellers and gossips themselves, shape that group. It is the black characters who have become the family's oral archivists. And Cather herself aligns herself with these African–American griots (*SSG* 283). 'Her stories about the Master and Mistress were never mere repetitions, but grew more and more into a complete picture of those two persons' (*SSG* 285). Nancy has become the guide and the source of gossip. She talks from within the group as a social equal to the whites who once owned her. Her stories command attention; Cather presents her fictionalised younger self as an avid listener to fables of the Confederacy told by an African–American. The implication – a subtext also present in other late Cather works such as 'Old Mrs. Harris' – is that we are looking into the rich well of domestic storytelling out of which the young Cather emerged: a world of female storytelling, here glimpsed quasi-anthropologically. And the centre of these discursive exchanges – gossipy tales about death, illness and age – is the African–American speaker, and her command over white narratives.

The last few pages of the novel – effectively, Cather's concluding public words in a long writing life – are deceptively banal on first reading, but steadily reveal a complex rendering of word and corporeality, text and body. At the end of this intensely embodied narrative, the last six pages might seem strangely *dis*-embodied.

Cather now shifts from a precise moment-by-moment creation of a sensorium to a narrative where characters' lives are simply summarised through conversation. In an almost parodic version of a narrative summing-up, Nancy's and Till's exchanges encompass the post-Emancipation lives of Sampson, Lizzie, Bluebell, Tap. And then, finally, we have the Colberts themselves, whose deaths (Henry died in an agricultural accident; Sapphira naturally, sitting in her chair as a heart attack took her) form a powerful contrasting diptych.

Now let us turn to a song that recurs in the novel and becomes central to these exchanges: the 'cane-brake song' or 'Nancy Till.'

'Down by de cane-brake, close by de mill,
Dar lived a yaller gal, her name was Nancy Till' (SSG, 177)

The song first appears in the crucial scene when Martin Colbert approaches Nancy amongst the cherry trees, on his way to assault her. 'He came through the wet grass straight toward the cherry trees, his straw hat in his hand, singing that old darky song' (*SSG* 177). When Nancy returns, Cather – writing in the first person – remembers the song. 'Ever since I could remember anything, I had heard about Nancy,' she adds, and quotes the couplet again, noting that her mother sang it to send her to sleep (*SSG* 274). There is a third quotation of song, after which we are told: 'That was the picture I had carried in my mind. The stranger who came to realize that image was forty-four years old' (*SSG* 277).

Ann Romines's annotations, in her 'Explanatory Notes' to the Scholarly Edition, suggest that these moments in the text reveal the origins of the song, and also give a sense of Cather's interest in African–American speech. 'Nancy Till' was a 'minstrel song published in 1851 ... Cather wrote to Dorothy Canfield Fisher that she had especially liked writing the idioms and patterns of African American speech, which she remembered clearly from her Virginia childhood' (*SSG* 492–3).

And the ballad is written and uttered in dialect – Cather using an African–American idiom which, as Janis Stout has shown, parallels and enters into dialogue with 1930s folklorists' interest in the black vernacular. In this most detailed account of Cather's rendering of black speech, Stout traces the origins of the ballad 'Nancy Till'. She notes that this was 'a real song, not a folk song but a composed one first published in 1851 for piano and voice'. There are numerous printings of the song, and 'it would apparently have been very popular around the time when the epilogue to *Sapphira and the Slave Girl* is set, 1881'. Stout believes that Cather 'took the names of both Nancy and Till from the name in the song'.[19] The narrative deploys a dialect-based ballad on those three occasions, and on each occasion we seem to be seeing a form of minstrelsy where a white character positions/frames a black character through an appropriation of African–American speech. Stout's account of the 'racialized vernacular' certainly tends toward this kind of reading. At the same time, it is possible to read the novel's Epilogue, in particular, as an ambiguous and divided fable of appropriation where Nancy is still being framed in this way, but also achieves a certain escape into agency, not only from the South and slavery, but also from how her own story had been told by the Colberts (and Cather herself). Now, she speaks differently; now, she dresses differently; now, she lives in Canada, and is married to a man whose presence would have been inconceivable in prewar Virginia.

Conclusion: Cather's Entry

Ann Romines points out that one of the last changes Cather made to the text of *Sapphira* was the addition of an italicised note on the last page of the manuscript (after 'THE END'), an addition which dealt with the names she had used in the novel: a highly personal note that discussed her memories. '*In this story I have called several of the characters by Frederick County surnames, but in no case have I used the name of a person whom I ever knew or saw,*' and then mentioned her parents chatting about their acquaintants (*SSG* 288). The novel synthesises or hybridises two quite different approaches to historical fiction: history as documented and sourced material; and history as oral transmission, family story or folklore. The latter discourses are vital to the sensory project of the novel, since they directly draw processes of listening and observing into the narrative (as in Cather's comment about persons she 'knew or saw'). That is, the foregrounding of authorial presence, and the forging of a narrative partly out of gossip and anecdote, all help to expand the sensory dimensions of storytelling.

In the final pages of her last novel Cather turned the narrative toward herself, and toward her own sensory engagement with family history, regional history and the national past. These pages foreground her selfhood in terms of being a fiction-maker and memory-artist. Little apparently happens: Cather herself enters the story, as a little girl listening in to Nancy, Till and her own mother. *Sapphira and the Slave Girl*, especially in its final stages, acknowledged the African–American presence in a fuller way than Cather had managed to achieve in her earlier writing (think of Blind D'Arnault in *My Ántonia*): an imaginative recognition of lives that matter could be achieved only by Cather literally placing a version of herself into the text. These pages ask us to think about how the writer relates to her own materials, and to the contexts of a fictional work, by reflecting on the relationship between the writer's body and the bodies of others (in this case, fictional constructs). In doing this, Cather was fulfilling her own work's internal logic – work which had deployed 'real' figures (Helena Modjeska in *My Mortal Enemy*, for instance) as a means to deepen her fictional investigations into the habitus and the senses, and then to focus that investigation on relationships between very different identities of 'American'.

Was this narrative, as Toni Morrison has suggested, a form of 'delayed gratification' for the white child? Had Cather, in imagining herself listening to Till's voice (the final paragraph of the novel consists of Till's commentary on Sapphira's decision to live where she did – that is, it is a black commentary on white society and its class foibles), caught a transitional moment of white listening/ black utterance?

Cather's fiction had often been end-oriented – quite literally moving toward death in *Death Comes for the Archbishop* and *The Professor's House*, for instance. But memory had also been one of her central subjects. In *Sapphira and the Slave Girl* this narrative torque achieved its finest form, as Cather pushed her protagonists forward into the future, while pulling the narrative back into a neo-anthropological account of prewar Virginia and its habitus. What Cather had brought to narrative, through this shaping of story, was a profound attention to the senses, and through them to what finally seemed to be 'bodily time' itself. Working through this narrative logic, Cather then placed herself centrally into narrative, into sensory time itself.

Notes

1. Schueth, 'A Portrait of an Artist as a Cultural Icon: Edward Steichen, *Vanity Fair*, and Willa Cather', 54, 56.
2. Ibid. 59.
3. Cather, 'Literary. [Concerning Thos. Carlyle]', 3-4.
4. Cather, 'When I Knew Stephen Crane', 17-18.
5. O'Brien, *Willa Cather: The Emerging Voice*, 334-52.
6. Smith, 'Jewett's Unspeakable Unspoken: Retracing the Female Body through *The Country of the Pointed Firs*', 11.
7. Hicks, 'The Case Against Willa Cather'.
8. Cather, *Not Under Forty*, 820.
9. Ibid. 815.
10. Ibid. 828.
11. Ondaatje, 'Pale Flags: Reflections on Writing Anil's Ghost', 62.
12. Cather, *Not Under Forty*, 830.
13. Lewis, *Willa Cather Living: A Personal Record*, 13.
14. Romines, 'Historical Essay,' in the Scholarly Edition of *Sapphira and the Slave Girl*, 356.
15. Morrison, *Playing in the Dark*, 27-8.
16. Wolff, 'Time and Memory in *Sapphira and the Slave Girl*: Sex, Abuse, and Art', 212-13.
17. Jacobs, 'A (Slave) Girl's Life in Virginia Before the War: Willa Cather and Antebellum Nostalgia', 150-65: 161. See also: Merrill Maguire Skaggs, *After the World Broke in Two: The Later Novels of Willa Cather*, 165-81; Joseph Urgo, '"Dock Burs in Yo' Pants": Reading Cather through *Sapphira and the Slave Girl*', 24-37.
18. Gluckman, 'Gossip and Scandal', 307-16: 313. Two articles on Jane Austen and gossip might usefully be read alongside *Sapphira*. Casey Finch and Peter Bowen, '"The Tittle-Tattle of Highbury": Gossip and the Free Indirect Style in *Emma*', 1-18. Elaine Bander, 'Gossip as Pleasure, Pursuit, Power, and Plot Device in Jane Austen's Novels', 118-29. See also Patricia Mayer Spacks, *Gossip*.
19. Stout, '"Down by de Canebrake": Willa Cather, Sterling A. Brown, and the Racialized Vernacular', 37.

BIBLIOGRAPHY AND FURTHER READING

Adams, Henry, 'The Dynamo and the Virgin', in Adams, *The Education of Henry Adams* (Boston: Houghton Mifflin, 1918), 379–90.
Agee, James, *Let us Now Praise Famous Men* (Boston: Houghton Mifflin, 1941).
Al-Ghalith, Asad, 'Cather's Use of Light: An Impressionistic Tone', *Cather Studies*, 3 (1996), 267–82.
Ammons, Elizabeth, 'Cather and the New Canon: "The Old Beauty" and the Issue of Empire', *Cather Studies*, 3 (1996), 256–66.
Anonymous, 'Puvis de Chavannes', *The Art Critic*, 1.2 (1894), 30–1.
Antin, Mary, *The Promised Land: The Autobiography of Mary Antin* (Boston: Houghton Mifflin, 1912).
Archer, William, 'The Free Stage and the New Drama', *Fortnightly Review*, 50, New Series 56 (1891), 663–72.
—, *The Theatrical 'World' of 1894* (London: Walter Scott, 1895).
Aronoff, Eric, *Composing Cultures: Modernism, American Literary Studies, and the Problem of Culture* (Charlottesville: University of Virginia Press, 2013).
Aston, Elaine, 'Studies in Hysteria: Actress and Courtesan, Sarah Bernhardt and Mrs. Patrick Campbell', in Maggie Gale (ed.), *The Cambridge Companion to the Actress* (Cambridge: Cambridge University Press, 2007), 253–71.
Auerbach, Jonathan, *Body Shots: Early Cinema's Incarnations* (Berkeley: University of California Press, 2007).
Baker, Carlos (ed.), *Ernest Hemingway: Selected Letters 1917–1961* (New York: Scribner's, 1961).
Bander, Elaine, 'Gossip as Pleasure, Pursuit, Power, and Plot Device in Jane Austen's Novels', *Persuasions*, 23 (2001), 118–29.
Barker, Jennifer M., *The Tactile Eye: Touch and the Cinematic Experience* (Berkeley: University of California Press, 2009).
Barthes, Roland, *Camera Lucida: Reflections on Photography* (New York: Hill and Wang, 1981).
Baxter, Charles, *The Art of Subtext: Beyond Plot* (Minneapolis: Graywolf Press, 2007).
Berger, John, *Ways of Seeing* (London: Penguin Books, 1972).

Blanchard, Mary Warner, *Oscar Wilde's America: Counterculture in the Gilded Age* (New Haven: Yale University Press, 1988).
Blom, Philipp, *The Vertigo Years: Europe, 1900–1914* (New York: Basic Books, 2008).
Bloom, Edward A. and Lillian D. Bloom, *Willa Cather's Gift of Sympathy* (Carbondale: Southern Illinois University Press, 1962).
Bohlke, L. Brent (ed.), *Willa Cather in Person: Interviews, Speeches, and Letters* (Lincoln: University of Nebraska Press, 1986).
Bourne, Randolph, 'The Handicapped – By One of Them', *The Atlantic*, 108.3 (1911), 320–9.
Braswell, Suzanne, 'Mallarmé, Huysmans, and the Poetics of Hothouse Blooms', *French Forum*, 38.1–2 (2013), 69–87.
Butsch, Richard, 'Bowery B'hoys and Matinee Ladies: The Re-Gendering of Nineteenth-Century American Theatre Audiences', *American Quarterly*, 46.3 (1994), 374–405.
Capuano, Peter J., *Changing Hands: Industry, Evolution, and the Reconfiguration of the Victorian Body* (Ann Arbor: University of Michigan Press, 2015).
Carlin, Deborah, 'Cather's Jewett: Relationship, Influence, and Representation', *Cather Studies*, 10 (2015), 169–88.
Cather, Willa, 'Literary. [Concerning Thos. Carlyle]', *The Hesperian*, 20.11 (1891), 3–4.
—, 'Peter', *The Hesperian*, 22.4 (24 November 1892), 10–12.
—, 'The Tale of the White Pyramid', *The Hesperian*, 22.5 (22 December 1892), 8–11.
—, 'One Way of Putting It', *Nebraska State Journal* (3 December 1893), 13.
—, 'One Way of Putting It', *Nebraska State Journal* (17 December 1893), 13.
—, 'With Plays and Players', *Nebraska State Journal* (25 February 1894), 9.
—, 'Amusements', *Nebraska State Journal* (13 September 1894), 5.
—, 'Utterly Irrelevant', *Nebraska State Journal* (16 September 1894), 13.
—, 'Utterly Irrelevant', *Nebraska State Journal* (23 September 1894), 13.
—, 'Utterly Irrelevant', *Nebraska State Journal* (28 October 1894), 13.
—, 'As You Like It', *Nebraska State Journal* (11 November 1894), 13.
—, 'The Fear That Walks By Noonday', *The Sombrero* (1895), 224–31.
—, 'The Passing Show', *Nebraska State Journal* (2 February 1896), 1.
—, *The Home Monthly*, 6 (November 1896), 11.
—, [signed Elizabeth L. Seymour], 'Nursing as a Profession for Women', *The Home Monthly*, 6 (1897), 3–5.
—, Pittsburgh *Leader* (2 December 1898), 13.
—, [signed Henry Nicklemann], 'When I Knew Stephen Crane', *The Library* (23 June 1900), 17–18.
—, [signed Henry Nicklemann], 'Popular Pictures: Favorites at the Carnegie Art Exhibit as Viewed by a Connoisseur – "The Hour Glass"', *Pittsburgh Gazette* (24 November 1901), 6.
—, 'Paul's Case: A Study in Temperament', *McClure's Magazine*, 25.1 (1905), 74–83.
—, 'On the Gulls' Road', *McClure's Magazine*, 32.2 (1908), 145–52.
—, *Alexander's Bridge* (1912), Willa Cather Scholarly Edition. Historical essay and explanatory notes by Thomas Quirk, textual essay and editing by Frederick M. Link (Lincoln: University of Nebraska Press, 2007).

—, *O Pioneers!* (1913), Willa Cather Scholarly Edition. Historical essay and explanatory notes by David Stouck (Lincoln: University of Nebraska Press, 1992).

—, 'Training for the Ballet: Making American Dancers', *McClure's Magazine*, 41.6 (1913), 85–95.

—, 'Three American Singers: Louise Homer, Geraldine Farrar, Olive Fremstad', *McClure's Magazine*, 42.2 (1913), 33–48.

—, *The Song of the Lark* (1915), Willa Cather Scholarly Edition. Historical essay and explanatory notes by Ann Moseley, textual essay and editing by Kari A. Ronning (Lincoln: University of Nebraska Press, 2012).

—, 'Mesa Verde Wonderland Is Easy To Reach', *The Denver Times* (31 January 1916), 7.

—, *My Ántonia*, with illustrations by W. T. Benda (1918), Willa Cather Scholarly Edition. Edited by Charles Mignon with Kari A. Ronning, historical essay by James Woodress, with contributions by Ronning, Kathleen Danker and Emily Levine (Lincoln: University of Nebraska Press, 1995).

—, 'Roll Call on the Prairies', *The Red Cross Magazine*, 14.7 (1919), 27–31.

—, 'Light on Adobe Walls', in *Willa Cather on Writing: Critical Studies of Writing as an Art* (Lincoln: University of Nebraska Press, 1920).

—, *Youth and the Bright Medusa* (1920), Willa Cather Scholarly Edition. Historical essay and explanatory notes by Mark J. Madigan, and textual essay and editing by Frederick M. Link, Charles W. Mignon, Judith Boss and Kari Ronning (University of Nebraska Press, 2009).

—, 'The Novel Démeublé' (1922), in *Willa Cather on Writing: Critical Studies on Writing as an Art* (Lincoln: University of Nebraska Press, 1988).

—, 'Nebraska: End of the First Cycle', *The Nation*, 117.3035 (5 September 1923), 236–8.

—, *A Lost Lady* (1923), Willa Cather Scholarly Edition. Historical essay by Susan J. Rosowski with Kari A. Ronning, explanatory notes by Ronning, textual editing by Charles W. Mignon and Frederick M. Link, with Kari A. Ronning (Lincoln: University of Nebraska Press, 1997).

—, *One of Ours* (1925), Willa Cather Scholarly Edition. Historical essay and explanatory notes by Richard C. Harris, textual essay and editing by Frederick M. Link with Kari A. Ronning (Lincoln: University of Nebraska Press, 2006).

—, *The Professor's House* (1925), Willa Cather Scholarly Edition. Historical essay by James Woodress, explanatory notes by Woodress with Kari A. Ronning, textual editing by Frederick M. Link (Lincoln: University of Nebraska Press, 2002).

—, *My Mortal Enemy* (New York: Alfred A. Knopf, 1926).

—, *Death Comes for the Archbishop* (1927), Willa Cather Scholarly Edition. Historical essay and explanatory notes by John J. Murphy, textual editing by Charles W. Mignon with Frederick M. Link and Kari A. Ronning (Lincoln: University of Nebraska Press, 1999).

—, *Shadows on the Rock* (1931), Willa Cather Scholarly Edition. Historical essay and explanatory notes by John J. Murphy and David Stouck, textual editing by Frederick M. Link (Lincoln: University of Nebraska Press, 2006).

—, *Obscure Destinies* (1932), Willa Cather Scholarly Edition. Historical essay and explanatory notes by Kari A. Ronning, textual essay by Frederick M. Link, with Kari A. Ronning and Mark Kamrath (Lincoln: University of Nebraska Press, 1998).

—, *Lucy Gayheart* (1935), Willa Cather Scholarly Edition. Historical essay by David Porter, explanatory notes by Kari A. Ronning and Porter, textual essay and editing by Frederick M. Link and Ronning (Lincoln: University of Nebraska Press, 2015).

—, *Sapphira and the Slave Girl* (1940), Willa Cather Scholarly Edition. Historical essay and explanatory notes by Ann Romines, textual essay and editing by Charles W. Mignon, Kari A. Ronning and Frederick M. Link (Lincoln: University of Nebraska Press, 2009).

—, Letter to Langston Hughes (1901-67), 15 April 1941, Beinecke Library, Yale University, New Haven, CT.

—, 'On *Death Comes for the Archbishop*', in *Willa Cather on Writing: Critical Studies on Writing as an Art* (Lincoln: University of Nebraska Press, 1988), 3-13.

—, *Willa Cather on Writing: Critical Studies on Writing as an Art* (Lincoln: University of Nebraska Press, 1988).

—, *Not Under Forty*, in Sharon O'Brien (ed.), *Willa Cather: Stories, Poems, and Other Writings* (New York: Library of America, 1992), 811-83.

Cather, Willa and Georgine Milmine, *The Life of Mary Baker G. Eddy and the History of Christian Science* (Lincoln: University of Nebraska Press, 1993).

Cheng, Anne Anlin, *Second Skin: Josephine Baker and the Modern Surface* (Oxford: Oxford University Press, 2011).

Chopin, Kate, *The Awakening* (New York: Herbert S. Stone, 1899).

Clarke, Graham, 'The Body in Photography', in Clarke, *The Photograph* (Oxford University Press, 1997), 123-43.

Classen, Constance, *Worlds of Sense: Exploring the Senses in History and Across Cultures* (New York: Routledge, 1993).

—, 'Engendering Perception: Gender Ideologies and Sensory Hierarchies in Western History', *Body and Society*, 3.2 (1997), 1-19.

— (ed.), *The Book of Touch* (Oxford: Berg, 2005).

—, David Howes and Anthony Synnott, *Aroma: The Cultural History of Smell* (London and New York: Routledge, 1994).

Clere, Sarah, *Troubling Bodies in the Fiction of Willa Cather* (PhD diss., University of North Carolina at Chapel Hill, 2011).

— 'Thea's "Indian Play" in *The Song of the Lark*', *Cather Studies*, 9 (2011), 21-44.

Cochran, Robert, *Louise Pound: Scholar, Athlete, Feminist Pioneer* (Lincoln: University of Nebraska Press, 2009).

Cohen, Debra Rae, 'Culture and the "Cathedral": Tourism as Potlatch in *One of Ours*', *Cather Studies*, 6 (2006), 184-204.

Colglazier, Douglas J., 'Willa Cather on Henrik Ibsen's Realism: The Protest Against Lies', *American Literary Realism*, 33.2 (2001), 99-103.

Collingham, Lizzie, *Curry: A Tale of Cooks and Conquerors* (Oxford: Oxford University Press, 2007).

Connor, Steven, *The Book of Skin* (Ithaca, NY: Cornell University Press, 2004).

Corbin, Alain, *The Foul and the Fragrant: Odor and the French Social Imagination* (Cambridge, MA: Harvard University Press, 1986).

Counihan, Carole M. (ed.), *Food in the USA: A Reader* (London and New York: Routledge, 2002).
Crane, Joan, *Willa Cather: A Bibliography* (Lincoln: University of Nebraska Press, 1982).
Curtin, William (ed.), *The World and the Parish, Volume II: Willa Cather's Articles and Reviews 1893–1902* (Lincoln: University of Nebraska Press, 1970).
Davidson, Michael, *Invalid Modernism: Disability and the Missing Body of the Aesthetic* (Oxford: Oxford University Press, 2019).
Davis, Lennard, *Enforcing Normalcy: Disability, Deafness, and the Body* (London: Verso, 1995).
Dent, Peter (ed.), *Sculpture and Touch* (London: Routledge, 2014).
Dixon, Mary Marie, 'Willa Cather's Immigrants: An Aesthetics of Food Strategies in Negotiating Displacement Anxieties', *Journal of American Culture*, 40.3 (2017), 227–34.
Dolezal, Joshua, 'Cather's Medical Icon: Euclide Auclair, Healing Art, and the Cultivated Physician', *Cather Studies*, 7 (2007), 229–52.
Douglas, Mary, *Purity and Danger: An Analysis of Concepts of Pollution and Taboo* (New York: Routledge & Kegan Paul, 1966, 2013).
Dumas, Alexandre, fils, *La Dame aux camélias* (Paris: Michel Lévy Frères, 1848), trans. and Introduction David Coward (Oxford: Oxford University Press, 1986).
Du Maurier, George, *Trilby* (New York: Harper and Brothers, 1894).
Earle, Rebecca, *The Body of the Conquistador: Food, Race and the Colonial Experience in Spanish America, 1492–1700* (Cambridge: Cambridge University Press, 2012).
Edmonds, Jill, 'Princess Hamlet', in Vivien Gardner and Susan Rutherford (eds), *New Woman and Her Sisters: Feminism and Theatre 1850–1914* (Ann Arbor: University of Michigan Press, 1992).
Facknitz, Mark A. R., 'Character, Compromise, and Idealism in Willa Cather's Gardens', *Cather Studies*, 5 (2003), 291–307.
—, 'Changing Trains: Metaphors of Transfer in Willa Cather', *Cather Studies*, 9 (2011), 67–92.
Fara, Patricia, *An Entertainment for Angels: Electricity in the Enlightenment* (London: Icon Books, 2003).
Finch, Casey and Peter Bowen, '"The Tittle-Tattle of Highbury": Gossip and the Free Indirect Style in *Emma*', *Representations*, 31 (1990), 1–18.
Fishkin, Shelly Fisher, *Is Huck Black?: Mark Twain and African-American Voices* (Oxford: Oxford University Press, 1994).
Fitzgerald, F. Scott, *Flappers and Philosophers* (New York: Charles Scribner's Sons, 1920).
Flannigan, John H., 'Cather's Evolving Ear: Music Reheard in the Late Fiction', *Cather Studies*, 12 (2020), 68–88.
Frederic, Harold, *The Damnation of Theron Ware* (Chicago: Stone and Kimball, 1896).
Freedman, Jonathan, 'An Aestheticism of Our Own: American Writers and the Aesthetic Movement', in Doreen B. Burke (ed.), *In Pursuit of Beauty: Americans and the Aesthetic Movement* (New York: Rizzoli, 1986), 385–99.
Freud, Sigmund, *Civilization and its Discontents* (London: Penguin, 2002).
Funda, Evelyn, '"The Crowning Flight of Egotism": Willa Cather, Sarah Bernhardt,

and the Cult of Celebrity', *Willa Cather Newsletter & Review*, 55.2 (Fall 2011), 25–30.
Gale, Maggie B. and John Stokes (eds), *The Cambridge Companion to the Actress* (Cambridge: Cambridge University Press, 2007).
Garland-Thomson, Rosemarie, *Staring: How We Look* (Oxford: Oxford University Press, 2009).
Garrington, Abbie, *Haptic Modernism: Touch and the Tactile in Modernist Writing* (Edinburgh: Edinburgh University Press, 2015).
Geurts, Kathryn Linn, *Culture and the Senses: Bodily Ways of Knowing in an African Community* (Berkeley: University of California Press, 2003).
Giannone, Richard, *Music in Willa Cather's Fiction* (Lincoln: University of Nebraska Press, 2001).
Gigante, Denise, *Taste: A Literary History* (New Haven: Yale University Press, 2005).
Giorcelli, Cristina, 'Willa Cather and Pierre Puvis de Chavannes: Extending the Comparison', *Literature and Belief*, 23.2 (2003), 70–88.
—, 'Writing and/as Weaving: *Shadows on the Rock* and *La Dame à la licorne*', *Cather Studies*, 8 (2010), 262–81.
Gluckman, Max, 'Gossip and Scandal', *Current Anthropology*, 4.3 (1963), 307–16.
Hamilton, Erika, 'Advertising Cather during the Transition Years (1914–1922)', *Cather Studies*, 7 (2007), 13–26.
Hamilton, Roger, Roger Hargreaves and the National Portrait Gallery (Great Britain), *The Beautiful and the Damned: The Creation of Identity in Nineteenth Century Photography* (Aldershot: Lund Humphries, London: National Portrait Gallery, 2001).
Harbison, Sherill, 'Cather, Fremstad, and Wagner', in Merrill Maguire Skaggs (ed.), *Willa Cather's New York: New Essays on Cather in the City* (Madison, NJ: Fairleigh Dickinson University Press, 2001), 144–58.
Hardy, Thomas, *Far From the Madding Crowd* (London: Smith, Elder, 1874).
Hargreaves, Roger, 'Putting Faces to the Names: Social and Celebrity Photography', in Peter Hamilton, Hargreaves, and the National Portrait Gallery (Great Britain), *The Beautiful and the Damned: The Creation of Identity in Nineteenth Century Photography* (Aldershot: Lund Humphries; London: National Portrait Gallery, 2001), 16–56.
Harrell, David, 'Willa Cather's Mesa Verde Myth', *Cather Studies*, 1 (1990), 130–43.
Hemingway, Ernest, 'Camping Out: When You Camp Out, Do It Right', *Toronto Star Weekly* (6 June 1920), 20.
—, *In Our Time* (New York: Boni & Liveright, 1925).
Herring, Scott, 'Catherian Friendship; or, How Not To Do the History of Homosexuality', *Modern Fiction Studies*, 52.1 (2006), 66–91.
Hicks, Granville, 'The Case Against Willa Cather', *The English Journal*, 22.9 (1933), 703–10.
Hillman, David and Ulrika Maude (eds), 'Introduction', *The Cambridge Companion to the Body in Literature* (Cambridge: Cambridge University Press, 2015), 3–9.
Hollander, Anne, *Seeing Through Clothes* (Berkeley: University of California Press, 1975).
Homestead, Melissa J. and Anne L. Kaufman, 'Nebraska, New England, New York:

Mapping the Foreground of Willa Cather and Edith Lewis's Creative Partnership', *Western American Literature*, 43.1 (2008), 41-69.

hooks, bell, 'The Oppositional Gaze: Black Female Spectators', in hooks, *Black Looks: Race and Representation* (Boston: South End Press, 1992), 115-31.

Hoover, Sharon, 'Reflections of Authority and Community in *Sapphira and the Slave Girl*', *Cather Studies*, 3 (1996), 238-55.

Houchin, John. H., *Censorship of the American Theatre in the Twentieth Century* (Cambridge: Cambridge University Press, 2003).

Humphrey, Mary Jane, '"The White Mulberry Tree" as Opera', *Cather Studies*, 3 (1996), 51-66.

Hyde, Alan, 'Offensive Bodies', in Jim Drobnick (ed.), *The Smell Culture Reader* (Oxford: Berg, 2006), 53-8.

Jacobs, John, 'A (Slave) Girl's Life in Virginia before the War: Willa Cather and Antebellum Nostalgia', *Cather Studies*, 10 (2015), 150-65.

James, Henry, 'On the Occasion of *Hedda Gabler*' (1891), *Essays in London and Elsewhere* (New York: Harper, 1893), 230-52.

Jewell, Andrew, 'Chocolate, Cannibalism, and Gastronomical Meaning in *Shadows on the Rock*', *Cather Studies*, 8 (2010), 282-94.

— and Janis Stout (eds), *The Selected Letters of Willa Cather* (New York: Alfred A. Knopf, 2013).

Jewett, Sarah Orne, *Country of the Pointed Firs* (Boston: Houghton Mifflin, 1896).

Johnson, Katie N., *Sisters in Sin: Brothel Drama in America, 1900-1920* (Cambridge: Cambridge University Press, 2006).

Jones, Amelia (ed.), *The Feminism and Visual Culture Reader* (London and New York: Routledge, 2003).

Joyce, Simon, 'Sexual Politics and the Aesthetics of Crime: Oscar Wilde in the Nineties', *ELH*, 69.2 (2002), 501-23.

Kaplan, Amy, *The Anarchy of Empire in the Making of U. S. Culture* (Cambridge, MA: Harvard University Press, 2005).

Keeler, Clinton, 'Narrative without Accent: Willa Cather and Puvis de Chavannes', *American Quarterly*, 17.1 (1965), 119-26.

Kelly, Veronica, 'Beauty and the Market: Actress Postcards and Their Senders in Early Twentieth-Century Australia', *New Theatre Quarterly*, 20.2 (May 2004), 99-116.

Kennicott, Philip, 'Wagner, Place, and the Growth of Pessimism in the Fiction of Willa Cather', *Cather Studies*, 5 (2003), 190-8.

Kessler, Joyce, '"The Cruelty of Physical Things": Picture Writing and Violence in Willa Cather's "The Profile"', *Cather Studies*, 9 (2011), 244-65.

Kittler, Friedrich, *Gramophone, Film, Typewriter* (Redwood City: Stanford University Press, 1999).

Knausgaard, Karl Ove, *Boyhood Island: My Struggle* (New York: Random House, 2014).

Kot, Paula, 'Speculation, Tourism, and *The Professor's House*', *Twentieth Century Literature*, 48.4 (2002), 393-426.

Largey, Gale and Rod Watson, 'The Sociology of Odors', in Jim Drobnick (ed.), *The Smell Culture Reader* (Oxford: Berg, 2006), 29-40.

Lavin, Matthew J., 'Reciprocity and the "Real" Author: Willa Cather as S. S. McClure's Ghostwriter', *a/b: Auto/Biography Studies*, 31.2 (2016), 233-60.
Lawrence, D. H., 'Odour of Chrysanthemums', *The English Review*, 8.3 (1911), 415-33.
—, *Studies in Classic American Literature* (New York: Thomas Seltzer, 1923).
Lears, T. J. Jackson, *No Place of Grace: Antimodernism and the Transformation of American Culture 1880-1920* (New York: Pantheon Books, 1981).
Lee, Hermione, *Willa Cather: Double Lives* (New York: Pantheon Books, 1990).
Lewis, Edith, *Willa Cather Living: A Personal Record* (New York: Alfred A. Knopf, 1953).
Lindemann, Marilee, *Willa Cather: Queering America* (New York: Columbia University Press, 1999).
— (ed.), *The Cambridge Companion to Willa Cather* (Cambridge: Cambridge University Press, 2005).
Lutz, Tom, *American Nervousness 1903: An Anecdotal History* (Ithaca, NY: Cornell University Press, 1991).
McClure, S. S., *My Autobiography* (New York: McClure Publications, 1913).
MacDougall, David, *The Corporeal Image: Film, Ethnography, and the Senses* (Princeton: Princeton University Press, 2006).
MacInerney, Dorothy McLeod, William Warren Rogers and Robert David Ward, 'Oscar Wilde Lectures in Texas, 1882', *The Southwestern Historical Quarterly*, 106.4 (2003), 550-73.
Manguel, Alberto, *Reading Pictures: What We Think About When We Look at Art* (New York: Random House, 2000).
Marks, Laura U., *The Skin of the Film: Intercultural Cinema, Embodiment, and the Senses* (Durham, NC: Duke University Press, 1999).
Marra, Kim, 'Clyde Fitch's Too Wilde Love', in Marra and Robert A. Schanke (eds), *Staging Desire: Queer Readings of American Theatre History* (Ann Arbor: University of Michigan Press, 2002), 23-54.
—, *Strange Duets: Impresarios and Actresses in the American Theatre, 1865-1914* (Iowa City: University of Iowa Press, 2006).
Marshall, Gail, *Actresses on the Victorian Stage: Feminine Performance and the Galatea Myth* (Cambridge: Cambridge University Press, 1998).
—, 'Cultural Formations: The Nineteenth Century Touring Actress and Her International Audiences', in Maggie B. Gale and John Stokes (eds), *The Cambridge Companion to the Actress* (Cambridge: Cambridge University Press, 2007), 52-73.
Martin, Terence, '"Grande [sic] Communications avec Dieu": The Surrounding Power of *Shadows on the Rock*', *Cather Studies*, 3 (1996), 31-50.
Mauss, Marcel, 'Techniques of the Body', trans. Ben Brewster, *Economy and Society*, 2.1 (1973), 70-88.
Mayer, David, 'The Actress as Photographic Icon: From Early Photography to Early Film', in Maggie B. Gale and John Stokes (eds), *The Cambridge Companion to the Actress* (Cambridge: Cambridge University Press, 2007), 74-94.
Meisel, Martin, *Realizations: Narrative, Pictorial and Theatrical Arts in Nineteenth-Century England* (Princeton: Princeton University Press, 1983).

Merrill, Flora, 'A Short Story Course Can Only Delay, It Cannot Kill an Artist, Says Willa Cather', *Nebraska State Journal* (25 April 1925), 11.

Meyer, Susan, 'Craniometry, Race, and the Artist in Willa Cather', *Prospects*, 27 (2002), 341–58.

—, 'Coughing Girls in *The Song of the Lark*: Willa Cather, Breathing, and the Health of the Artist', *Willa Cather Newsletter & Review*, L.2 (2006), 27–30.

—, 'On the Front and at Home: Wharton, Cather, the Jews, and the First World War', *Cather Studies*, 6 (2006), 205–27.

—, 'Sanitary Piggeries and Chaste Hens: Willa Cather and the Pure Food Movement', *Willa Cather Newsletter & Review*, 54.2 (2010), 38–47.

—, 'Contamination, Modernity, Health, and Art in Edith Wharton and Willa Cather', *Cather Studies*, 10 (2015), 97–132.

Michaels, Michael Benn, 'The Vanishing American', *American Literary History*, 2 (1990), 220–41.

Millington, Richard H., 'Willa Cather and "The Storyteller": Hostility to the Novel in *My Ántonia*', *American Literature*, 66.4 (1994), 689–717.

—, 'Where is Willa Cather's Quebec? Anthropological Modernism in *Shadows on the Rock*', *Cather Studies*, 4 (1999), 23–44.

—, '*Shadows on the Rock*: Against Interpretation', *Cather Studies*, 7 (2007), 165–73.

Mintz, Sidney W., *Sweetness and Power: The Place of Sugar in Modern History* (London: Penguin Books, 1986).

Mitchell, Margaret, *Gone With the Wind* (New York: Macmillan, 1936).

Modjeska, Helena, *Memories and Impressions of Helena Modjeska* (New York: MacMillan, 1910).

Moeran, Brian, 'Marketing Scents and the Anthropology of Smell', *Social Anthropology/Anthropologie Sociale*, 15.2 (2007), 153–68.

Moers, Ellen, *Literary Women: The Great Writers* (Oxford: Oxford University Press, 1977).

Morley, Catherine, 'Crossing the Water: Willa Cather and the Transatlantic Imaginary', *European Journal of American Culture*, 28.2 (2009), 125–40.

Morrison, Toni, *Playing in the Dark: Whiteness and the Literary Imagination* (Cambridge, MA: Harvard University Press, 1992).

Moseley, Ann, 'Spatial Structures and Forms in *The Professor's House*', *Cather Studies*, 3 (1996), 197–211.

—, 'The Creative Ecology of Walnut Canyon: From the Sinagua to Thea Kronborg', *Cather Studies*, 5 (2003), 216–36.

Mulvey, Laura, 'Visual Pleasure and Narrative Cinema', *Screen*, 16.3 (1975), 6–18.

—, *Visual and Other Pleasures* (Bloomington: Indiana University Press, 1989).

Murphy, John J., 'The Art of *Shadows on the Rock*', *Prairie Schooner*, 50.1 (1976), 37–51.

Nettels, Elsa, 'Youth and Age in the Old and New Worlds: Willa Cather and A. E. Housman', *Cather Studies*, 4 (1999), 284–93.

North, Michael, *Reading 1922: A Return to the Scene of the Modern* (Oxford: Oxford University Press, 1999).

Oates, Joyce Carol, 'Inspiration and Obsession in Life and Literature', *New York Review of Books*, 62.13 (2015), 80–5.

O'Brien, Sharon, *Willa Cather: The Emerging Voice* (Oxford: Oxford University Press, 1986).
Olin, Margaret, *Touching Photographs* (Chicago: University of Chicago Press, 2012).
Ondaatje, Michael, 'Pale Flags: Reflections on Writing Anil's Ghost', *Wasafiri*, 19.42 (2004), 61-2.
O'Reilly, Sally, *The Body in Contemporary Art* (London: Thames & Hudson, 2009).
Peterman, Michael A. and Robert Thacker, 'Gazing Down from Cap Diamant: Cather's Canadian and Old World Connections', *Cather Studies*, 4 (1999), 1-6.
Porteous, J. Douglas, 'Smellscape', *Progress in Physical Geography: Earth and Environment*, 9.3 (1985), 356-78.
Porter, David, 'Historical Essay', in Willa Cather, *Lucy Gayheart* (1934), Willa Cather Scholarly Edition. Historical essay by David Porter, explanatory notes by Kari A. Ronning and Porter, textual essay and editing by Frederick M. Link and Ronning (Lincoln: University of Nebraska Press, 2015), 251-347.
Porter, David H., 'Chance Meetings in Southern France', *Cather Studies*, 8 (2010), 193-207.
Price, Aimée Brown, *Pierre Puvis de Chavannes: The Artist and His Art* (New Haven: Yale University Press, 2010).
Reynolds, Guy J., 'The Transatlantic Virtual Salon: Cather and the British', *Studies in the Novel*, 45.3 (2013), 349-68.
Roberts, Mary Louise, *Disruptive Acts: The New Woman in Fin-de-siècle France* (Chicago: University of Chicago Press, 2002).
Romines, Ann, 'Her Mortal Enemy's Daughter: Cather and the Writing of Age', *Cather Studies*, 3 (1996), 100-14.
—, 'Admiring and Remembering: The Problem of Virginia', *Cather Studies*, 5 (2003), 273-90.
—, 'Cather's Civil War: A Very Long Engagement', *Cather Studies*, 6 (2006), 1-27.
—, 'Historical Essay', in Willa Cather, *Sapphira and the Slave Girl* (1940). Willa Cather Scholarly Edition. Historical essay and explanatory notes by Ann Romines, textual essay and editing by Charles W. Mignon, Kari A. Ronning and Frederick M. Link (Lincoln: University of Nebraska Press, 2009), 297-404.
—, 'Losing and Finding Race: Old Jezebel's African Story', *Cather Studies*, 8 (2010), 396-411.
—, 'The Double Bind of Southern Food in Willa Cather's *Sapphira and the Slave Girl*', in David A. Davis and Tara Powell (eds), *Writing in the Kitchen: Essays on Southern Literature and Foodways* (Jackson: University Press of Mississippi, 2014), 86-104.
Roosevelt, Theodore, *Hunting Trips of a Ranchman* (New York and London: G. P. Putnam's Sons, 1885).
Rosowski, Susan J., *The Voyage Perilous: Willa Cather's Romanticism* (Lincoln: University of Nebraska Press, 1986).
—, 'Willa Cather's Subverted Endings and Gendered Time', *Cather Studies*, 1 (1990), 68-88.
Rutherford, Susan, 'The Voice of Freedom: Images of the Prima Donna', in Vivien Gardner and Rutherford (eds), *The New Woman and Her Sisters: Feminism and Theatre 1850-1914* (Ann Arbor: University of Michigan Press, 1992), 95-113.

Salamensky, S. I., 'Re-Presenting Oscar Wilde: Wilde's Trials, "Gross Indecency" and Documentary Spectacle', *Theatre Journal*, 54.4 (2002), 575–88.

Savage, Jon, *Teenage: The Creation of Youth Culture* (New York: Viking Press, 2007).

Saxon, Theresa, 'Sexual Transgression on the American Stage: Clyde Fitch, *Sapho* and the "American Girl"', *Literature Compass*, 10.10 (2013), 735–47.

Schamus, James, *Carl Theodor Dreyer's 'Gertrude': The Moving Word* (Seattle: University of Washington Press, 2008).

Schueth, Michael, 'Taking Liberties: Willa Cather and the Film Adaptation of *A Lost Lady*', in Janis Stout (ed.), *Willa Cather and Material Culture* (Tuscaloosa: University of Alabama Press, 2005), 113–24.

—, 'A Portrait of an Artist as a Cultural Icon: Edward Steichen, *Vanity Fair*, and Willa Cather', *Cather Studies*, 7 (2007), 46–67.

Sebald, W. G., *Austerlitz* (Munich: Carl Hanser, 2001), trans. Anthea Bell (New York: Random House, 2001).

Siebers, Tobin, *Disability Aesthetics* (Ann Arbor: University of Michigan Press, 2010).

Simmel, Georg, 'Sociology of the Senses: Visual Interaction', *Introduction to the Science of Sociology* (Chicago: University of Chicago Press, 1921), 356–61.

Skaggs, Merrill Maguire, *After the World Broke in Two: The Later Novels of Willa Cather* (Charlottesville: University Press of Virginia, 1990).

Slote, Bernice, *The Kingdom of Art: Willa Cather's First Principles and Critical Statements, 1893–1896* (Lincoln: University of Nebraska Press, 1966).

Smith, George, 'Jewett's Unspeakable Unspoken: Retracing the Female Body through *The Country of the Pointed Firs*', *Modern Language Studies*, 24.2 (1994), 11–19.

Sontag, Susan, *In America* (New York: Farrar, Straus and Giroux, 1999).

Spacks, Patricia Mayer, *Gossip* (New York: Alfred A. Knopf, 1985).

Stokes, John, 'Peacocks and Pearls: Oscar Wilde and Sarah Bernhardt', in Stokes, *The French Actress and Her English Audience* (Cambridge: Cambridge University Press, 2005), 138–58, 203–07.

—, 'Varieties of Performance at the Turn of the Century', in Gail Marshall (ed.), *The Cambridge Companion to the Fin de Siècle* (Cambridge: Cambridge University Press, 2007), 207–22.

Stouck, David, 'Willa Cather and the Russians', *Cather Studies*, 1 (1990), 1–20.

—, '"Willa Cather's Canada": The Border as Fiction', *Cather Studies*, 4 (1999), 7–22.

Stout, Janis P., *A Calendar of the Letters of Willa Cather* (Lincoln: University of Nebraska Press, 2002).

—, 'Observant Eye, the Art of Illustration, and Willa Cather's *My Ántonia*', *Cather Studies*, 5 (2003), 128–52.

—, 'Daughter of a War Lost, Won, and Evaded: Cather and the Ambiguities of the Civil War', *Cather Studies*, 10 (2015), 133–49.

—, '"Down by de Canebrake": Willa Cather, Sterling A. Brown, and the Racialized Vernacular', *Cather Studies*, 12 (2020), 37–59.

Swift, John, 'Unwrapping the Mummy: Cather's Mother Eve and the Business of

Desire', in Swift and Joseph R. Urgo (eds), *Willa Cather and the American Southwest* (Lincoln: University of Nebraska Press, 2002), 12–31.

Taussig, Michael, *What Color Is the Sacred?* (Chicago: University of Chicago Press, 2009).

Thomas, Keith, 'Magical Healing: The King's Touch', in Constance Classen, *Book of Touch* (Oxford: Berg, 2005), 354.

Tittle, Walter, 'Glimpses of Interesting Americans', *The Century Magazine*, 110.3 (1925), 305–20.

Titus, Mary, 'Cather's Creative Women and Du Maurier's Cozy Men: *The Song of the Lark* and *Trilby*', *Modern Language Studies*, 24.2 (1994), 27–37.

Trilling, Lionel, 'Willa Cather', *The New Republic*, 90 (10 February 1937), 10–13.

Trowse, Nadeane, 'Willa Cather's Condition: Disease, Doctors, and Diagnoses as Social Action', *Cather Studies*, 4 (1999), 205–24.

Tsank, Stephanie, 'Under the White Mulberry Tree: Food and Artistry in Cather's Orchards', *Cather Studies*, 12 (2020), 152–70.

Urgo, Joseph, '"Dock Burs in Yo' Pants": Reading Cather through *Sapphira and the Slave Girl*', in Ann Romines (ed.), *Southern Connections: New Essays on Cather and the South* (Charlottesville: University Press of Virginia, 2000).

—, 'Cather's Secular Humanism: Writing Anacoluthon and Shooting Out into the Eternities', *Cather Studies*, 7 (2007), 186–202.

Vester, Katharina, *A Taste of Power: Food and American Identities* (Oakland: University of California Press, 2015).

Vulliamy, Ed, 'Sontag Pleads Poetic Licence in Using Uncredited "scraps of history"', *The Guardian* (27 May 2000), <https://www.theguardian.com/world/2000/may/28/books.booksnews> (last accessed 28 July 2016).

Walker, Julia A., *Expressionism and Modernism in the American Theatre: Bodies, Voices, Words* (Cambridge: Cambridge University Press, 2005).

Wallach, Jennifer Jensen, *How America Eats: A Social History of U. S. Food and Culture* (Lanham: Rowman & Littlefield, 2012).

Weinstein, Arnold, *Northern Arts: The Breakthrough of Scandinavian Literature and Art, from Ibsen to Bergman* (Princeton: Princeton University Press, 2008).

Welsch, Roger L. and Linda K. Welsch, *Cather's Kitchens: Foodways in Literature and Life* (Lincoln: University of Nebraska Press, 1987).

West, Rebecca, 'The Classic Artist', in *The Strange Necessity* (London: Virago, 1987), 215–28.

Wilde, Oscar, *The Picture of Dorian Gray* (1890) (Oxford: Oxford University Press, 1998).

—, *Decorative Art in America* (New York: Brentano's, 1906).

Williams, Deborah Lindsay, 'Losing Nothing, Comprehending Everything: Learning to Read Both the Old World and the New in *Death Comes for the Archbishop*', *Cather Studies*, 4 (1999), 80–96.

Williams, William Carlos, *Spring and All* (Paris: Contact, 1923).

Wolff, Cynthia Griffin, 'Time and Memory in *Sapphira and the Slave Girl*: Sex, Abuse, and Art', *Cather Studies*, 3 (1996), 212–37.

Woodress, James, *Willa Cather: A Literary Life* (Lincoln: University of Nebraska Press, 1987).

Yerxa, Donald A., 'The Deepest Sense: An Interview with Constance Classen', *Historically Speaking*, 14.3 (2013), 27–8.

Young, Sarah, 'The Singer as Artist: Willa Cather, Olive Fremstad and the Artist's Voice', *Cather Studies*, 12 (2020), 44–67.

INDEX

'WC' stands for 'Willa Cather'; all other abbreviations are from page viii.

accidents and injuries
 industrialised, 73–4, 122–3, 152, 189, 191, 221
 non-industrialised, 75, 150, 156
actresses
 bodies, 44–5, 46–7, 48–50, 210–11
 dramatic roles, 34, 35, 40, 44
 expressive style, 41–2, 43, 49–50
 voices, 42, 114, 122
Adams, Nick (fictional character), 67, 166–7, 168
Aestheticism
 ALL, 192, 193
 'Coming, Aphrodite!' 76–9
 MME, 55–6, 129
 'Paul's Case', 71–4, 189–91
 SOL, 56, 64, 80–3, 121, 130
 TPH, 34, 62, 65, 74, 157, 174
 WC's views on, 19, 20, 33–5, 60–4, 68–71, 75
 see also males: aesthetes; Wilde, Oscar
African–American identities, 102–4, 219–20, 222–5; *see also* slavery
ageing, 11, 64, 211, 215–16
Alexander's Bridge, 81, 95, 96, 191
American national identities
 food, 163–5, 167–9
 language, 53–4, 118–19
 and masculinities, 66, 67, 74, 167
American Upper South, 157–8, 199–200
American West (Southwest)
 clothes, 66, 211–12
 food, 163, 164–6, 168, 169–71
 sensorium, 14–15, 23, 51
 smellscapes, 194–6
 sound, 116–17
 touch and landscape, 147–50, 154
anacoluthon, 13, 175–7, 179
anthropology
 anthropologists, 3–4, 78, 82, 187
 in WC's fiction, 158, 160, 163, 177, 195, 222–3, 226
Archer, William, 34–5, 40
Archie, Doctor Howard (fictional character), 96, 120–2, 123
Arizona, 194, 195
Aronoff, Eric, 147
art
 art galleries, 90–1
 painters and paintings, 18, 66, 76–9, 100–1, 110–12, 147
 writing as art, 13–15
 see also crafts (handwork); Puvis de Chavannes, Pierre

asceticism, 179–80
Atkins, Frederick, 48
Atkins, Henry (fictional character), 170
Auclair, Cécile (fictional character), 11, 12, 108–10, 155, 177–8, 179, 181–2
Auclair, Euclide (fictional character), 107, 153–6, 176–8, 179, 183
Auerbach, Jonathan, 25
Augusta (fictional character), 143, 144, 148, 150
Awakening, The, 66–7, 80
Ayrshire, Kitty (fictional character), 52, 92, 155

Barker, Jennifer, 25
Barthes, Roland, 47
Beard, George Miller, 45
Beardsley, Aubrey, 213
Berger, John, 95–7, 106
Bergson, Emil (fictional character), 93
Bernhardt, Sarah, 40, 41–2, 44, 54, 117, 122
Birdseye, Nellie (fictional character), 54–5, 100, 112, 128–9, 141
Blake, Roddy (fictional character), 170
Blanchard, Mary Warner, 64–5, 66
Blind D'Arnault (fictional character), 101, 102–4, 109, 130, 219, 226
Blinker (fictional character), 11, 12, 108–10
Blom, Philipp, 49
Bloom, Edward and Lillian, 90
Bloom, Harold, 213
Blue Eyes on the Platte, 94; *see also Lucy Gayheart*
bodies (embodiment) *see* actresses: bodies; female bodies; males: bodies; performative bodies; singers' bodies; writers' bodies
Bohemian national identity, 10, 93, 134, 178
Boston, 80, 95

Bourdieu, Pierre, 3
Bourne, Randolph, 7, 9–11, 12–13, 109, 178
Bower, Eden (fictional character), 23, 48, 76–7, 78–9
Braswell, Suzanne, 189
Burden, Jim (fictional character), 37, 89, 94, 101–2, 104–5, 131, 134

Camille (Dumas), 40
Canada, 12, 177, 222, 225; *see also* Quebec
Capuano, Peter J., 25
Cather, Willa
 appearance/body/identity, 88–90, 209–11, 213–14
 high school/college, 10, 19, 28, 35, 41, 43–4, 60
 living in Lincoln, 1, 19–20, 37, 41, 70
 living in New York, 87, 118, 164, 165, 218
 living in Pittsburgh, 33, 42, 72, 91, 195
 living in Red Cloud, 35, 70, 102, 189
 mother's illness, 151
 theatre reviewer and 'gazer', 1, 19, 21, 36, 38–9, 86–7, 128
 visiting Europe, 34, 213, 215
 visiting the Southwest, 14, 23, 116–17, 164–6, 169, 194–5
Catholicism, 93–4, 135, 173, 178
'Chance Meeting, A', 215–16
Charron, Pierre (fictional character), 177, 180–2
Cheng, Anne Anlin, 46
Chicago, 41, 83, 123, 132
Chopin, Kate, 66–7, 80, 81, 192
Christian Science, 7–8, 10
cinema, 6, 17, 25–6, 48, 50, 73–4, 76–9
Civil War
 ante-bellum (pre-Civil War), 158, 199–200, 220–1, 226–7
 post-Civil War, 65, 221–4
Classen, Constance, 137
Clere, Sarah, 12

Cliff City/cliff dwellings, 65, 147, 149, 150, 168, 169
clothes
  male aesthetes, 65–6, 70–1, 73
  real singers/actresses, 49–50, 68, 210
  WC, 210–11
  WC's fictional characters, 22, 70–1, 73, 92–3, 102, 222–3
Colbert, Henry (fictional character), 97, 159, 206, 224
Colbert, Martin (fictional character), 159, 180, 203–5, 221, 224
Colbert, Sapphira (fictional character)
  disability/illness, 11, 12, 180, 221, 224
  hands, 158, 159
  whiteness, 201, 205, 221
Collingham, Lizzie, 162–3
colonists/European settlers
  food, 163, 171–4, 176–8, 179–83
  sight/gaze, 106–10, 153–4
  smellscapes, 195–9, 201–6
  sound, 107
  touch, 153–9
colour, 92, 94–5, 107
'Coming, Aphrodite!' ('Coming, Eden Bower!'), 19, 23, 47–8, 75–7, 78–9, 172
Commonweal, 1927 letter to, 14–17, 28, 174
Corbin, Alain, 200, 205
Cornell, Katharine, 210
corporealism, definition, 2–3
Counihan, Carole, 164
Courier, 62, 63
crafts (handwork), 14–15, 143–7, 148–50, 157
Crane, Stephen, 13, 213
Crazy Ivar (fictional character), 26, 155, 202
crime, 71–2, 73, 93, 150–1, 173, 175

'Critical Studies on Writing as an Art' *see On Writing*

Damnation of Theron Ware, The, 66, 80
dancing, 98, 101–2, 103
D'Arnault, Samson 'Blind' (fictional character), 101, 102–4, 109, 219, 226
Daudet, Alphonse, 40, 44
Davidson, Michael, 25
Davis, Lennard, 25, 109
death
  deaths depicted, 12, 82–3, 99, 123, 224
  end-oriented narratives, 76, 226
  mourning/memory, 133–4, 155, 193
  transcendence of, 8
  WC's mother, 151
  see also mummification; murder; suicide
Death Comes for the Archbishop
  food, 162, 163, 168, 171–4, 178, 182
  gaze, 93–4
  narrative structures, 8, 14–17, 127, 174–5, 226
  smellscapes, 130, 188, 194, 195, 197–9, 202
  violence, 111, 173
  see also Commonweal, 1927 letter to
decoration *see* clothes; furniture and domestic objects
'Decorative Arts, The' (Wilde), 63, 65–6
Deleuze, Gilles, 25
Dent, Peter, 25–6
Diego, Juan (fictional character), 198
disabilities, 9–13, 24–5, 75, 108–9, 110, 216; *see also* accidents and injuries; illness
Dolezal, Joshua, 178
domestic settings, 158–9, 199–200, 211, 220, 223; *see also* furniture and domestic objects

Douglas, Mary, 82, 156
Du Maurier, George, 60, 68–70, 80, 131
Dumas, Alexandre, *fils*, 40, 42
Duncan, Therese, 210
Duse, Eleonora, 41–2

Earle, Rebecca, 171
Ebbing, Alexandra (fictional character), 22
Eddy, Mary Baker, 7–8, 10, 74, 178
Edmonds, Jill, 122
Education of Henry Adams, The, 73
Egypt, Ancient, 142
embodiment (bodies) *see* actresses: bodies; female bodies; males: bodies; performative bodies; singers' bodies; writers' bodies
England, 35, 41, 48
English national identity, 42–3, 44, 53–4, 118–19, 201
Eusabio (fictional character), 198
eyes
　character/selfhood, 94–5, 97, 100, 107, 109, 215
　damaged/missing, 103, 109, 123
　WC's eyes, 88–9

faces, 47, 93–4, 96–7, 108, 111, 210; *see also* eyes
Fara, Patricia, 78
Farrar, Geraldine, 45, 47, 48, 49
fashion *see* clothes
female aesthetes, 66, 69
female autonomy
　fictional characters, 51–2, 69–70, 104–6, 131, 134
　real women, 40–1, 44, 210–11, 213–16
female bodies
　actresses' bodies, 44–5, 46–7, 49–50, 210–11
　dressmaker's forms, 144
　objectified by the male gaze, 39, 77–9, 95–6, 106, 131
　sexual assault, 158, 204–5
　WC's body, 209–11, 213–14

see also female hands; singers' bodies
female gaze, 39, 91, 96–8, 109, 112, 141
female hands
　crafts, 143–7, 148–50, 157
　nursing, 151–3, 160
　Sapphira Colbert, 158, 159
　singers, 55, 56, 121
female voice
　achievement of, 50–2, 114, 118–19, 122–5, 131–2, 134
　actress's voices, 42, 114, 122
　male control of, 69–70, 81, 133–4
First World War, 2, 3, 149, 164, 167, 184
Fitch, Clyde, 40, 44
Fitzgerald, F. Scott, 41, 45, 67, 212
Flaubert, Gustave, 215–16
flowers
　language of, 187–91, 191–4, 197–8
　sensory abundance/mix, 132, 139, 196, 202–3
folk music, 124–5
food
　American national identity, 163–5, 168, 169
　asceticism, 179–80
　campfire cooking/masculinity, 166–7, 170–1, 181
　communality, 169–71, 177
　evolution of food cultures, 14–15, 162–3, 171–3, 176–8, 181–2
　food smells, 196–7
Ford, Ford Maddox, 213
Forrester, Marian (fictional character), 127, 191–3, 206
Foucault, Michel, 25
France, 155, 182, 189, 215; *see also* Paris
Frederic, Harold, 66, 80
Fremstad, Olive, 45, 48
French national identity, 42–3, 44, 54, 168, 171, 178, 189
French symbolism, 60–1
Frontenac, Count, 107, 177, 182–3

furniture and domestic objects
  beauty/cleanliness, 65, 177, 181–2
  preparing food, 169, 170
  touch, 139–42, 150, 155

Garbo, Greta, 210–11
Garland-Thomson, Rosamond, 24
Garrington, Abbie, 25
Gayheart, Lucy (fictional character), 5, 12, 52, 74, 98–101, 131–5, 180
gaze
  covert glances, 22, 109
  otherness objectified, 2, 87, 90, 92–3
  and social connection, 86, 89–91, 94
  WC as theatre reviewer and 'gazer', 1, 19, 21, 38–9, 86–7, 128
  see also female gaze; male gaze
gender
  food, 163, 165–7, 169–71
  narrators and addressees, 22–3, 138
  and national identity, 42–3, 67, 167
  nursing/care, 142–3, 152–3, 156–7
  WC's male acting roles, 35
  WC's male pseudonym, 90–1
  see also female autonomy; female bodies; female hands; female voice; male gaze; males; singers' bodies
German national identity, 116
Geurts, Kathryn Linn, 3–4
Giannone, Richard, 136n
Gilman, Charlotte Perkins, 51, 81
Giorcelli, Cristina, 16
Glover, Mrs *see* Eddy, Mary Baker
Gluckman, Max, 223
'Gold Slipper, A', 5, 45, 91–2, 126, 186
Goody, Jack, 187
Gordon, Harry (fictional character), 5, 98–101, 131, 132–5, 180

Grout, Madame, 215–16
Guattari, Pierre-Félix, 25

habitus, definition, 3–6
Hall, Gertrude, 13, 115–17
'Handicapped – By One of Them, The' (Bourne), 7, 9–10, 109
hands
  indigenous cultures, 147, 149–50
  slavery, 157, 158, 159–60
  Steichen's photographs, 210
  see also female hands
haptic modernism, 139, 143
Harsanyi, Andor (fictional character), 123
Hedger, Don (fictional character), 23, 76–7, 78–9
Hemingway, Ernest
  contemporary of WC, 153
  food/cooking, 166–7, 168, 170, 171, 181
Henshawe, Myra (fictional character), 100, 109, 112, 126, 129, 141
Herbert, Niel (fictional character), 191–3
Hesperian, The, 10, 33, 142
Hicks, Granville, 14, 215
Hillman, David, 25
Hispanic national identities, 168, 171–2, 195
historical figures in WC's fiction, 52–6, 117, 127–9, 226
Homer, Louise, 45, 48
Hoover, Herbert, 164, 184
Hooverizing, 163, 164–5, 184
Housman, A. E., 213

Ibsen, Henrik, 31–5, 36, 118
illness, 11, 82, 120, 123, 151–3, 155, 220–1; *see also* neurasthenia
immigration, 10, 53–4, 118–19, 163, 171–4, 181; *see also* colonists/European settlers

Indian (Amerindian) cultures, 147, 156, 170, 172–3, 175, 181, 198–9; *see also* Pueblo cultures
indigenous cultures
    food, 163, 168, 169, 170, 171, 172–3, 196–7
    hands, 147, 149–50
    language, 181
    smellscapes, 195–8
Ivar, 'Crazy' (fictional character), 26, 155, 202

Jacinto (fictional character), 197, 198
Jacobs, John, 220
James, Henry, 32
Jewell, Andrew, 163
Jewett, Sarah Orne, 13, 213–15
Jewish identity, 54, 56, 130
Jezebel (fictional character), 111, 159, 205, 218–19
Johnson, Katie N., 40, 44
Juschereau de Sainte-Ignace, Mother, 156, 188

Kaplan, Amy, 67
Kelly, Veronica, 46
Kennedy, Ray (fictional character), 122
Kennicott, Philip, 116
Kingdom of Art, The, 60–1
Kittler, Friedrich, 6, 135
Knausgaard, Karl Ove, 86
Kot, Paula, 148
Kronberg, Peter (fictional character), 118–19
Kronberg, Thea (fictional character)
    autonomy, 51–2, 70, 80–1
    body, 50–2, 83, 119–23, 142, 195–7
    female gaze, 96
    voice, 50–2, 118–19, 122–5, 131
Künstlerroman, 82, 123–4

Lady Windermere's Fan, 63
languages and accents, 53–4, 118–19, 134, 181, 196, 222–5

Latour, Father Jean Marie (fictional character)
    food, 168, 171, 173, 178, 182
    gaze, 93–4
    ideals, 8
    smellscapes, 197, 198–9, 202
Lawrence, D. H., 167
Le Ber, Jeanne (fictional character), 179–81, 182
Lears, Jackson, 45, 51, 65
Lemoine-Montigny, Adolphe, 139
Lewis, Edith, 42, 87–90, 218, 220
Life of Mary Baker G. Eddy and the History of Christian Science, The, 7–8
'Light on Adobe Walls', 15, 18–19
Lincoln, Nebraska
    setting for WC's fiction, 19–20, 37, 60, 63, 68, 70–1
    theatre, 1, 36–8, 40, 41, 43, 44
Lindemann, Marilee, 26
Lingard, Lena (fictional character), 5, 37, 96, 101–2, 103
London, 32, 41, 48, 213
Lost Lady, A, 106, 127–8, 141, 187–8, 191–3, 206
Loti, Pierre, 62
Lucy Gayheart
    bodies, 12, 52, 74, 180
    sight/gaze, 5, 92, 94, 98–101, 106, 110
    touch, 138–9, 151
    voice/sound, 27, 114–15, 130–6

McClure's Magazine, 7, 31, 45, 71, 98, 214
McKann, Marshall (fictional character), 91–2, 125–6
male gaze
    AB, 95–6
    'Coming, Aphrodite!' 77–9
    LG, 5, 98–101
    MA, 104–6, 131
    photographic portraits, 210–11
    reversed by WC, 39, 91, 96–8, 112
    SOR, 106–8, 153–4
    TPH, 148–9

males
  aesthetes, 65–6, 70–4, 77, 84, 189–90
  bodies, 22, 74–5, 91, 96–8, 123
  narrators, 22–3
  singing voice, 133
  traditional masculinity, 67–8, 75, 166–7, 170–1, 181
Manguel, Alberto, 100
Mansfield, Katherine, 217–18
Marlowe, Julia, 41–2
Marshall, Gail, 48, 54
Martin, Terence, 178, 179
Maude, Ulrika, 25
Mauss, Marcel, 3, 4–5
Mayer, David, 50
Merrill, Flora, 127, 206–7
Mesa Verde, 148, 169, 170–1, 195
Mexican national identity, 93, 124–5, 172, 199
Mexico, 194, 197
Meyer, Susan, 82
Millington, Richard, 101
Milmine, Georgine, 7–8
Mintz, Sidney, 164
Mockford, James (fictional character), 12
Modernism
  ALL, 191
  haptic modernism, 25, 139, 143
  ignored/rejected aspects, 14, 18, 35
  MME, 55–6, 128–30
  SOL, 80, 120, 196
  SOR/late fiction, 108, 160
  TPH, 139, 143, 145
  trajectory, 2, 7, 15, 26–7, 46
  WC's early stories, 19–20
  WC's non-fiction, 13, 17, 35, 140
  WC's portrait, 211
Modjeska, Helena, 52–6, 117, 126, 128, 129–30, 226
Moeran, Brian, 186–7
Montigny (Adolphe Lemoine-Montigny), 139
Montoya, Friar (Fray) Baltazar (fictional character), 111, 168, 172–3
Morrison, Toni, 219, 226

Mother Eve, 83, 139, 142, 143, 150, 175
Mulvey, Laura, 78
mummification, 75, 120, 139, 142–3, 150
murals, 15–17, 27, 79
murder, 93, 150–1, 173, 175
music
  effect on listeners, 27, 72, 101, 103, 125–6
  folk music, 124–5
  loss of, 10, 132–4
  opera, 115–17
  pre-linguistic, 196
  see also female voice; singers' bodies
My Ántonia
  flowers, 187, 193–4
  food, 178
  narrative structures, 88–9, 90, 92, 112, 130–1, 199, 226
  setting, 21, 37, 174
  sight/gaze, 96, 101–6, 112, 130–1
  sound/voice, 134
  suicide, 1, 94–5
'My First Novels (There Were Two)', 191
My Mortal Enemy
  historical figures, 52, 54–6, 117, 126–7, 128–30, 226
  realism, 35
  sight/gaze, 109, 112, 141

Nancy (fictional character), 12, 110–11, 158, 200, 203–6, 222–5
'Nancy Till' ballad, 224–5, 226
narrative structures
  anacoluthon, 13, 175–7, 179
  death/end-oriented, 76, 226
  embedded narratives, 23, 148–50, 174–5
  epiphany, 129–30
  Künstlerroman, 82, 123–4
  micro-narratives, 21–4, 77, 105, 142, 183, 215
  use of new technologies, 21, 22, 73, 122–3
  Victorian forms, 81–2
  see also 'panel method' narratives

national identities
  clothes, 66, 74, 93
  food, 162–5, 167–9, 171–4, 178, 180, 182, 221
  and gender identity, 42–3, 67, 167
  habitus, 3–5
  language and accent, 53–4, 118–19, 134, 181, 222–5
  music, 116, 124–5
Nebraska, 80, 86, 105, 117, 139, 148, 195; *see also* Lincoln, Nebraska; Red Cloud, Nebraska; University of Nebraska
Nebraska State Journal, 19–21, 33, 38–9, 41, 61
Nethersole, Olga, 40–4, 114
neurasthenia, 45, 51, 142, 143
New Mexico, 116–17, 194
New York
  'Paul's Case', 71, 190
  theatre, 32, 41, 44, 49, 87
  WC's home, 87, 118, 164, 165, 218
Nicklemann, Henry, 90–1
North, Michael, 35
Not Under Forty, 21, 213, 217
'Novel Démeublé, The', 13, 140–1, 218
nursing, 142–3, 151–3, 156–7, 160, 205, 221
'Nursing as a Profession for Women', 152

O Pioneers!
  narrative structures, 81, 92, 93, 174–5
  outsiders, 26, 155, 202
Oates, Joyce Carol, 86
O'Brien, Sharon, 213
Old Jezebel (fictional character), 111, 159, 205, 218–19
'Old Mrs Harris', 15, 155, 215, 223
Olin, Margaret, 105
'On the Gulls' Road', 19, 22–3
On Writing, 13–15, 217; *see also* Commonweal, 1927 letter to; 'Light on Adobe Walls'; 'My First Novels (There Were Two)'; 'Novel Démeublé, The'; *Wagnerian Romances, The* (preface)
Ondaatje, Michael, 216
One of Ours, 74–5, 152
'One Way of Putting It', 38–9
opera, 37, 115–17
O'Reilly, Sally, 111
otherness
  outsiders in WC's fiction, 51, 72, 82–3, 155, 187, 194, 202–3
  smellscapes, 78, 82, 187, 194, 197, 201–2, 204–5
  sympathy for, 89–90, 217
  white writing of black characters, 103–4, 218–20, 225, 226
  see also disabilities; race and racism
Outland, Tom (fictional character), 37, 83, 89, 139, 147–50, 170

'panel method' narratives
  across multiple WC works, 11, 27, 45, 201–2
  definition, 16–17
  embedded narratives, 23, 148–50, 174–5
  within single WC works, 79, 83, 106, 134, 157, 172, 179
Paris, 16, 43, 47, 60, 69, 186
'Paul's Case', 10–11, 63, 71–4, 122, 187, 189–91
performative bodies
  performance of selfhood, 9, 43–4, 45, 49–50, 95, 109
  recurring motif, 1–2, 20–1, 36, 52–3, 118, 128–30, 132
  see also actresses: bodies; Blind D'Arnault (fictional character); female aesthetes; males: aesthetes; singers' bodies
Peters, Ivy (fictional character), 192–3
photography
  portrait of WC, 209, 211–12
  sight, 6, 46–50, 77, 98–9, 104–6, 126–7

sound, 126–7
touch, 105
Pittsburgh
  'Paul's Case', 60, 71, 72, 80, 187, 190
  WC's home, 33, 42, 72, 91, 195
Polish national identity, 54
'Popular Pictures', 90–1
Porteous, J. Douglas, 187
Porter, David, 99
Portrait of Dorian Gray, The, 64, 71
Price, Aimee Brown, 15
Professor's House, The
  aestheticism, 34, 62, 65, 74, 157, 174
  food, 163, 167, 169–71
  gaze/eyes, 88–9, 95, 97
  touch, 13, 139, 141, 143–7, 157
Protestantism, 93–4, 201, 220
Pueblo cultures, 14, 166, 168, 195, 197
Puvis de Chavannes, Pierre, 15–17, 27, 79, 118, 149, 175

Quebec, 106–7, 153–4, 168, 175–6, 179, 181, 201
queer identity/queer studies, 26, 63, 68, 90–1, 188

race and racism, 11, 54, 56, 125, 130, 219–20, 225; *see also* slavery; whiteness
realism
  in WC's fiction, 75, 120, 199
  WC's views on, 31, 33–5, 127–8, 139–41, 188
Red Cloud, Nebraska, 35, 70, 102, 189
'Roll Call on the Prairies', 164
Romines, Ann, 199, 218–19, 224, 225
Roosevelt, Theodore, 67, 75, 123, 166–8, 171, 181
Rosowski, Susan, 68

St Peter, Professor Godfrey (fictional character)
  aestheticism, 34, 74, 157
  food, 169, 170–1

gaze/eyes, 89, 95, 97, 109
touch, 142, 143–7, 148–50, 157
Salamensky, S. I., 65
Sapho (Daudet), 40, 44
Sapphira and the Slave Girl
  disability/illness/death, 11, 12, 180, 205, 218–19, 220–1, 224
  domestic settings, 5, 158–9, 199–200
  sight/gaze, 97, 110–11, 222
  smellscapes, 158, 188, 200–5
  time/temporality, 200, 205–6
  violence, 157–60, 204–5, 220
  WC in narrative, 219–20, 223–4, 225–6
  WC's final novel, 15, 130, 174, 177, 209, 226–7
Savage, Jon, 71
Saxon, Theresa, 44
'Scandal', 45
Schamus, James, 127
Schueth, Michael, 211
'Sculptor's Funeral, The', 41
Sebastian, Clement (fictional character), 12, 100, 133, 138
sensorism
  definition, 18–19, 63–4
  focus on the 'sensorium', 4, 6
  sensory hierarchy, 78, 186–7, 194
  sensory politics, 130
  sensory time, 226–7
  see also sight; smell; sound; taste; touch
sexual assault, 158, 204–5
Shabata, Frank and Maria (fictional characters), 93
Shadows on the Rock
  disability/injury, 11, 12, 25, 108–10, 151, 156
  flowers, 188
  food, 163, 168, 176–8, 179–82, 182–3
  narrative structures, 13, 106, 112, 160, 175–6
  sight/gaze, 25, 90, 92, 106–10, 112, 153–4
  touch, 139, 141, 151, 153–7, 221
Shaw, George Bernard, 133

Shimerda, Ántonia (fictional character), 89, 101, 104–5, 118, 131, 134
Shimerda, Mr (fictional character), 1, 94–5
Siebers, Tobin, 25
sight
  impact of cinema, 6, 17, 25–6, 48, 50, 76–9
  impact of photography, 6, 46–50, 77, 98–9, 104–6
  painters and paintings, 18, 66, 76–9, 90–1, 100–1, 110–12
  and smell, 196
  and sound, 61, 126, 222
  and touch, 25–6, 33, 78, 105, 120–1, 153–5, 222
  see also female gaze; gaze; male gaze
Simmel, Georg, 78
singers' bodies
  fictional female singers, 50–2, 55, 69, 74, 77, 83, 119–23
  real female singers, 44–6, 49–50, 55, 56, 117, 129, 130
slavery
  ballads, 224–5
  domestic settings, 5, 158–9, 199–200
  smellscapes, 158, 201–5
  time/temporality, 200, 205–6
  touch/violence, 157–60, 204–5
  WC's research, 218–19
Slote, Bernice, 60–1
Smart Set, 23, 75, 211
smell
  otherness, 78, 82, 187, 194, 197, 201–2, 204–5
  primitive connotations, 1, 187, 196, 205
  sensory hierarchy, 78, 186–7, 194
  and sight, 196, 205
  and taste, 169
  and touch, 1, 158
  see also flowers
Smith, George, 214
Song of the Lark, The

aestheticism, 56, 64, 80–3, 121, 130
'The Ancient People', 50–2, 169, 188, 195–7
female performer, 50–2, 53, 118–19, 122–5
see also Kronberg, Thea (fictional character)
Sontag, Susan, 47, 52
sound
  impact of new technologies, 6, 77, 135–6
  and sight, 61, 126, 222
  silence, 116, 132–5
  and touch, 133, 138, 222
  see also female voice; languages and accents; music
Spanish Johnny (fictional character), 124–5
Spanish national identity, 124–5, 171
Steichen, Edward, 209–12
Stokes, John, 31–2, 139
Stout, Janis, 224–5
suicide
  The Awakening (Chopin), 67, 80
  'Paul's Case', 71, 73–4, 189, 190
  WC's other fiction, 1, 10, 82, 94–5, 148
Susanna (fictional character), 202
Svengali (fictional character), 69–70

'Tale of the White Pyramid, A', 142
Tansy Dave (fictional character), 202–3
tapestries, 16–17, 107, 146
taste, 162, 169; see also food
Taussig, Michael, 92
technological innovations
  impact on sight, 6, 17, 25–6, 46–50, 76–9, 98–9, 104–6
  impact on sound, 6, 77
  impact on touch, 25–6, 105
  as settings/narrative devices, 21, 22, 73, 122–3

Tellamantez, Juan 'Spanish Johnny' (fictional character), 124–5
theatre
  metropolitan theatres, 32, 41, 44, 49, 87
  provincial theatres, 1, 36–8, 39, 40, 42–4, 86
  WC as theatre reviewer and 'gazer', 1, 19, 21, 36, 38–9, 86–7, 128
  see also actresses; Ibsen, Henrik; performative bodies
'Three American Singers', 45, 47–50, 129
Till (fictional character), 110–11, 224–5, 226
time/temporality, 47–8, 149, 176, 200, 205–6
'Tom Outland's Story'
  embedded narrative, 23, 148–50, 174–5
  food, 166, 168, 169–70
  touch, 139, 142, 143, 147–50
touch
  furniture and domestic objects, 139–42, 150, 155
  impact of new technologies, 25–6, 105
  miraculous healing, 137
  mummification, 142–3, 150
  and sight, 25–6, 33, 78, 105, 120–1, 153–5, 222
  and smell, 1, 158
  and sound, 133, 138
  see also female hands; hands; nursing; violence
'Training for the Ballet: Making American Dancers', 98
trains, 21, 73, 122–3
tramps, 82–3
Trilby (Du Maurier), 68–70, 131
Trilling, Lionel, 163–4, 169, 182, 184
Tuke, Henry Scott, 90–1

University of Nebraska, 10, 28, 31, 36, 37, 60

Vaillant, Father Joseph (fictional character), 168, 171, 197
Vanity Fair portrait, 209, 211–12
Vester, Katharina, 166–7
Victorian culture
  narrative structures, 81–2
  trajectory, 2, 7, 15, 31, 48–9, 50
  see also Aestheticism; Realism
violence
  murder, 93, 150–1, 173, 175
  slavery, 157–60, 204–5, 220
Virginia, 187, 200–2, 206, 224, 225, 226
voice see female voice; languages and accents

Wagner, Richard, 115–17, 118
'Wagner Matinée, A', 41, 80
Wagnerian Romances, The (preface), 13, 115–17
Walker, Julia A., 6
Wallach, Jennifer Jensen, 164
Weinstein, Arnold, 34
West, Rebecca, 1–2, 33, 115
Wetherill, Richard, 148, 169, 195
Wheeler, Claude (fictional character), 74–5, 152
whiteness
  black stories of white characters, 223, 226
  narration/focalisation, 102–3, 200
  reconciliation, 221
  settlers' whiteness, 106, 108, 110, 156–7, 195–7, 205–6
  white response to blackness/slaves, 159, 201–2, 204–5
  white transcendence/superiority, 102, 125
  white writing of black characters, 103–4, 218–20, 225, 226
Wilde, Oscar, 37, 60, 62–8, 71, 80, 189, 192–3
Willa Cather Living, 218
Willa Cather on Writing see *On Writing*
Wilson, Professor Lucius (fictional character), 95

Wolff, Cynthia Griffin, 220
World War One, 2, 3, 149, 164, 167, 184
writers' bodies, 210, 211–12, 213–18

Wunsch (fictional character), 121, 122

Young, Sarah L., 119
Yourcenar, Marguerite, 172

EU representative:
Easy Access System Europe
Mustamäe tee 50, 10621 Tallinn, Estonia
Gpsr.requests@easproject.com